Enterprise Risk and Opportunity Management

Concepts and Step-by-Step Examples for Pioneering Scientific and Technical Organizations

ALLAN S. BENJAMIN

WILEY

Published by John Wiley & Sons, Inc., Hoboken, New Jersey.
Published simultaneously in Canada.

For general information on our other products and services or for technical support, please contact our Customer Care Department within the United States at (800) 762-2974, outside the United States at (317) 572-3993 or fax (317) 572-4002.

Wiley publishes in a variety of print and electronic formats and by print-on-demand. Some material included with standard print versions of this book may not be included in e-books or in print-on-demand. If this book refers to media such as a CD or DVD that is not included in the version you purchased, you may download this material at http://booksupport.wiley.com. For more information about Wiley products, visit www.wiley.com.

Library of Congress Cataloging-in-Publication Data:

Names: Benjamin, Allan S., author.
Title: Enterprise risk and opportunity management : concepts and step-by-step
    examples for pioneering scientific and technical organizations / Allan S.
    Benjamin.
Description: Hoboken : Wiley, 2017. | Series: Wiley finance | Includes index.
Identifiers: LCCN 2016031019 (print) | LCCN 2016055611 (ebook) | ISBN
    9781119288428 (hardback) | ISBN 9781119318729 (ePDF) | ISBN 9781119318712
    (ePub)
Subjects: LCSH: Risk management. | Information technology—Management. |
    Strategic planning. | BISAC: BUSINESS & ECONOMICS / Finance.
Classification: LCC HD61 .B46 2017 (print) | LCC HD61 (ebook) | DDC
    658.15/5—dc23
LC record available at https://lccn.loc.gov/2016031019

Cover design: Wiley
Cover images: Modern business center, Toronto © PhotoSerg/Shutterstock;
Businessman on tight rope © i-works/amanaimagesRF/Getty Images, Inc.

Printed in the United States of America

10 9 8 7 6 5 4 3 2 1

Contents

Figures

Tables

Preface

In one form or another, I have been preparing to write this book for many years. In the most recent of those years, my focus has been on collaborating with NASA personnel on producing detailed guidance about potential ways that the agency could apply enterprise risk and opportunity management to help ensure its success as its mission becomes more complex. This collaboration has resulted in the publication of the NASA special publication report, *Organizational Risk and Opportunity Management: Concepts and Processes for NASA Consideration.*

In the process of writing that report, my thinking has evolved into considering two extensions of the original NASA purpose. First is how EROM can be applied to other pioneering technical organizations, both nonprofit and commercial, some of whom I have previously worked with on matters of risk and opportunity assessment and management. Second is how EROM can be integrated with the identification, implementation, and evaluation of internal controls, complying with new requirements from the federal government. This book, therefore, builds on the NASA work by extending it to be generally applicable to organizations of all sorts that are concerned with performing pioneering technical research, integrating and operationalizing that research into complex technical systems, and satisfying externally mandated requirements.

One might ask, "Why yet another guidebook on EROM when there have been several others produced during the past 10 or 15 years?" The answer is that the vast majority of the work that has appeared before now has been oriented toward business and financial organizations, whose objectives center on ultimate monetary gain for their company and their stockholders. In contrast, organizations whose principal objective is to develop and implement risky technologies for scientific and technical gain are faced with different kinds of risks and different kinds of opportunities. In many ways, their risks and opportunities are broader and more challenging than those of the traditional commercial business/financial sector, because their successes may produce breakthroughs that benefit the entire world while their failures may correspondingly have negative global implications. Yet they, like commercial business/financial companies, are also faced with the pressure of tight schedules, decreasing budgets, and political vagaries.

Another reason for writing this book is to fill a gap that exists in explaining how the high-level principles of EROM that others have presented (for example, COSO) can be converted into fine-tuned methods and tools. The practice of EROM in pioneering technical enterprises involves working with mostly qualitative data in a realm that is characterized by high uncertainties. The rigorous part of EROM in such an environment is in the strength of the arguments that are made to reach conclusions about how the enterprise should proceed. Thus, a large part of the effort concerns the derivation of the tasks and templates needed to assist in ensuring that the rationale behind the arguments is both sound and comprehensive. Fulfilling this need is one of the focuses of the book.

Government offices like the office of Management and Budget (OMB), the Government Accountability Office (GAO), and the President's Management Council (PMC) are beginning to encourage and even require the use of EROM in federal agencies, while many top-notch educational and research centers are beginning or have already begun to incorporate EROM into their strategic planning. It is hoped that this book will be of particular value in encouraging and informing these efforts.

In the words of Thomas H. Stanton, past president of the Association of Federal Enterprise Risk Management (AFERM), [quoting from the second quarter 2015 AFERM newsletter]: "Among those agencies that face serious budget cuts, those with strong risk management processes are likely to fare much better—in terms of protecting their core missions and the well-being of their constituents and employees—than those lacking the ability to identify, prioritize, and address major risks that may arise without the protections that effective ERM provides."

Before commencing, I would like to express my special thanks to Dr. Homayoon Dezfuli, Technical Fellow for System Safety and Risk Management at the NASA office of Safety and Mission Assurance, and Chris Everett, Manager of the Technology Risk Management office at Information Systems Laboratories, Inc. (ISL), with whom I collaborated in the formulation of an integrated EROM framework and in the development of the antecedent NASA report through a NASA/ISL blanket purchase agreement (BPA). Special thanks are also due to the following professionals at NASA for reviewing that work and helping to improve its content: Julie Pollitt (retired), Chet Everline, Martin Feather, Sharon Thomas, Emma Lehnhardt, Jessica Southwell (now with the Department of Labor), Prince Kalia, Harmony Myers, Anthony Mittskus, Sue Otero, Wayne Frazier, Kimberly Ennix Sandhu, and Pete Rutledge (retired and now with Quality Assurance and Risk Management Inc.).

Introduction

Enterprise risk and opportunity management (EROM), also known as enterprise risk management (ERM), concerns the means by which organizations apply risk and opportunity considerations in developing their strategic goals and objectives, in implementing them through a portfolio of programs, projects, institutional assets, and activities, and in managing them through internal controls. The overall purpose of EROM is to help reach an optimal balance between minimizing the potential for loss (risk) while maximizing the potential for gain (opportunity).

The principal focus of this book is on the development of an EROM framework and overall approach that serves the interests of organizations that are charged with pioneering the development of new technology and applying it to complex systems (henceforth referred to as "Technical Research, Integration, and Operationalizing enterprises," or TRIO enterprises). The framework is developed first for nonprofit and government organizations whose interests are specifically in achieving technical gains and performing services in the interest of the public. That framework is then extended to provide an EROM framework for commercial TRIO enterprises that develop and apply technology as a means for achieving their stakeholders' financial goals.

The book discusses the philosophical underpinnings of EROM for TRIO enterprises, the integration of EROM with existing management processes, and the nature of the activities that are performed to implement EROM within this context. It also provides concrete examples to illustrate all of these topics. The framework includes a set of core principles and examples that would be pertinent to any successful EROM approach, along with some features that are specific to TRIO enterprises.

The book also provides guidance that is intended to help federal agencies comply with the requirements of the Office of Management and Budget (OMB), expressed in their most recent updates to Circulars A-11 and A-123. The July 2016 update of Circular A-123 directs agencies of the federal government to fully integrate risk management and internal control activities into an EROM framework, proceeding incrementally according to a "maturity model approach." This book discusses organizational structures and analytical tools that are consistent with reaching that point.

Chapters 1 and 2 are intended mainly for high-level managers and their administrative staff who wish to understand the organizational aspects of EROM and the broad concepts of how it could be applied at TRIO enterprises. Chapter 1 is presented in the form of a primer on EROM, answering fundamental questions about how EROM works at a high level, how EROM is particularly relevant to pioneering technical enterprises, how it operates in tandem with existing management structures, how it facilitates interactions with external agencies, and how it can be applied both across the enterprise as a whole and within individual management units of the enterprise. Chapter 2 discusses how EROM coordinates with the major management functions within most technically oriented enterprises, how it helps to shape and corroborate the information that flows within, between, and out of these management functions, how it may be practiced in TRIO enterprises that interact with many partners, both domestic and international, and how it helps to satisfy requirements mandated by governing federal entities.

Chapters 3 and 4 are directed more toward technical managers and practitioners who wish to gain an understanding of some of the more important technical details and the fine points of implementing EROM at TRIO enterprises. Chapter 3 provides guidance on the activities that are conducted within an EROM analysis for TRIO enterprises, including advice on how risk tolerances and opportunity appetites can be established, how risk and opportunity scenarios can be formulated and categorized, how indicators of the potential importance of risks and opportunities can be identified, tracked, and evaluated, how the overall degree of achievement for each objective can be inferred from the indicators, how the potential for unknown and/or underappreciated (UU) risks can be evaluated, how risk and opportunity drivers can be derived, and how responses including risk mitigation, opportunity exploitation, and internal controls can be identified and evaluated. Chapter 4 provides helpful templates for conducting EROM within TRIO enterprises, and using a real example derived from the NASA James Webb Space Telescope (JWST) project, shows how the templates may be populated and exploited for purposes of evaluating overall performance and planning strategy.

Chapter 5 focuses on how EROM may be applied within major technical units of a TRIO enterprise (i.e., technical centers or technical directorates). Sections 5.1 and 5.2 speak about the managerial aspects of EROM at the center or directorate level, emphasizing the various roles that each center or directorate plays in executing its programmatic and institutional responsibilities, the nature of the strategic objectives that require technical centers and directorates to manage multiple partnerships, the ways in which a center or directorate can use an EROM approach to facilitate its management responsibilities, and the organizational aspects of EROM that permit effective communication between a technical center or directorate and its various partnering organizations. Section 5.3 discusses the technical activities that may be conducted within an EROM analysis for technical centers and directorates, emphasizing the types of risks and opportunities and associated indicators that pertain to its core competencies and the development, allocation, and retirement of its resources and assets. Section 5.3 also provides additional templates, which, together with those in Chapter 4, can be of significant use for planning the strategies and evaluating the overall performance of technical centers and directorates.

Chapter 6 augments the approaches discussed in the preceding chapters to establish a framework for commercial TRIO enterprises, where the primary objectives are the optimization of financial gains for its stakeholders over short-term, mid-term, and long-term time frames. One of the primary intents of Chapter 6 is to incorporate the qualitative aspects of EROM developed in earlier chapters with the quantitative aspects of financial planning and accounting. For this purpose, the treatment of risks and opportunities in the financial model is informed by the risk and opportunity scenarios developed in the templates of Chapters 4 and 5, and the key variables in the financial model are informed by the leading indicators and risk/opportunity drivers identified through the use of the templates. The process is illustrated using, as an example, a fictional prime contractor that manufactures products and develops systems for the aerospace and defense markets. The example focuses on developing risk and opportunity scenario taxonomies and event sequence diagrams that depict the choices that the company has to make and the risks and opportunities that each choice entails with respect to its financial goals. Financially oriented risk and opportunity matrices are introduced to facilitate the decision-making process and the derivation of internal controls.

Chapter 7 deals with the application of EROM results to assist top management in making risk acceptance decisions at key decision points when there are competing objectives at the top level of the organization with correspondingly different levels of risk tolerance. It uses two examples, one based on the DoD Ground-based Missile Defense (GMD) program and the other based on the NASA Commercial Crew Transportation System (CCTS) program, to illustrate the processes involved.

Chapter 8 provides evaluation guidance for independent appraisers who are responsible for auditing the EROM practices and processes employed at a TRIO enterprise and for determining the viability of results obtained from the EROM analyses. The chapter presents a template containing a list of queries whose answers are designed to supply TRIO enterprise management and governing authorities with reliable information about the strength of the EROM analysis, the robustness of the internal controls relative to the principal risks, and the degree to which reasonable opportunities for progress have been availed. The guidance is intended to be of use to both government and commercial auditors and auditees.

Chapter 9 provides a brief discussion of how EROM in general and the EROM templates in particular can potentially interact with important strategic initiatives and other enterprise-wide activities currently practiced within TRIO enterprises, including technical capabilities assessment (TCA) processes, strategic annual review (SAR) processes, and portfolio performance review (PPR) processes.

Finally, Chapter 10 presents an integrated framework for deriving hierarchies of internal controls based on results from the EROM process. The approach taken here differs philosophically from the approach taken by others (e.g., COSO), where internal controls are derived separately from EROM but used as input to EROM. The fully integrated approach allows for the internal controls to be responsive to the drivers of aggregate risk and opportunity. The hierarchical formulation enables different levels of internal controls to be matched to different levels in the organizational hierarchy. The fully integrated, hierarchical approach is especially suitable for organizations whose objectives are more technical in nature than financial.

Enterprise Risk and Opportunity Management

An EROM Primer for Organizations Concerned with Technical Research, Integration, and Operations (TRIO Enterprises)

1.1 EROM SCOPE AND OBJECTIVES FOR TRIO ENTERPRISES

1.1.1 What Is EROM?

Enterprise risk and opportunity management (EROM) refers to the methods and processes used by organizations to manage risks and seize opportunities related to the achievement of their objectives. It is a means by which organizations identify and implement their strategic goals, objectives, and priorities, subject to imposed constraints, through a process of strategic planning, execution, and performance evaluation.

Quoting from a report by the Committee of Sponsoring Organizations (COSO) of the Treadway Commission (2004), "Enterprise risk management encompasses:

- "*Aligning risk appetite and strategy*—Management considers the entity's risk appetite in evaluating strategic alternatives, setting related objectives, and developing mechanisms to manage related risks.[1]
- "*Enhancing risk response decisions*—Enterprise risk management provides the rigor to identify and select among alternative risk responses—risk avoidance, reduction, sharing, and acceptance.
- "*Reducing operational surprises and losses*—Entities gain enhanced capability to identify potential events and establish responses, reducing surprises and associated costs or losses.

- *"Identifying and managing multiple and cross-enterprise risks*—Every enterprise faces a myriad of risks affecting different parts of the organization, and enterprise risk management facilitates effective response to the interrelated impacts, and integrated responses to multiple risks.
- *"Seizing opportunities*—By considering a full range of potential events, management is positioned to identify and proactively realize opportunities.
- *"Improving deployment of capital*—Obtaining robust risk information allows management to effectively assess overall capital needs and enhance capital allocation."

The overall objectives of EROM are to facilitate the successful development of the strategic plan, to promote an overall best approach for implementing the plan, and to evaluate performance with respect to the plan. The means for doing this is to seek an optimal balance between minimizing the potential for loss (risk) while maximizing the potential for gain (opportunity) with respect to the organization's overall mission. The focus on the overall mission is the reason for the "E" in "EROM." It implies an integration of risk and opportunity management over all programs, projects, initiatives, and activities in the organization's portfolio. Achievement of an *optimal* balance implies the involvement of the decision maker(s) in setting maximum tolerable levels for risk, minimum desirable levels for opportunity, and the trade-offs between them.

1.1.2 Why Is EROM Important to TRIO Enterprises?

Organizations that perform pioneering technical work must continually assess whether their strategic objectives continue to be achievable as conditions evolve, whether the balance between the risks and the opportunities has changed with time so as to require a recalibration of the strategic plan or a reassessment of how it is being implemented, and whether the funding agencies have introduced new requirements or constraints that need to be addressed.

For example, NASA, in response to new directions advocated by the executive branch of the US government, announced its intentions in 2013 to embark on new space exploration missions that necessitate a change in philosophy from strict risk minimization to a balanced combination of risk control and opportunity exploitation. This direction was enunciated in the following statements made by NASA Administrator Charles Bolden in a letter addressed to all NASA employees (Bolden 2013):

> …*throughout our history NASA's explorer spirit has led us deeper into the unknown where we continue to learn as much from our failures as our successes. One of the things that impress me most*

*about our workforce is the willingness of so many to dream big, think outside the box, and take risks.... We have to be willing to do daring things. Put another way, **risk intolerance is a guarantee of failure to accomplish anything of significance** [emphasis is the Administrator's].*

...As long as we ensure that our people are protected we can manage and tolerate failures as part of the price of progress.... As we prepare to undertake the many challenges offered in the President's 2014 budget for our agency, I ask you to continue to think about how we can identify and seize opportunities to make progress quickly and affordably, identify and manage risks, learn fast and adapt our plans to take the next steps. While we do this, we must constantly balance our risks and rewards and always, always put the lives and safety of our people first.

This change in philosophy has infused not only NASA but also other TRIO enterprises. Because of it, there is a need to expand our thinking regarding enterprise risk management from one that is centered on reducing risks to one that includes recognizing, cultivating, and exploiting opportunities. EROM is a rational, structured approach toward reaching an optimal balance between minimizing the potential for loss (risk) while maximizing the potential for gain (opportunity).

Finally, EROM is important to government technical organizations because the July 2016 update of OMB Circular A-123 specifically requires that all federal agencies use enterprise risk management as an integral part of deriving, implementing, and managing internal controls.

1.1.3　What Kinds of Risk and Opportunity Are Considered within EROM for TRIO Enterprises?

EROM in general is concerned with the enterprise-wide management of strategic and performance risks, which for purposes of this book are characterized as follows:

- Strategic risk refers to shortfalls in the ability of an organization to adequately achieve the long-term goals of its stated mission. In part, strategic risk may be equated with the potential for an organization to fail in accomplishing one or more of its strategic objectives. Inferentially, it additionally includes the potential for an organization to fail to formulate its strategic objectives in a manner that best serves its overall mission.
- Performance risk refers to shortfalls in the ability of an organization to achieve its shorter-term performance plan. Performance risk in part concerns the potential for an organization to fail to accomplish one or

more of the performance objectives in its performance plan. It additionally includes the potential for an organization to fail to formulate its performance objectives in a manner that best serves its strategic objectives.

Strategic and performance risks are considered to consist of the enterprise-wide aggregation of several categories of risk, including (for purposes of this book) program/project risks, institutional risks, requirement risks, and reputational risks. These risk categories may be defined as follows (COSO 2004; International Standards 2008; NASA 2008, 2016a):

- Program/project risk is the potential for performance shortfalls, which may be realized in the future, with respect to achieving explicitly established and stated program/project performance requirements. Performance shortfalls for programs/projects may be related to any or all of the following mission execution domains: safety, technical, cost, and schedule.
- Institutional risk concerns risks to infrastructure, information technology, resources, personnel, assets, processes, occupational safety, environmental management, or security. They affect capabilities and resources necessary for mission success, including institutional flexibility to respond to changing mission needs and compliance with external requirements such as government regulations.
- Requirement risk is the risk of not satisfying the requirements of the organization's stakeholders and regulators. Requirements to be satisfied may include environmental safety and health (ES&H) protection, protection against fraud and misconduct, equal opportunity and other labor requirements, and in the case of federal agencies, federal mandates directed at achieving specific goals in the areas of public education, international cooperation, and commercial partnerships.
- Reputational risk concerns risks that could jeopardize the viability of the organization, and includes risks to financial health, legal risks, and public confidence risks. The latter category includes the risk of a catastrophic accident or other high-profile loss attributable to mismanagement or malfeasance.

1.1.4 How Does EROM for Nonprofit and Government TRIO Enterprises Differ from EROM for Typical Commercial Enterprises?

The last 10 to 15 years has seen a steadily expanding development of processes and standards for conducting EROM within commercial enterprises, for example, COSO (2004) and ISO-31000 (2008). While these frameworks have undoubtedly provided impetus for the acceptance and practice of EROM, they have tended to emphasize monetary risks and opportunities as would be paramount for profit-making companies. EROM to this point has been used less widely for nonprofit or government TRIO enterprises. For EROM to be effective at such enterprises, it must focus on the more qualitative, multidimensional objectives and constraints that noncommercial TRIO enterprises are required to satisfy, including:

- Achievement of scientific and technical gains in the public interest, over both short-term and long-term horizons
- Exploration of new frontiers and knowledge development
- Partnerships with other nations, commercial enterprises, and academia
- Public education and outreach
- Objectives common to both commercial and nonprofit enterprises, including institutional development and maintenance, legal and reputational protection, and financial health
- Specific annual outcomes mandated by funding entities (e.g., in the case of federal agencies, Congress, and the White House)
- Outcomes specified by oversight bodies such as independent advisory groups and inspectors general
- Satisfaction of government requirements and policies such as, for federal agencies, those prescribed within GPRAMA (2011), OMB Circular A-11 (OMB 2016a), and OMB Circular A-123 (OMB 2004, 2016b), among others[2]

In addition, these objectives must be met within financial, schedule, and political constraints that are subject to periodical change due to changing administrations and changing public priorities.

Thus, the EROM framework for TRIO enterprises may utilize ideas from COSO, ISO-31000, and standardized quality management systems where applicable, but also must include the capability of addressing strategic objectives that are fundamental to the mission of the organization and should build on its culture and history of performance management and risk management. Furthermore, it should adhere to the basic principles in its directives, requirements, and standards. These documents typically address roles and responsibilities pertaining to risk management and the functions to be addressed by risk-informed decision making (RIDM) and continuous risk management (CRM).

1.1.5   To What Extent Does EROM Work within the Existing Management Structure of a TRIO Enterprise?

For any well-established organization, the EROM approach is framed and structured to synchronize with and facilitate the philosophy and management processes that already exist within that organization. EROM does not fundamentally alter the existing management approach for setting strategic direction, goals, architectures, requirements, and policies, establishing metrics, setting mission and budget priorities, and approving major new initiatives, although it may result in adjustments to some of the processes. Rather, it generally supports the existing approach for overseeing and approving risk plans and mitigation strategies, reviewing progress, overseeing internal controls, identifying deficiencies, and reviewing corrective actions.

Over time, TRIO enterprises evolve a set of processes for establishing enterprise-level strategic objectives and desired outcomes while developing their core institutional and technical capabilities and tailoring their programmatic initiatives to support these objectives. In facilitating these processes and helping make them more effective, the EROM framework for TRIO enterprises should support decisions made within the strategic management, mission support management, and program management functions of the organization. Simultaneously, it should support existing high-level reviews and decision forums conducted within the organization, such as meetings of management councils, acquisition planning and procurement meetings, and portfolio performance review meetings.[3]

The EROM process facilitates management activities by providing some of the key data and insights needed to make informed decisions. These processes are guided by information obtained from both external and internal sources. The needed information includes knowledge and understanding of the constraints that are imposed by government and other sources, as well as recognition of the problems that occur during the execution of the strategic plan, the opportunities that present themselves, the risks from potential adverse events that have not yet occurred, and the leading indicators that portend emerging problems, opportunities, and risks.[4]

1.1.6   How Does EROM Facilitate Negotiations between a TRIO Enterprise and the Entities That Provide Funding and Governance?

Although strategic planning is performed within the enterprise that is responsible for executing the strategic plan, external stakeholders often mandate many of the strategic objectives that the executing enterprise must achieve. EROM has a role to play in informing external stakeholders and funding entities about the achievability of various strategic objective alternatives so that these stakeholders can make informed decisions about which objectives to mandate. EROM does this by determining the overall risk of not being able to meet each strategic objective, taking into account all the individual risks and opportunities that accompany the objective. While stakeholders like Congress, the White House, and nongovernment funding entities may have different views from the TRIO enterprise about what constitutes gain and what level of opportunity is significant, a majority can agree on whether the risk of not being able to achieve an objective is intolerably high so long as the case is laid out plainly and accurately. The justification of the case is the role that EROM plays. When a TRIO enterprise determines through EROM analysis that the aggregate risk of not being able to achieve an objective is steep and there are few opportunities for reducing it, it makes these findings known to all stakeholders to help discourage them from mandating unachievable objectives and from having unrealistic expectations.

1.1.7 Can Various Management Units within the Organization Separately Apply EROM as Though Each Were an Enterprise?

Although EROM is intended to apply to an autonomous, self-contained enterprise such as an agency, an institution, or a company, it can also be applied separately to management units within an enterprise so long as the objectives of each management unit are consistent with the objectives of the enterprise as a whole, and the cross-cutting risks and opportunities are handled consistently. For example, a typical TRIO enterprise management structure may consist of its administration and supporting offices providing its executive management, a set of program directorates providing its programmatic management, and a set of technical centers and facilities providing its institutional and technical management as well as program/project support. Each of the program directorates, technical centers, and facilities has its own top objectives and lower-level performance objectives, each with its own set of risks, opportunities, and associated indicators. Therefore, the EROM framework can be applied to each unit separately. However, the EROM processes applied for management units will not be successful unless there are both formal and informal communication channels to ensure that the top objectives of each program directorate, technical center, and facility support the strategic objectives developed at the executive level, and that the technical performance objectives of the technical centers and facilities support the program/project performance objectives of the program directorates. Such communication channels must also ensure that risks, opportunities, and associated indicators that cut across management units are identified and accounted for by all affected parties in a consistent manner.[5]

1.1.8   In What Areas Does EROM Facilitate Strategic Planning, Implementation, and Evaluation of Performance for TRIO Enterprises?

Following are examples of the planning, implementation, and evaluation processes that benefit from an EROM approach:[6]

- Developing the organization's strategic plans and performance management plans by selecting options that maximize the likelihood of successfully advancing the organization's fundamental mission. In the case of federal agencies, EROM provides traceable and documented evidence for justifying the selections of objectives in a manner that is consistent with the constraints placed by the government.
- Developing a portfolio of programs, projects, research initiatives, institutional assets, and other activities and resources by selecting alternatives that maximize the likelihood of successful achieving the strategic objectives. EROM uses a risk- and opportunity-informed decision making process to help the decision makers within the enterprise select the most viable portfolio.
- Promoting creative technologies and new processes and/or leveraging legacy systems for advancing the organization's mission in a manner that promotes a more optimal trade-off between risk and opportunity while working within the reality of a limited and sometimes shrinking budget.
- Allocating the organization's budgets, facilities, infrastructure, and human resources in a manner that promotes a more optimal balance between the probability of success and the cost of implementation. In concert with the organization's ongoing technology capabilities assessment processes, EROM identifies enterprise-level risks and opportunities that pertain to staffing requirements, the qualifications of the staff, test facility requirements, information technology needs, and other program/project support needs, thereby providing focus for institutional and mission support functions and initiatives.
- Tracking and controlling risks, opportunities, and leading indicators so as to facilitate evaluation of performance relative to the strategic and performance management plans. EROM provides traceable and documented evidence of how well the programs, projects, and other portfolio items are being implemented and the degree to which that implementation is satisfying the strategic and nearer-term objectives.
- Updating and amending the strategic and performance management plans at selected (usually different) intervals to reflect status changes and the emergence of new risks and opportunities.

■ Complying with federal and other regulations on risk and internal controls, and in the case of federal agencies, producing the Statement of Assurance required by the Federal Managers Financial Integrity Act (FMFIA). For federal agencies, EROM also supports the requirements and guidelines contained in the GPRA Modernization Act (GPRAMA) and in OMB Circulars A-11 and A-123.

■ Informing portfolio performance reviews (PPRs) and strategic assessment reviews (SARs).[7] EROM interacts with PPRs and SARs by helping to identify risk and opportunity indicators that each program needs to track and internal controls that each program needs to manage; by informing these reviews about how the indicators and controls cross programmatic boundaries; by helping to provide a logical basis for self-assessing performance relative to the strategic plan; and by helping to generate results that are required by external entities, including self-assessment results and rankings.

■ Enabling an agile response to pervasive new conditions, either positive or negative, that require immediate action. By treating risks and opportunities that cut across programs, projects, entities, and organizational units in a consistent and integrated fashion, EROM helps ensure that the means are in place to develop timely responses to newly developing cross-cutting issues that require an integrated response.

■ Facilitating risk acceptance decisions at key decision points. Results obtained from EROM include an aggregation of risk and opportunity information from lower to higher levels, allowing decision makers to obtain insight into the overall level of concern or confidence attributable to the organization's chances of satisfying each of its top objectives.

The benefits that derive from using an EROM approach are particularly significant for complex missions that involve difficult choices between alternative pathways.

1.2   EROM DEFINITIONS AND TECHNICAL ATTRIBUTES FOR TRIO ENTERPRISES

1.2.1   What Is Meant by *Risk* and *Opportunity* within the Context of EROM?

Within the context of EROM, we define *risk* and *opportunity* as follows:

■ *Risk* is the possibility of future performance shortfalls with respect to achieving explicitly established and stated objectives at all organizational levels, including the organization's strategic objectives.

- *Opportunity* is the possibility of future performance improvements with respect to achieving the explicitly established objectives and accomplishing the mission of the organization.

Risks and opportunities are always possible occurrences that may take place in the future. Once a risk is realized, it becomes a problem and is no longer a risk. Once an opportunity is realized, it becomes a gain and is no longer an opportunity.

Although the realization of a risk is viewed as negative and the realization of an opportunity is viewed as positive, risk and opportunity are two sides of the same coin. We speak of "the risk of missing an opportunity" to emphasize that missing an opportunity is a form of risk. In the same way, we speak of "the opportunity of mitigating a risk" to emphasize the fact that mitigating a risk is a form of seizing an opportunity. Both risk and opportunity require an action to achieve the best possible outcome (i.e., mitigate a risk or seize an opportunity). The actions must occur within an acceptable time frame to be effective.

That said, the fundamental difference between a risk and an opportunity is that the action is intrinsic to the definition of an opportunity but extrinsic to the definition of a risk. The potential negative outcomes that are the basis for identifying a risk exist as concerns prior to any intervention, whereas the potential benefits of an opportunity that are the basis for identifying a circumstance as an opportunity only exist in the context of some action(s) that could be taken to realize those benefits.

In the present context, opportunity has two dimensions. The first applies to the potential to reduce the risk of not meeting one or more already-stated strategic goals or desired outcomes. For example, an emerging opportunity for an organization that has begun execution on a project to share a research and development task with a partner organization that has specialized expertise in that area might result in a reduction of the risk of the originating organization failing in that task. The event that leads to the possibility of a partnership (e.g., the partnering organization expressing a willingness to participate) is an opportunity because it offers the promise of leading to a positive outcome. (In contrast, a risk leads to the possibility of a negative, or unwanted, outcome.)

The second dimension applies to an opening for changing strategic objectives or desired outcomes to align them better with the TRIO enterprise's vision and mission. For example, the emergence of a new technology might open up possibilities for the originating organization to achieve strategic benefits that were not previously considered possible. The latter type of opportunity pertains to promoting accomplishment of the TRIO enterprise's mission through strategic re-planning, rather than reducing the risk of not meeting its existing strategic objectives.[8]

Risks and opportunities may both have a time frame associated with them, a *window of opportunity*, after which response to the risk or seizure of the opportunity is no longer possible. This is one reason that an enterprise must be agile.

Significant gains in advancement or progress may involve proactively searching for opportunities, such as putting resources into basic or applied research, with the expectation that on the whole these efforts will bear fruit and speed the rate of progress toward long-term goals. In the words of Francis Bacon (1612): "A wise man will make more opportunities than he finds."

1.2.2   How Do We Differentiate between Risks and Opportunities during Strategic Planning versus during Plan Implementation and Performance Evaluation?

EROM is concerned with enterprise-wide risks and opportunities during strategic planning, during development of the TRIO enterprise's portfolio of programs, projects, initiatives, and other activities, and during evaluation of performance. Strategic planning often occurs when the functions to be performed have been conceived but the specifics of the system design, and even the system architecture, have not yet been decided on. In that case, the identification of risks and opportunities derives from historical experience, tempered with expert judgment, gained from missions that have preceded the present one but are in some ways similar to it. For example, in the case of space exploration, the identification of risks for a low-earth-orbit mission using some future, as-yet undefined system may, for preliminary purposes, be considered to be informed by the risks that were identified for the space shuttle. These are risks that may or may not remain applicable as the system design matures, but that the organization needs to be aware of in making strategic decisions.

Obviously, the state of definition of risks and opportunities for future missions without a specific system design will be less mature than for missions that have well-defined system designs. Correspondingly, the state of risk and opportunity definition during strategic planning will generally be less mature than during implementation and performance evaluation.

1.2.3   How Does EROM Help Achieve an Optimal Balance between Risk and Opportunity?

The concept of balancing risk against opportunity is illustrated schematically in Figure 1.1. As shown in the figure, the balance is a reflection of the decision maker's sense of the risk relative to his/her sense of the opportunity. In this context, *sense of the risk* is equivalent to one's tolerance for

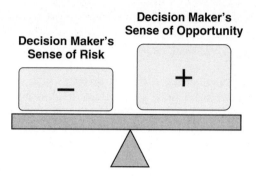

FIGURE 1.1 Decision making is a balance between risk and opportunity

the risk as presently perceived, and *sense of the opportunity* is equivalent to one's appetite for the opportunity as currently perceived. Factors such as the availability of resources or assets, together with other fixed constraints, enter into the decision maker's sense of risk or opportunity.

The balance between tolerating risks and seizing opportunities is informed by guidance provided at the executive level, such as the NASA Administrator's comments cited in Section 1.1.2, which imply that the organization must manage risks and opportunities in a graded manner across its portfolio of activities. As shown in Figure 1.2, most organizations have stricter standards (low tolerance for risk) relative to preserving their core capabilities and human lives and safety, while at the same time having more lenient standards (tolerating higher risk) relative to accepting the possibility of losing hardware in the pursuit of pioneering or capability-expanding activities that create new opportunities to more effectively advance the

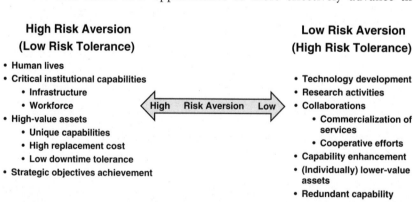

FIGURE 1.2 Risk tolerance relative to diverse goals and objectives

organization's mission. This considered grading of risk tolerance during strategic planning and during execution of the plan sets the ground rules for *strategic risk taking* that is essential for progress and success over the long term. It creates areas where the organization learns rapidly, in part through acceptable setbacks, as well as promoting areas where the gains made through high-risk activities are consolidated and institutionalized into a more capable organization.[9]

There is a well-known tendency for such balances to be made based on psychological factors that are not always in the interest of making the optimum decision. A variety of treatises on risk aversion point out that when people are confronted with two choices where the balance between opportunity for success and risk of loss is neutral or even moderately favorable to the opportunity, they will tend to choose the path with lower risk. This aversion is related to the so-called Ellsberg paradox (Ellsberg 1961), which concerns people's choice between situations that exhibit different levels of certainty (they have *ambiguity aversion*). Use of EROM in a structured approach helps to counter risk aversion and ambiguity aversion by ensuring that strategic decisions are made more objectively.

The decision to pursue an opportunity in one area invariably involves exposure to risk in another area. For example, a major revision to a design may provide an opportunity to increase technical performance but simultaneously introduce risks to cost and schedule. EROM provides an objective means for determining the break even point between the opportunity and the risk. It does this by examining the degree to which the opportunity meets or exceeds the decision maker's minimum expectation for an opportunity to be worthwhile, and comparing it to the degree to which the concomitant risk meets or exceeds the decision maker's tolerance for risk. In other words, EROM makes an objective assessment of the likelihood and magnitude of benefit and the likelihood and magnitude of loss relative to each of the agency's strategic objectives, and the decision maker's stated risk tolerance and opportunity appetite determine whether the former justifies the latter.

Ultimately, the decision maker has the responsibility to define risk tolerance levels rather than simply accept a risk-averse stance.

1.2.4   What Is Meant by the Terms *Risk Scenario, Opportunity Scenario, Cumulative Risk,* and *Cumulative Opportunity?*

The EROM process identifies specific concerns that are perceived as presenting a risk to the ability to achieve one or more strategic objectives. Each concern implies a scenario of events that must happen in order for the risk to come true. Collectively, these individual scenarios comprise the cumulative, or aggregate, risk of not being able to achieve the objective.

It is common practice to use the term *risk* to denote both the individual concern, or scenario, and the cumulative likelihood of not meeting the objective. The differentiation between the two is provided by the context, but sometimes, this dual usage leads to confusion when the context is not clear. In such cases, we refer to the specific concerns as being *risk scenarios* and the effect on the strategic objective as being *cumulative risk* or *aggregate risk*. For example, the possibility of staffing shortages in a crucial technical area due to higher-than-expected retirements is a risk scenario, and the likelihood of not being able to complete the projects that are critical to a strategic objective or goal as a result of this and other risk scenarios is a cumulative risk.

Likewise, the EROM process identifies specific scenarios that, if they should occur, would lead to an opportunity to either increase the likelihood of achieving a strategic objective or open the possibility of defining a new objective that coincides with the TRIO enterprise's mission. Therefore, we sometimes use the term *opportunity scenario* to differentiate the individual context for opportunity from the cumulative context. For example, the possibility of a breakthrough in the development of a new technology, opening the possibility of taking a positive action to reap the benefit, is an opportunity scenario. The prospect of translating that development, along with other opportunistic developments and directed actions, into higher performance for strategically critical programs and projects is a cumulative opportunity.[10]

1.2.5 How Does EROM Incorporate Risk-Informed Decision Making and Continuous Risk Management within the Organization as a Whole and within Different Management Units?

EROM is operationalized within a TRIO enterprise through the introduction of risk- and opportunity-informed decision making and continuous risk and opportunity management into the organization's management processes. In both the program/project domain and the institutional/technical domain, they are denoted as risk-informed decision making (RIDM) and continuous risk management (CRM). The RIDM and CRM processes are documented, for example, in NASA (2011) and Alberts et al. (1996), and as shown in Figure 1.3, they are executed at each of the management levels of the organization.

For the TRIO enterprise as a whole, risk- and opportunity-informed decision making is applicable to strategic planning activities and the selection of the organization's portfolio of programs, projects, and other initiatives. It is similar to its counterpart for programs/projects, RIDM,

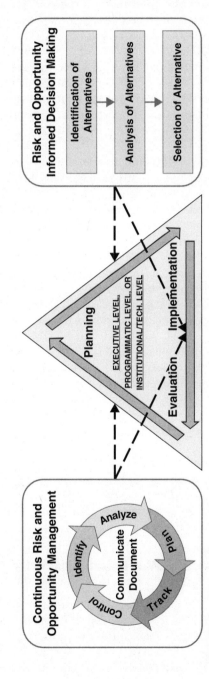

FIGURE 1.3 The elements of RIDM and CRM applied to the TRIO enterprise's management activities at various levels

but it is expanded to make opportunity a more major component of the decision-making process. It is used first to help executive management select from among various alternative sets of long-term strategic objectives and nearer-term programmatic objectives in formulating a strategic plan, subject to external constraints, that supports the mission of the TRIO enterprise. It is then used to help executive management select from among various alternative portfolios of programs, projects, institutional initiatives, and other major initiatives to support the achievement of the strategic objectives. Like the RIDM process that it is derived from, it is composed of the following three steps: (1) identification of alternatives, (2) analysis of alternatives, and (3) the selection of an alternative.

Continuous risk and opportunity management, for the TRIO enterprise as a whole, is applicable to implementation of the portfolio approved at the executive level and to evaluation of the organization's performance relative to the strategic objectives. The process of managing risks and opportunities on a continuing basis is similar to the CRM process exercised for programs/projects, except again for the expansion to make opportunity a more major component in the management process. Like its CRM counterpart, it consists of the following five basic actions: (1) identify, (2) analyze, (3) plan, (4) track, and (5) control. This five-step process is supported by robust communication and documentation.

In incorporating RIDM and CRM into EROM for different management units, the areas of emphasis tend to differ according to the responsibilities assigned to each unit. At the executive level, emphasis is on strategic objectives and meeting the overall goals of the TRIO enterprise. For management units within the programmatic level (e.g., program directorates), the emphasis shifts to programmatic objectives and meeting project milestones within established schedules and costs. For management units within the institutional/technical level (e.g., technical centers), there is an increased emphasis on the development and maintenance of the workforce, facilities, and support systems. While the areas of emphasis may differ, however, the general approach for incorporating RIDM and CRM into EROM is basically the same whether applied at the executive level, the programmatic level, or the institutional/technical level.

1.2.6   Is the Analysis in EROM Principally Qualitative or Quantitative?

EROM uses a mixture of qualitative and quantitative methods. On the one hand, quantitative models are used for assessing and predicting specific outcomes that are amenable to quantitative analysis (e.g., matters of budget and schedule). On the other hand, there is a greater reliance on qualitative methods for EROM than there is for program/project risk management.

That is because EROM involves assessments of strategic goals and objectives that are largely subjective in their interpretation and for which there are no easily formed quantitative models (e.g., increase human knowledge; promote the development of groundbreaking new technology; etc.). To assess the status or potential for achieving such goals and objectives, EROM relies on risk and opportunity leading indicators,[11] which serve as surrogates for the identified risks and opportunities. Although the leading indicators are in themselves quantifiable, their relationship to the actual risks and opportunities is qualitative, and hence the EROM analysis itself is more qualitative than quantitative.

1.2.7 Can EROM Account for Unknown and Underappreciated (UU) Risks?

Unknown and underappreciated (UU) risks are risk scenarios that either have not been identified and are therefore unknown at the time of analysis, or have been correctly identified but for which the likelihood of occurrence and/or potential severity of harm or loss are underestimated. By definition, it is not possible to identify unknown scenarios before they are revealed, or to be aware that a known scenario is underappreciated before it has occurred. It is possible, however, to be aware of various types of indicators that can be correlated with the likelihood of unknown and underappreciated risks, based on experiences that have been reported in the literature. These indicators tend to be associated with organizational shortcomings, questionable managerial practices, and certain design approaches. As will be discussed shortly, EROM analyses are able to include these indicators in the assessment of whether UU risks are likely to be a large contributor to the overall risk of not achieving the organization's objectives.

Recent work reported in NASA (2015) and Benjamin et al. (2015) has demonstrated that for complex systems, the probability of loss from UU risks early in a program/project or during the initial stages of operation can be several times greater than the probability of loss from known risks, not only for space systems but also for other systems such as commercial nuclear and military. The presence of UU risks can therefore significantly affect the ability of an organization to achieve its strategic objectives.

In addition, sizable UU risks extend not only to safety concerns but also to concerns related to technical performance, cost, and schedule (NASA 2015; Benjamin et al. 2015). An understanding of the potential magnitude of UU risks in each area of concern, and the factors that are causing them to be of concern, is important for at least the following two reasons:

1. It helps inform external stakeholders about the achievability of various strategic objectives and portfolio alternatives so that these stakeholders can make informed decisions about how to allocate funding.

2. It helps identify ways for mitigating the design-related, organizational and programmatic causes of UU risks, thereby increasing the potential for achieving the agreed-upon strategic objectives.

It has *not* been common practice for UU risks to be considered as a part of an EROM analysis, but the approach described in this book goes beyond present practice by considering the organizational, programmatic, and design factors that can lead to UU risks. These factors, obtained largely from NASA (2015) and Benjamin et al. (2015), are treated as leading indicators of UU risk, and are included in the roll-up of leading indicators that is performed to estimate the aggregate risk of not being able to meet each strategic objective. The treatment of UU risks is itself qualitative, in keeping with the overall qualitative nature of EROM. The potential effects of UU risks are included both in the strategic planning, RIDM-based aspect of EROM, and in the performance evaluation, CRM-based aspect of EROM.[12]

NOTES

1. In the COSO reports, the term *risk appetite* has the same meaning as the term *risk tolerance* in this book. Contrarily, the term *risk tolerance* in the COSO reports has a different meaning, more akin to the use of the term *performance margin* in this book. The term *opportunity appetite* is not used in the COSO report, but is used in this book to convey the positive connotation of opportunity versus the negative connotation of risk (i.e., one has an appetite for opportunity versus a tolerance for risk).
2. A discussion of some of the principal requirements and policies contained in these documents will be provided in Section 2.5.
3. These roles of EROM will be discussed further in Section 2.3 and Chapter 9.
4. Leading indicators are traceable measures that are quantifiable, can be correlated with the likelihood of success of one or more of the TRIO enterprise's objectives, and are actionable. Leading indicators will be discussed in more detail in Sections 3.4, 3.5, 4.4, 4.5, and 5.3.
5. Communication channels and protocols for EROM will be discussed in Sections 2.4, 4.8, and 5.2.
6. Further elaboration on these points will be provided throughout the report.
7. In some organizations, strategic assessment reviews are referred to as *strategic objectives assessment reviews,* or SOARs, and portfolio performance reviews (PPRs) are referred to as *baseline performance reviews,* or BPRs.
8. In Webster's online dictionary, *opportunity* is defined as: (1) a favorable juncture of circumstances, and (2) a good chance for advancement or progress. Although not strictly parallel, the two-dimensional definition in this book can roughly be considered to be an application of Webster's definitions, in that an opportunity to reduce risk emanates from "a favorable juncture of circumstances" and an opportunity to expand the strategic objectives constitutes "a good chance for advancement or progress."

9. The subjects of risk tolerance, opportunity appetite, and the break even point between them will be discussed further in Sections 3.3, 4.5, 7.2, and 7.3.
10. The concept of cumulative risks and cumulative opportunities will be discussed in considerably more detail in Sections 3.5 and 4.6.
11. We use the term *risk leading indicator* in the same sense that COSO uses the term *risk indicator*. Both terms refer to a possible future development that is indicated by a present condition that is evolving with time. We include the word *leading* to emphasize that these indicators may be changing with time, and that one needs to track not only their present values but also their trends to infer potential future values.
12. The treatment of UU risks within the EROM framework will be discussed further in Sections 3.4.5 and 4.6.5.

REFERENCES

Alberts, C. J., et al. January 1996. *Continuous Risk Management Guidebook*. New York: Software Engineering Institute, Carnegie Mellon University.

Bacon, Francis. 1612. *The Essays, or, Counsels Civil and Moral of Francis Bacon, 2nd ed. Reprinted with an Introduction by Henry Morley*. London: George Routledge and Sons, 1884.

Benjamin, A., Dezfuli, H., and Everett, C. 2015. "Developing Probabilistic Safety Performance Margins for Unknown and Underappreciated Risks," *Journal of Reliability Engineering and System Safety*. Available online from ScienceDirect.

Bolden, Charles. 2013. Internal email from NASA Administrator to all NASA employees (April 19). The text of the entire email may be found in Appendix A of NASA (2016).

Committee of Sponsoring Organizations of the Treadway Commission (COSO). 2004. *Enterprise Risk Management—Integrated Framework: Application Techniques*.

Ellsberg, Daniel. 1961. "Risk, Ambiguity, and the Savage Axioms." *Quarterly Journal of Economics* 75 (4).

International Standard ISO/FDIS 31000. 2008. *Risk Management—Principles and Guidelines*.

National Aeronautics and Space Administration (NASA). 2008. NPR 8000.4A. "Agency Risk Management Procedural Requirements" (Revalidated January 29, 2014). http://nodis3.gsfc.nasa.gov/npg_img/N_PR_8000_004A_/N_PR_8000_004A_.pdf

National Aeronautics and Space Administration (NASA). 2011. NASA/SP-2011-3422. *NASA Risk Management Handbook*. Washington, DC: National Aeronautics and Space Administration. http://www.hq.nasa.gov/office/codeq/doctree/NHBK_2011_3422.pdf

National Aeronautics and Space Administration (NASA). 2015. NASA/SP-2014-612. *NASA System Safety Handbook, Volume 2: System Safety Concepts, Guidelines, and Implementation Examples*. Washington, DC: National Aeronautics and Space Administration. http://www.hq.nasa.gov/office/codeq/doctree/NASASP2014612.pdf

National Aeronautics and Space Administration (NASA). 2016a. (In Publication). SP-2014-615. "Organizational Risk and Opportunity Management: Concepts and Processes for NASA Consideration" (June).

Office of Management and Budget (OMB). 2004. OMB Circular A-123. "Management's Responsibility for Internal Control." https://www.whitehouse.gov/omb/circulars_a123_rev

Office of Management and Budget (OMB). 2016a. OMB Circular A-11. "Preparation, Submission, and Execution of the Budget." (July). https://www.whitehouse.gov/sites/default/files/omb/assets/a11_current_year/a11_2014.pdf

Office of Management and Budget (OMB). 2016b. OMB Circular A-123. "Management's Responsibility for Enterprise Risk Management and Internal Control." (July). https://www.whitehouse.gov/sites/default/files/omb/memoranda/2016/m-16-17.pdf

Public Law 11-352. 2011. "GPRA (Government Performance and Results Act) Modernization Act of 2010."

CHAPTER 2

Coordination of EROM with Organizational Management Activities

Although the need for EROM in TRIO enterprises may be driven by a need to provide innovative technical solutions to complex problems, it is also desirable, and often necessary, to implement EROM within the current management framework of the organization. This chapter describes the high-level structure of most TRIO enterprises, the interfaces between the principal entities of these enterprises in the areas of strategic planning, implementation, and evaluation, and the manner in which EROM activities interface with these traditional management activities.

2.1   THE EXECUTIVE, PROGRAMMATIC, AND INSTITUTIONAL/TECHNICAL MANAGEMENT FUNCTIONS AND THEIR INTERFACES

While the detailed organizational and management structure of individual organizations differs, most TRIO enterprises share common top-level organizational entities, management processes, and activities. Generally, as illustrated in Figure 2.1, a TRIO enterprise may be described as comprising three management organizational levels: (1) an executive level that sets and manages the direction and strategy for the enterprise; (2) a programmatic level that develops and manages the programs and projects that support the strategic plan; and (3) an institutional/technical level that develops and manages the institutional and technical resources that support the programs and projects. Decision making involves robust communication within and among all levels.

Each of these organizational levels performs a similar set of management activities, as shown in Figure 2.2. These activities include planning, plan implementation, and performance evaluation. At the executive level, management sets the overall strategic objectives, goals, and desired outcomes for the enterprise; develops a plan for implementation, including the

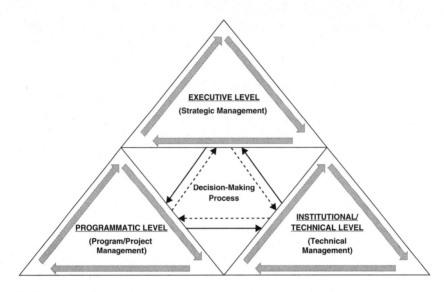

FIGURE 2.1   The three levels of management within a typical enterprise

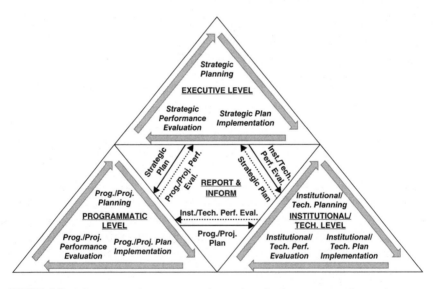

FIGURE 2.2   The principal activities and transfer of information within and between levels of management

definition of major programs and projects and specification of institutional support requirements; evaluates performance in terms of the degree to which its strategic objectives are being realized; and makes major course correction or course resetting decisions when conditions warrant. At the programmatic level, program/project management provides the same goal setting and execution oversight with respect to the programs and projects that the executive level initiates. At the institutional/technical level, technical management does the same for the institutional and technical capabilities of the enterprise, including the sufficiency of the workforce, availability of facilities, and integrity of procurement and quality control practices. The transfer of information between the organizational levels is bidirectional, with the results of the planning activities being communicated in general from executive to programmatic to institutional/technical level, and the results of the evaluation activities being communicated in general from institutional/technical to programmatic to executive level (although the direction of communication may vary according to the nature of the organization).

2.2 EROM-RELEVANT MANAGEMENT ACTIVITIES

2.2.1 Activities within Each Management Level

At the executive level, the processes of strategic planning, strategic plan implementation, and strategic performance evaluation are guided by information obtained from both external and internal sources, as shown in Figure 2.3. The information to be gleaned from external sources includes:

- Mission priorities, programs/projects, schedules, and budgets that are mandated by external stakeholders and funding authorities, such as Congress and the US president in the case of federal agencies
- Supply constraints such as the availability of suppliers, parts, and materials
- Marketplace constraints such as inflation rates and competition from other entities, both domestic and foreign
- Political constraints, such as the prospects for changes in the federal administration, the makeup of Congress, restrictions on certain foreign entities, or the leadership of nongovernment funding agencies
- Legal constraints, such as new enactments with new requirements or threats of litigation
- The emergence of new technology that may open opportunities for undertaking new objectives or achieving faster progress toward current objectives, or conversely pose new threats (e.g., cyber-security)

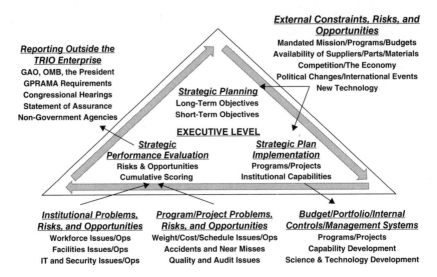

FIGURE 2.3 Activities within the executive level and transfer of information from/to external and internal sources

In addition, information is transferred from the executive level to entities external to or independent from the TRIO enterprise management structure, such as (for federal agencies) the GAO, the OMB, inspectors general, and Congress, in the form of presentations and reports. The scope and contents of information provided to OMB has to comply with the requirements of GPRAMA as detailed in various OMB circulars.

Information to be received from internal sources (programmatic and institutional/technical levels) includes:

- The status of risks and opportunities for programs/projects, including safety concerns, technical performance concerns, cost concerns, and schedule concerns
- The status of risks and opportunities at the institutional/technical level, including workforce concerns, concerns with facilities and equipment, IT concerns, and security concerns
- Identification and evaluation of risks and opportunities that cut across programs, projects, and institutional/technical entities
- The status of concerns within the programmatic and institutional/technical levels that have evolved from risks to problems, and the status of corrective actions

Correspondingly, information is transferred from the executive level to the programmatic and institutional/technical levels via the strategic plan, and associated back-up material, including in particular the specifications for the agency's portfolio of programs, projects, institutional initiatives, research and development initiatives, resource expectations, schedules and budgets, and so on.

The activities and transfer of information at the programmatic or program directorate level parallel the activities and transfer of information at the executive level, but with the following differences as shown in Figure 2.4:

- The top objectives are programmatic and, for the most part, are received from the executive level as part of its strategic planning and plan implementation activities.
- The results from the programmatic planning, implementation, and performance evaluation activities are presented to the various governing councils within the TRIO enterprise, which may include (for example) a strategic management council, an executive council, a program management council, and/or a mission support council.
- The results from the programmatic performance evaluation also provide input to portfolio performance reviews.
- Implementation of the programmatic planning activity includes feedback to and from other program directorates, particularly regarding concerns that cut across program directorates.

FIGURE 2.4 Activities within a program directorate (programmatic level) and transfer of information from/to external and internal sources

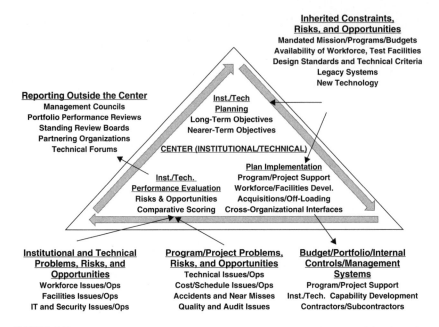

FIGURE 2.5 Activities within a technical center (institutional/technical level) and transfer of information from/to external and internal sources

By and large, the program directorates operate as enterprises, so from a practical point of view, the principles of EROM apply to them as well as to the executive level.

The same is true for the technical centers or directorates,[1] as shown in Figure 2.5. The activities and transfer of information at the center level parallel the activities at the program directorate level, except that the top objectives concern institutional and technical capability development as well as support of the programs/projects. These top objectives require the technical centers to concentrate, in their planning processes, upon how to achieve an efficacious balance between services provided directly by them versus services acquired from other entities such as commercial companies, universities, and other agencies.

2.2.2 Roles and Responsibilities within and between Each Management Level

Ensuring that managerial roles and responsibilities are clearly defined and that there are no gaps in the assignment of these roles and responsibilities is a major element of enterprise risk management and internal controls. Table 2.1 presents a representative list of roles and responsibilities at the

TABLE 2.1 Typical Executive, Program Directorate, and Technical Directorate Managerial Roles and Responsibilities (Adapted from NASA 2014a, Table D-1)

Category	Responsibility of Executive Management	Responsibility of Executive Management Staff and Advisory Groups	Responsibility of Program Directorates	Responsibility of Technical Directorates (I = Institutional Development, Strategic Support, Program/Project Support, T = Technical Authority)
Strategic Planning	Establish enterprise strategic priorities and direction. Approve enterprise strategic plan, programmatic architecture, and top-level guidance. Approve implementation plans developed by program directorates.	Lead development of enterprise strategic plan. Lead development of annual performance plan.	Support enterprise strategic planning. Develop program directorate Implementation plan and cross-directorate architecture plans consistent with enterprise strategic plan, programmatic architecture, and top-level guidance.	Support enterprise and program directorate strategic planning and supporting studies (I).
Program/Project Concept Studies		Provide technical expertise for advanced concept studies, as required.	Develop direction and guidance specific to concept studies for formulation of programs and noncompeted projects.	Develop direction and guidance specific to concept studies (I).
Development of Programmatic Requirements			Establish, coordinate, and approve high-level program requirements. Establish, coordinate, and approve high-level project requirements, including success criteria.	Provide support to program and project requirements development (I). Provide assessments of resources with regard to facilities (I).

(continued)

TABLE 2.1 (*Continued*)

Category	Responsibility of Executive Management	Responsibility of Executive Management Staff and Advisory Groups	Responsibility of Program Directorates	Responsibility of Technical Directorates (I = Institutional Development, Strategic Support, Program/Project Support, T = Technical Authority)
				Approve changes to and deviations and waivers from those requirements that are the responsibility of the technical authority and have been delegated to the technical directorate (T).
Development of Institutional Requirements	Approve enterprise-level policies and requirements for programs and projects.	Develop policies and procedural requirements for programs and projects and ensure adequate implementation. Approve/disapprove waivers and deviations to requirements under their authority.	Develop cross-cutting mission support policies and requirements for programs and projects and ensure adequate implementation. Approve/disapprove waivers and deviations to requirements under their authority.	Develop technical directorate policies and requirements for programs and projects and ensure adequate implementation (I). Develop technical authority policies and requirements for programs and projects and ensure adequate implementation (T). Approve/disapprove waivers and deviations to requirements under their authority (I, T).
Budget and Resource Management	Determine relative priorities for use of enterprise resources (e.g., facilities). Establish budget planning controls for program directorates and mission support offices.	Manage and coordinate enterprise annual budget guidance, development, and submission. Analyze program directorate submissions for consistency with program and project plans and performance.	Develop workforce and facilities plans with implementing technical directorates. Provide guidelines for program and project budget submissions consistent with approved plans.	Confirm program and project workforce requirements (I). Provide the personnel, facilities, resources, and training necessary for implementing assigned programs and projects (I). Support annual program and project budget submissions, and validate technical directorate inputs (I).

(continued)

	Develop enterprise operating plans and enterprise execute budget.		Allocate budget resources to technical directorates for assigned programs and projects. Conduct annual program and project budget submission reviews.	Provide resources for review, assessment, development, and maintenance of the core competencies required to ensure technical and program/project management excellence (T). Ensure independence of resources to support the implementation of technical authority (T).
Program/ Project Performance Assessment	Assess program and major project technical, schedule, and cost performance through status reviews. Chair enterprise performance management councils. Chair enterprise-wide baseline program performance reviews.	Conduct special studies for executive management. Provide independent performance assessments. Administer the enterprise-wide baseline program performance review process.	Assess program technical, schedule, and cost performance and take action, as appropriate, to mitigate risks. Chair program directorate performance management council. Support the enterprise-wide baseline program performance reviews.	Assess program and project technical, schedule, and cost performance against approved plans as part of ongoing processes and forums. Chair technical directorate management council (I). Provide summary status to support the enterprise-wide baseline program performance review process and other suitable forums (I).
Program Performance Issues	Assess project programmatic, technical, schedule, and cost through performance management council and enterprise-wide baseline program performance review.	Maintain issues and risk performance information. Track project cost and schedule performance. Manage project performance reporting to external stakeholders.	Communicate program and project performance issues and risks to executive management and present plan for mitigation or recovery.	Monitor the technical and programmatic progress of programs and projects to help identify issues as they emerge (I). Provide support and guidance to programs and projects in resolving technical and programmatic issues and risks (I).

TABLE 2.1 *(Continued)*

Category	Responsibility of Executive Management	Responsibility of Executive Management Staff and Advisory Groups	Responsibility of Program Directorates	Responsibility of Technical Directorates (I = Institutional Development, Strategic Support, Program/Project Support, T = Technical Authority)
				Proactively work with the program directorates, programs, projects, and other institutional authorities to find constructive solutions to problems (I). Direct corrective actions to resolve performance Issues (I).
Key Decision Points (KDPs)	Authorize program and major projects to proceed past KDPs.	Provide executive secretariat function for KDPs, including preparation of final decision memorandum.	Authorize programs and major projects to proceed past KDPs. Provide recommendation for programs and major projects at KDPs, including proposing cost and schedule commitments.	Perform supporting analysis to confirm readiness leading to KDPs for programs and all projects (I). Conduct readiness reviews leading to KDPs for all projects (I). Present technical directorate's assessment of readiness to proceed past KDPs, adequacy of planned resources, and ability of technical directorate to meet commitments (I). Engage in major replanning or rebaselining activities and processes, ensuring constructive communication and progress between the time it becomes clear that a replan is necessary and the time it is formally put in place (I).

executive, program directorate, and technical directorate levels for a typical TRIO enterprise. The entries in the table were adapted from NASA (2014a) (Table D-1), and they elaborate further on the information conveyed in Figures 2.3 through 2.5.[2]

2.3 COORDINATION OF EROM WITH MANAGEMENT ACTIVITIES

2.3.1 Organizational Planning and Plan Implementation

The manner in which EROM assists management at all three levels in developing a responsive and achievable plan is illustrated in Figure 2.6. Following is a brief summary of the activities depicted in this figure:

Management activities that provide input to the EROM process include:

- Understand and comply with external constraints such as mandated missions and programs, mandated budgets, the availability of suppliers and parts or materials, and legal realities.
- Identify alternative objectives hierarchies that comply with the external constraints and have the potential for achieving the organization's mission in all time frames.

EROM activities that provide input to the management activity of selecting among alternative objectives and preparing the organizational plan include:

- Characterize and understand all relevant historical experience pertaining to failures, successes, precursors, anomalies, unexpected benefits, and lessons learned.
- Identify risks and opportunities for each alternative set of objectives based on the historical record and expert judgment.
- From past experience and current risk/opportunity leading indicators, assess the state of risks/opportunities as they pertain to the likelihood of achieving each objective.
- Risk-inform the selection and application of internal controls.

2.3.2 Evaluation of Organizational Performance and Replanning

The evaluation of performance at the various management levels also involves close coordination between management activities and EROM activities. From an EROM perspective, the activities that support performance evaluation are similar to the activities that support organizational

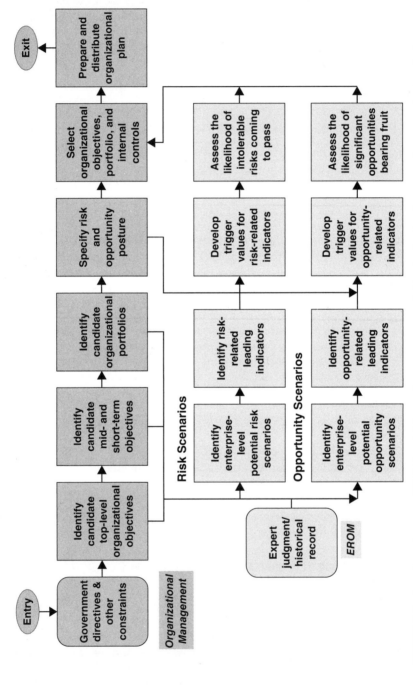

FIGURE 2.6 Interfaces between EROM activities and management activities in the development of an organizational plan

planning in the sense that both involve the identification and evaluation of risks and opportunities. As discussed in Section 1.2.2, the key difference is in the level of maturity that exists in the definition of risks and opportunities.

The manner in which EROM assists management in evaluating organizational performance is illustrated in Figure 2.7. Following is a brief summary of the activities depicted in that figure:

Management activities that provide input to the EROM process include:

- Track progress on individual programs, projects, institutional initiatives, and other activities in the portfolio with respect to meeting the mid- and short-term objectives in the organizational objectives hierarchy.
- Conduct a portfolio performance review (PPR) at periodic intervals to assess overall adherence to the performance plan and to identify and evaluate cross-cutting issues.

EROM activities that provide input to the management activity of conducting the portfolio performance review include:

- Track leading indicators that pertain to organizational risks and opportunities. (Note that executive-level risks and opportunities generally emanate from external sources such as political, economic, or regulatory changes, whereas risks and opportunities at lower management units generally emanate from internal sources such as the depletion of reserves and margins in any of the mission execution domains: safety, technical performance, schedule, and cost.)
- From the current values of the leading indicators, assess the significance of the risks and opportunities at each level in the organizational objectives hierarchy.

EROM activities that provide input to the management activity of evaluating organizational performance include:

- Identify and track internal performance measures and internal/external leading indicators of risks and opportunities that pertain to the mid- and short-term organizational objectives.
- From the current values of the performance measures and leading indicators and their observed trends, assess the state of risks and opportunities as they pertain to the likelihood of achieving the top organizational objectives.
- When risks are of concern, or when opportunities are attractive, perform an analysis to suggest options that may be pursued to mitigate risks or pursue opportunities and identify associated internal controls.

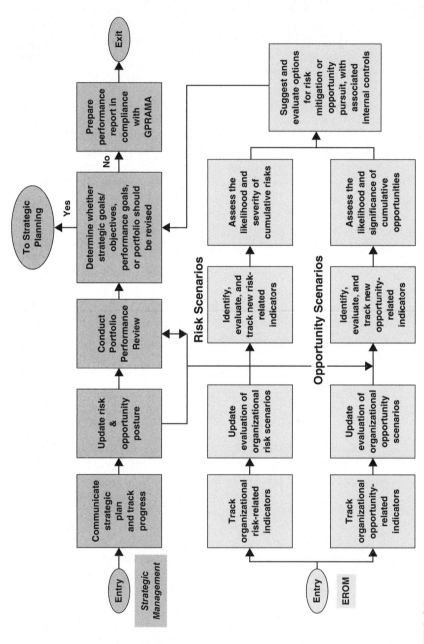

FIGURE 2.7 Interfaces between EROM activities and management activities in the evaluation of performance relative to the organizational plan

With these inputs in hand, management has a solid basis for determining whether the organization's objectives are being achieved and whether there are imposing reasons (either positive or negative) for amending or changing some of the objectives and/or portfolio elements. The organization also is in a better position to prepare performance reports and presentations of the type required by the external stakeholders and funding agencies.

2.3.3   Alignment with Management-Level Roles and Responsibilities

Table 2.2 provides a more detailed itemization of EROM activities to support the various management levels of a TRIO enterprise consistent with the roles and responsibilities listed in Table 2.1. The entries in the table elaborate further on the information conveyed in Figures 2.6 and 2.7.

2.4   COMMUNICATION ACROSS EXTENDED PARTNERSHIPS

2.4.1   Nature of the Strategic Objectives That Require Extended Partnerships

Large not-for-profit and government TRIO organizations tend to have a diversity of strategic objectives that go beyond technical and scientific accomplishments related to the prime mission to geopolitical, macroeconomic, and societal objectives that require extensive collaboration. Following, for example, are several strategic objectives (S.O.s) from NASA's strategic plan that fall into this category (emphasis added to highlight the point):

[S.O. 1.1] Expand human presence into the solar system and to the surface of Mars to advance exploration, science, innovation, benefits to humanity, and *international collaboration*.

[S.O. 1.2] Conduct research on the International Space Station (ISS) to enable future space exploration, *facilitate a commercial space economy*, and advance the fundamental biological and physical sciences for the benefit of humanity.

[S.O. 1.3] Facilitate and utilize US *commercial capabilities* to deliver cargo and crew to space.

[S.O. 1.7] Transform NASA missions and advance the Nation's capabilities by maturing *crosscutting and innovative technologies*.

[S.O. 2.4] Advance the Nation's STEM education and workforce pipeline by working *collaboratively with other agencies* to engage students, teachers, and faculty in NASA's missions and unique assets.

TABLE 2.2 Executive, Program Directorate, and Technical Directorate Standards of Support to Be Provided by EROM Consistent with Roles and Responsibilities Outlined Previously

No.	Executive (E) Level	Program Directorate (PD) Level	Technical Directorate (TD) Level
1 (Strategic Planning)	When E-level strategic objectives have been formulated and enterprise-wide programmatic and mission support architectures are being considered: ■ Use historical experience and expert judgment to identify risks and opportunities affecting the ability to meet the E-level strategic objectives and estimate their potential significance. ■ Include risks and opportunities from sources internal to the enterprise and sources external to the enterprise. ■ Identify key risk and opportunity indicators to act as surrogates for E-level risks and opportunities that are qualitative in nature.	When PD-level objectives have been formulated and PD-level program/project architectures are being considered: ■ Use historical experience and expert judgment to identify risks and opportunities affecting the ability to meet the PD-level objectives and estimate their potential significance. ■ Include risks and opportunities from sources internal to the PD and sources external to the PD. ■ Identify key risk and opportunity indicators to act as surrogates for PD-level risks and opportunities that are qualitative in nature.	When TD-level objectives have been formulated and institutional and mission support architectures are being considered: ■ Use historical experience and expert judgment to identify risks and opportunities affecting the ability to meet the TD-level objectives and estimate their potential significance. ■ Include risks and opportunities from sources internal to the TD and sources external to the TD. ■ Identify key risk and opportunity indicators to act as surrogates for TD-level risks and opportunities that are qualitative in nature.
2 (Strategic Planning)	When PD-level and TD-level risks and opportunities have been identified and their significance has been estimated: ■ Use a roll-up process to integrate the PD-level and TD-level risks and opportunities to E level.	When program/project risks and opportunities have been identified and their significance has been estimated: ■ Use a roll-up process to integrate the program/project risks and opportunities to PD level.	When program/project and institutional risks and opportunities have been identified and their significance has been estimated: ■ Use a roll-up process to integrate the program/project and institutional risks and opportunities to TD level.

	E level	PD level	TD level
3 (Strategic Planning)	When the risks and opportunities have been rolled up to E level: ▪ Use an agreed-upon ranking scheme to assess the viability of the enterprise's programmatic and mission support architectures.	When the risks and opportunities have been rolled up to PD level: ▪ Use an agreed-upon ranking scheme to assess the viability of the PD program/project architectures.	When the risks and opportunities have been rolled up to TD level: ▪ Use an agreed-upon ranking scheme to assess the viability of the TD institutional and mission support architectures.
4 (Strategic Planning)	When the viability of each proposed enterprise programmatic and mission support architecture has been assessed: ▪ Prepare a report and presentation laying the technical basis for selecting or rejecting the E-level programmatic and institutional architecture. ▪ Use a format that is consistent with OMB requirements in Circulars A-11 and A-123.	When the viability of each proposed PD program/project architecture has been assessed: ▪ Prepare a report and presentation laying the technical basis for selecting or rejecting the PD-level program/project architecture. ▪ Use a format that is consistent with Management Council requirements.	When the viability of each proposed TD institutional and mission support architecture has been assessed: ▪ Prepare a report and presentation laying the technical basis for selecting or rejecting the TD-level institutional and mission support architecture. ▪ Use a format that is consistent with Management Council requirements.
5 (Program/ Project Concept Studies)	When programmatic and institutional architectures have been selected at all levels and concept studies are occurring: ▪ Use risk and opportunity results integrated at E level to provide guidance on the types of skills and resources needed to conduct advanced concept studies.	When program/project architectures have been selected and concept studies are occurring: ▪ Use risk and opportunity results integrated at PD level to provide guidance on the types of skills and resources needed to conduct advanced concept studies and the planning of analyses for the PD's programs and noncompeted projects.	When institutional and mission support architectures have been selected and concept studies are occurring: ▪ Use risk and opportunity results integrated at TD level to provide guidance on the types of skills and resources needed to conduct advanced concept studies and the planning of analyses that integrate performance and risk considerations.

(continued)

TABLE 2.2 (*Continued*)

No.	Executive (E) Level	Program Directorate (PD) Level	Technical Directorate (TD) Level
6 (Development of Programmatic and Institutional Requirements)	When programmatic and institutional requirements are being developed: ■ Help the enterprise ensure that relevant best practices and lessons learned from historical experience are incorporated into the enterprise's policies and procedural requirements for programs and projects. ■ Use risk and opportunity results integrated at E level to assess the relative importance of each high-level requirement relative to the enterprise's likelihood of success in meeting its strategic objectives. ■ Use risk and opportunity results integrated at E level to help ensure that proposed deviations and waivers do not significantly diminish the enterprise's likelihood of success in meeting its strategic objectives.	When programmatic and institutional requirements are being developed: ■ Help the PD ensure that relevant best practices and lessons learned from historical experience are incorporated into the establishment of high-level program and project requirements. ■ Use risk and opportunity results integrated at PD level to assess the relative importance of each high-level requirement relative to the PD's likelihood of success in meeting its objectives. ■ Use risk and opportunity results integrated at PD level to help ensure that proposed deviations and waivers do not significantly diminish the PD's likelihood of success in meeting its objectives.	When programmatic and institutional requirements are being developed: ■ Help the TD ensure that relevant best practices and lessons learned from historical experience are incorporated into the TD's policies and procedural requirements for programs and projects and for institutional initiatives. ■ Use risk and opportunity results integrated at TD level to assess the relative importance of each high-level requirement relative to the TD's likelihood of success in meeting its objectives and the objectives of each mission assigned to the TD. ■ Use risk and opportunity results integrated at TD level to help ensure that proposed deviations and waivers do not significantly diminish the TD's likelihood of success in meeting its objectives and the objectives of each mission assigned to the TD.

	When E-level budgets are being established and resources are being allocated:	When MD-level budgets are being established and resources are being allocated:	When TD-level budgets are being established and resources are being allocated:
7 (Budget and Resource Management)	■ Use risk and opportunity results integrated at E level to help ensure that the prioritization of enterprise resources and the budget guidance and operating plans for executing the budget are consistent with optimizing the enterprise's likelihood of success in meeting its strategic objectives.	■ Use risk and opportunity results integrated at PD level to help ensure that the workforce and facilities plans, the allocation of budget resources within the PD, and the allocation of budget resources to TDs are consistent with optimizing the PD's likelihood of success in meeting its objectives.	■ Use risk and opportunity results integrated at TD level to help ensure that the workforce and facilities plans and the allocation of budget resources within the TD are consistent with optimizing the TD's likelihood of success in meeting its objectives and the objectives of each mission assigned to the TD.
8 (Enterprise and Program/Project Performance Assessment and Issue Management)	When the enterprise's performance relative to its established strategic objectives is being assessed: ■ Identify and evaluate the significance of changes in the risks and opportunities that have occurred at E level since the last performance review or, if there has been no previous review, since the strategic plan was developed and approved. ■ Include risks and opportunities from sources internal to the enterprise and sources external to the enterprise. ■ Identify any new key indicators needed to act as surrogates for new E-level risks and opportunities that are qualitative in nature. ■ Develop processes for tracking the key E-level indicators and continually assessing the degree of concern represented by their present values and trends.	When the PD's performance relative to its established objectives is being assessed: ■ Identify and evaluate the significance of changes in the risks and opportunities that have occurred at PD level since the last performance review or, if there has been no previous review, since the strategic plan was developed and approved. ■ Include risks and opportunities from sources internal to the PD and sources external to the PD. ■ Identify any new key indicators needed to act as surrogates for new PD-level risks and opportunities that are qualitative in nature. ■ Develop processes for tracking the key PD-level indicators and continually assessing the degree of concern represented by their present values and trends.	When the TD's performance relative to its established objectives is being assessed: ■ Identify and evaluate the significance of changes in the risks and opportunities that have occurred at TD level since the last performance review or, if there has been no previous review, since the strategic plan was developed and approved. ■ Include risks and opportunities from sources internal to the TD and sources external to the TD. ■ Identify any new key indicators needed to act as surrogates for new TD-level risks and opportunities that are qualitative in nature. ■ Develop processes for tracking the key TD-level indicators and continually assessing the degree of concern represented by their present values and trends.

(continued)

TABLE 2.2 (*Continued*)

No.	Executive (E) Level	Program Directorate (PD) Level	Technical Directorate (TD) Level
9 (Enterprise and Program/ Project Performance Assessment and Issue Management)	When PD-level and TD-level risks and opportunities have been updated and their significance has been estimated: ■ Use a roll-up process to integrate the PD-level and TD-level risks and opportunities to E level.	When program/project risks and opportunities have been updated and their significance has been estimated: ■ Use a roll-up process to integrate the program/project risks and opportunities to PD-level.	When program/project and institutional risks and opportunities have been updated and their significance has been estimated: ■ Use a roll-up process to integrate the program/project and institutional risks and opportunities to TD level.
10 (Enterprise and Program/ Project Performance Assessment and Issue Management)	When the risks and opportunities have been rolled up to E level: ■ Identify performance issues that affect the enterprise's ability to meet its strategic objectives. ■ Identify performance issue solution or control options and assess the advantages and disadvantages of each option.	When the risks and opportunities have been rolled up to PD level: ■ Identify performance issues that affect the PD's ability to meet its objectives. ■ Identify performance issue solution or control options and assess the advantages and disadvantages of each option.	When the risks and opportunities have been rolled up to TD level: ■ Identify performance issues that affect the TD's ability to meet its objectives and the objectives of each mission assigned to the TD. ■ Identify performance issue solution or control options and assess the advantages and disadvantages of each option.

11 (Enterprise and Program/Project Performance Assessment and Issue Management)	When the viability of each proposed solution or control option for E-level performance issues has been assessed: ■ Prepare a report and presentation stating the results of the enterprise performance evaluation and laying the technical basis for selecting solution or control options at E level. ■ Use a format that is consistent with OMB requirements in Circs. A-11 and A-123.	When the viability of each proposed solution or control option for PD-level performance issues has been assessed: ■ Prepare a report and presentation stating the results of the PD-level performance evaluation and laying the technical basis for selecting solution or control options at PD level. ■ Use a format that is consistent with Management Council requirements.	When the viability of each proposed solution or control option for TD-level performance issues has been assessed: ■ Prepare a report and presentation stating the results of the TD-level performance evaluation and laying the technical basis for selecting solution or control options at TD level. ■ Use a format that is consistent with MSC requirements.
12 (Acceptance Criteria for Key Decision Points)	When the enterprise has to make decisions about risk acceptance at key decision points: ■ Help develop risk acceptance criteria relevant to risks that affect the enterprise's strategic objectives.	When the PD has to make decisions about risk acceptance at key decision points: ■ Help develop risk acceptance criteria relevant to risks that affect the PD's objectives.	When the TD has to make decisions about risk acceptance at key decision points: ■ Help develop risk acceptance criteria relevant to risks that affect the TD's objectives and the objectives of each mission assigned to the TD.

Objectives such as these require TRIO enterprises to work collaboratively with other US agencies, foreign agencies, commercial entities, and educational entities. Most of the collaboration takes place within projects, programs, and special activities (such as new technology development) that are designed to satisfy the strategic objectives of the managing organization.

2.4.2　The Challenges of Conducting EROM across Extended Partnerships

Implementing an effective EROM process within an enterprise that depends on extended partnerships can be challenging. For example, according to a deputy director for US Department of Defense's National Geospatial-Intelligence Agency (Holzer 2006), writing about the practice of EROM across extended partnerships: "Culture resistance to change and unwillingness to share information viewed as negative prevail. There is additional complexity convincing people to adopt a process that is part of the bigger organization and sharing information regarding their ability to achieve program objectives."

In general, the following attitudinal and operational perspectives are needed to accomplish a satisfactory implementation of EROM when extended partnerships are involved (Holzer 2006; Perera 2002):

- Managers within each of the partners need to be convinced that making risk known to all participants in the extended partnership will be positively recognized and at times rewarded with an allocation of risk mitigation funds.
- Partners whose components or systems are being integrated with those of other partners need to be convinced that it is to their benefit to collaboratively and cooperatively manage risks evolving from the integrated relationships.
- When joining enterprises managed by distinctly different organizations to create an extended partnership, diverse leaderships, objectives, motivations, and other cultural views (and ways of doing risk management) need to be melded in accordance with proprietary, security, foreign dissemination (ITAR), and other considerations.

According to various sources, the single most important factor for achieving buy-in across an extended partnership is for senior leaders of each partnering organization, especially at the top level, to repeatedly voice their support and enforce accountability for an integrated risk and opportunity management process across the partnership.[3]

2.5 CONTRIBUTION OF EROM TO COMPLIANCE WITH FEDERAL REGULATIONS AND DIRECTIVES

This section describes how the implementation of an EROM approach for federal agencies is directly relevant to management and reporting requirements and guidelines that have been issued by the legislative and executive branches of the federal government through the GPRAMA Act and OMB Circulars A-11 and A-123.

2.5.1 OMB Circular A-11 and GPRAMA (Government Performance, Results, and Budgeting)

The July 2016 release of OMB Circular A-11 (OMB 2016a) has several new sections devoted to enterprise risk management. Following are three relevant quotations from these sections:

- Section 270.24 states that "Enterprise risk management (ERM) is an effective agency-wide approach to addressing the full spectrum of the organization's significant risks by understanding the combined impact of risks as an interrelated portfolio, rather than addressing risks only within silos. ERM provides an enterprise-wide, strategically-aligned portfolio view of organizational challenges that provides better insight about how to most effectively prioritize and manage risks to mission delivery."
- Section 270.25 states that "ERM is a strategic discipline that can help agencies to properly identify and manage risks to performance, especially those risks related to achieving strategic objectives. An organizational view of risk positions allows the agency to quickly gauge which risks are directly aligned to achieving strategic objectives, and which have the highest probability of impacting mission.... When well executed, ERM improves agency capacity to prioritize efforts, optimize resources, and assess changes in the environment."
- Section 270.26 states that "While agencies are not required to have a CRO [chief risk officer] or enterprise risk management function, they are expected to manage risks to mission, goals, and objectives of the agency. Where applicable, a CRO or other person designated with these responsibilities may serve as a strategic advisor to the COO [chief operating officer] and other staff on the integration of risk management practices into day-to-day business operations and decision-making."

GPRAMA and OMB Circular A-11 also talk about leading indicators that enable the agency to show that it is on track with respect to meeting its goals and objectives, and in cases where it is not on track, to understand the causes of difficulty and how they can be corrected. The GPRAMA legislation contains the following provisions that are relevant to this discussion:

- In Paragraph 306: "The head of each agency shall make available on the public website of the agency a strategic plan [that] shall contain...an identification of those key factors external to the agency and beyond its control that could significantly affect the achievement of the general goals and objectives."
- In Paragraph 1121: "Use...performance information to achieve agency priority goals...[and] for agency priority goals at greatest risk of not meeting the planned level of performance, identify prospects and strategies for performance improvement, including any needed changes to agency program activities, regulations, policies, or other activities.

Amplification provided in OMB Circular A-11 includes the following observations:

- In Section 200.21, "Other indicators [are] indicators not used in a performance goal or Agency Priority Goal statement but are used to interpret agency progress or identify external factors that might affect that progress."
- Also in Section 200.21, "Outcome [indicators are] a type of measure that indicates progress against achieving the intended result of a program [and that] indicates changes in conditions that the government is trying to influence."

The indicators referred to here may be inferred to be risk leading indicators because they focus on factors that impede progress toward future results.

In addition, OMB Circular A-11 talks about the desirability of pursuing opportunity. Quoting from the Executive Summary:

- "The Administration expects agencies to set a limited number of ambitious goals that encourage innovation and adoption of evidence-based strategies. Agency leaders at all levels of the organization are accountable for choosing goals and indicators wisely and for setting ambitious, yet realistic targets. Wise selection of goals and indicators reflects careful analysis of the characteristics of the problems and opportunities an agency seeks to influence to advance its mission."
- "As important as it is to sustain a strong performance culture through the practices described in the guidance, it is equally important to have reliable and effective processes which support continuous improvement and opportunities for capacity building."

The principal ways in which EROM helps ensure compliance with GPRAMA and with the OMB Circular is through the emphasis it provides in having a robust process for selecting goals and objectives both long-term and short-term, in considering risk and opportunity leading indicators to evaluate the likelihood of success, and in placing opportunity pursuit on an equal basis with risk control. These facets of EROM are apparent from Figures 2.6 and 2.7.

2.5.2 EROM and Internal Controls from the Viewpoint of Federal Regulations and Guidance

Under the new federal regulations and related guidance, the activities involved in conducting EROM are intimately related to and mutually supportive of the activities involved in specifying, implementing, and maintaining internal controls.

According to Circular A-11 (OMB 2016a), "Internal controls are the organization, policies, and procedures that [an] agency uses to reasonably ensure that:

- Programs achieve their intended results.
- Resources used are consistent with agency mission.
- Programs and resources are protected from waste, fraud, and mismanagement.
- Laws and regulations are followed.
- Reliable and timely information is obtained, maintained, reported and used for decision making."

Within the context of EROM, internal controls can be viewed as processes that the organization decides to implement to provide defense-in-depth against risks and to promote successful achievement of its strategic goals and objectives. The overall set of responses to risks and opportunities may include additions or modifications to the design, fabrication, assembly, testing, and operation of a system to mitigate risks and exploit opportunities within the framework discussed earlier. Internal controls focus on processes, procedures, and protocols that make it possible for the overall set of responses to succeed.

According to COSO (2004), "Internal control is encompassed within and an integral part of enterprise risk management. Enterprise risk management is broader than internal control, expanding and elaborating on internal control to form a more robust conceptualization focusing more fully on risk."

Some typical examples of internal controls are cited in the last previous version of OMB Circular A-123, as follows (OMB 2004):

- "Policies and procedures;
- Management objectives (clearly written and communicated throughout the agency);
- Planning and reporting systems;
- Analytical review and analysis;
- Segregation of duties (separate personnel with authority to authorize a transaction, process the transaction, and review the transaction);
- Physical controls over assets (limited access to inventories or equipment);
- Proper authorization;
- Appropriate documentation and access to that documentation."

These controls tend to focus heavily on protecting programs and resources from waste, fraud, and mismanagement and on protecting entities from legal liability. In addition to these, the identification, tracking, and analysis of risk leading indicators is another type of internal control that addresses an organization's strategic risk and helps the organization to achieve its mission. This type of internal control is addressed more fully in the most recent issuances of Circulars A-123 and A-11.

In the realm of strategic planning, there are risks pertaining to the setting of objectives (such as failing to have reliable information from external entities), and there are controls to manage those risks (such as ensuring that reliable information is obtained and provided to those responsible for setting the objectives). Failure to have the correct information may also affect the ability to conduct effective risk management once the objectives have been decided on. There should be controls to address these risks as well (Marks 2013).

In determining whether a particular control should be established, the risk of failure and the significance of the opportunity are considered along with the related costs (COSO 2004). For example, it may not be cost-effective for a TRIO enterprise to install sophisticated inventory controls to monitor levels of raw material if the cost of the raw material used in a production process is low, the material is not perishable, ready supply sources exist, and storage space is readily available. Excessive controls that do not address significant risks or opportunities are likely to be costly and unproductive. In addition, they may actually increase risk due to the added burden of having to implement an unnecessary control.

2.5.3 OMB Circular A-123 (Management's Responsibility for ERM and Internal Control) and the Required Statement of Assurance

OMB Circular A-123 (OMB 2016b) concerns management's responsibility for integrating internal control with enterprise risk management. The memorandum introducing the new circular to the various government agencies states that the intent of the changes from the previous version is "to modernize existing efforts by requiring agencies to implement an Enterprise Risk Management (ERM) capability coordinated with the strategic planning and strategic review process established by GPRAMA, and the internal control processes required by FMFIA [Federal Managers Financial Integrity Act] and Government Accountability Office (GAO)'s Green Book." The tenor of the new circular is intentionally at a high level to allow each agency the latitude of developing approaches that are applicable to it.

OMB (2016b) views internal controls as being contained within enterprise risk management, and the latter as being contained within governance

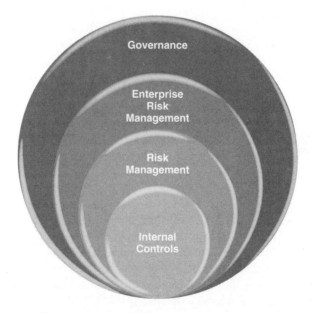

FIGURE 2.8 The relationship between governance, enterprise risk management, and internal controls according to the new OMB Circular A-123

(see Figure 2.8). As stated in OMB (2016b): "Most agencies should build their capabilities, first to conduct more effective risk management, then to implement ERM, rating those risks in terms of impact, and finally building internal controls to monitor and assess the risk developments at various time points." Furthermore: "To provide governance for the risk management function, agencies may use a Risk Management Council (RMC) to oversee the establishment of the Agency's risk profile, regular assessment of risk, and development of appropriate risk response."

The broad governance structure of the federal government is defined through a variety of sources, and in particular, according to OMB (2016b), the "core governance processes are defined by...OMB budget guidance, such as OMB Circular No. A-11, which defines the processes by which the Executive Branch develops and executes Strategic Plans, compiles the President's Budget request, assembles Congressional Budget Justifications, conducts performance reviews, and issues Annual Performance Plans and Annual Program Performance Reports."

According to OMB (2016b), each federal agency is required to submit a statement of assurance (SoA) that "represents the agency head's informed judgment as to the overall adequacy and effectiveness of internal control within the agency." According to NASA (2014b), "GAO and OMB are seeking to clarify existing guidance on internal controls...In the past, this review has been largely focused on financial [matters]...The clarifying guidance also seeks to more constructively focus on the concepts of integrated informed risk/risk-based system of internal controls that is not new but previously overshadowed by the financial focus."

OMB (2016b) emphasizes the importance of having appropriate enterprise risk management processes and systems to identify challenges early, to bring them to the attention of agency leadership, and to develop solutions. It synthesizes existing EROM material mainly from COSO and from the UK *Orange Book* (2004) while relying on the GAO Green Book (GAO 2014a) as the primary source for the principles relating to internal controls. As described earlier in Section 1.1.4 of this book, COSO provides an overarching EROM framework that is particularly relevant to private enterprise. The Orange Book, correspondingly, offers an EROM framework that is relevant to federal agencies especially in the United Kingdom. The technical references to the Orange book in the new OMB Circular A-123 mainly concern the derivation of risk profiles and the development of models of EROM defined largely in terms of the relationships between different entities.

The following statements are direct quotations (with emphasis added by the author) highlighting some of the new requirements placed by Circular A-123 on federal agencies:

- "[The circular] *requires* agencies to integrate risk management and internal control functions."
- "Federal leaders and managers are *responsible*…for implementing management practices that can effectively identify, assess, mitigate, and report on risks."
- "Annually, agencies *must* develop a risk profile coordinated with their annual strategic reviews."
- "[Risk profiles should] identify risks arising from mission and mission-support operations."
- "A portfolio view of risk [should provide] insight into all areas of organizational exposures to risk, such as reputational, programmatic, performance, financial, information technology, acquisitions, human capital, etc."
- "For those objectives for which formal internal control activities have been identified as part of the Risk Profile, assurances on internal control processes *must* be presented in its Annual Financial Report (AFR) or Annual Performance Report (APR), along with a report on identified material weaknesses and corrective actions."
- "Agencies should develop a "maturity model approach" to the adoption of an ERM framework."
- "For FY 2016, Agencies are encouraged to develop an approach to implement ERM. For FY 2017 and thereafter Agencies *must* continuously build risk identification capabilities into the framework to identify new or emerging risks, and/or changes in existing risks."

2.5.4   Example Risk Profile from OMB Circular A-123

One of the principles in Circular A-123 pertaining to the development of the risk profile is that the assessment should "ensure that there is a clearly structured process in which both likelihood and impact are considered for each risk." Table 1 of OMB (2016b) provides an example of a risk profile that specifically reports likelihood and impact as separate items for both inherent risk (the risk before instituting internal controls) and residual risk (the risk after instituting internal controls). The example is reproduced here in Table 2.3.

TABLE 2.3 Example Risk Profile from the New OMB-Circular A-123

STRATEGIC OBJECTIVE—Improve Program Outcomes

Risk	Inherent Assessment		Current Risk Response	Residual Assessment		Proposed Risk Response	Owner	Proposed Risk Response Category
	Impact	Likelihood		Impact	Likelihood			
Agency X may fail to achieve program targets due to lack of capacity at program partners.	High	High	REDUCTION: Agency X has developed a program to provide program partners technical assistance.	High	Medium	Agency X will monitor capacity of program partners through quarterly reporting from partners.	Primary—Program Office	Primary—Strategic Review

OPERATIONS OBJECTIVE—Manage This Risk of Fraud in Federal Operations

Risk	Inherent Assessment		Current Risk Response	Residual Assessment		Proposed Risk Response	Owner	Proposed Risk Response Category
	Impact	Likelihood		Impact	Likelihood			
Contract and Grant fraud.	High	Medium	REDUCTION: Agency X has developed procedures to ensure contract performance is monitored and that proper checks and balances are in place.	High	Medium	Agency X will provide training on fraud awareness, identification, prevention, and reporting.	Primary—Contracting or Grants Officer	Primary—Internal Control Assessment

Risk	Inherent Assessment		Risk Response	Residual Assessment		Proposed Action	Owner	Proposed Action Category
	Impact	Likelihood		Impact	Likelihood			
REPORTING OBJECTIVE—Provide Reliable External Financial Reporting								
Agency X identified material weaknesses in internal control.	High	High	REDUCTION: Agency X has developed corrective actions to provide program partners technical assistance.	High	Medium	Agency X will monitor corrective actions in consultation with OMB to maintain audit opinion.	Primary—Chief Financial Officer	Primary—Internal Control Assessment
COMPLIANCE OBJECTIVE—Comply with the Improper Payments Legislation								
Program X is highly susceptible to significant improper payments.	High	High	REDUCTION: Agency X has developed corrective actions to ensure improper payment rates are monitored and reduced.	High	Medium	Agency X will develop budget proposals to strengthen program integrity.	Primary—Program Office	Primary—Internal Control Assessment and Strategic Review

As stated in OMB (2016b), "While agencies can design their own appropriate categories, for the purposes of this guidance the following illustrative definitions can be used." For impact:

- "High: the impact could preclude or highly impair the entity's ability to achieve one or more of its objectives or performance goals;
- "Medium: the impact could significantly affect the entity's ability to achieve one or more of its objectives or performance goals; and
- "Low: the impact could not significantly affect the entity's ability to achieve each of its objectives or performance goals;"

and for likelihood:

- "High: the risk is very likely or reasonably expected to occur;
- "Medium: the risk is more likely to occur than unlikely; and
- "Low: the risk is unlikely to occur."

An alternative suggested ranking process more suitable for TRIO enterprises will be presented and discussed in Section 3.6.3.

NOTES

1. It should be noted that in addition to providing institutional and technical capabilities that support programs and projects, technical centers at some TRIOs also assume program/project management responsibilities that are assigned to them by program directorates. This role will be included in the discussion of EROM for technical centers that occurs in various later sections of this book.
2. Other management units covered in NASA (2014a) but not here include administrative staff, mission support directorate, program managers, and project managers.
3. More discussion on this subject will occur in Section 5.2 within the context of the extended partnerships that are managed within technical centers.

REFERENCES

Benjamin, A., Dezfuli, H., and Everett, C. 2015. "Developing Probabilistic Safety Performance Margins for Unknown and Underappreciated Risks," *Journal of Reliability Engineering and System Safety*. Available online from ScienceDirect.

Committee of Sponsoring Organizations of the Treadway Commission (COSO). 2004. *Enterprise Risk Management—Integrated Framework: Application Techniques.*

GAO-14-704G. 2014a. *The Green Book, Standards for Internal Control in the Federal Government.* Washington, DC: Government Accountability Accounting Office. (September).

Holzer, T. H. 2006. "Uniting Three Families of Risk Management—Complexity of Implementation x 3," *INCOSE International Symposium* 16 (1): 324–336. Also available from National Geospatial-Intelligence Agency. (July).

International Standard ISO/FDIS 31000. 2008. *Risk Management—Principles and Guidelines.*

Marks, Norman. 2013. "Is Risk Management Part of Internal Control or Is It the Other Way Around?" The Institute of Internal Auditors (May). www.theiia.org.

National Aeronautics and Space Administration (NASA). 2008. NPR 8000.4A. "Agency Risk Management Procedural Requirements." http://nodis3.gsfc.nasa .gov/displayDir.cfm?t=NPR&c=8000&s=4A

National Aeronautics and Space Administration (NASA). 2014a. NASA/SP-2014-3705. *NASA Space Flight Program and Project Management Handbook.* Washington, DC: National Aeronautics and Space Administration.

National Aeronautics and Space Administration (NASA). 2014b. "NASA Internal Control Program Statement of Assurance (SoA) Process Manual Fiscal Year 2014." (May 2).

Office of Management and Budget (OMB). 2004. OMB Circular A-123. "Management's Responsibility for Internal Control." https://www.whitehouse.gov/sites/ default/files/omb/assets/omb/circulars/a123/a123_rev.pdf

Office of Management and Budget (OMB). 2016a. OMB Circular A-11. "Preparation, Submission, and Execution of the Budget." (July) https://www.whitehouse .gov/sites/default/files/omb/assets/a11_current_year/a11_2016.pdf

Office of Management and Budget (OMB). 2016b. OMB Circular A-123. "Management's Responsibility for Enterprise Risk Management and Internal Control." (July) https://www.whitehouse.gov/sites/default/files/omb/memoranda/2016/m-16-17.pdf

The Orange Book, Management of Risk—Principles and Concepts. October 2004. United Kingdom: HM Treasury.

Perera, J. S. 2002. "Risk Management for the International Space Station." Joint ESA-NASA Space-Flight Safety Conference, European Space Agency, ESA SP-486. Also available from NASA Astrophysics Data System (ADS).

CHAPTER 3

Overview of EROM Process and Analysis Approach

This chapter discusses some of the main processes and analysis activities that are involved in conducting EROM in coordination with organizational planning, plan implementation, and organizational evaluation of performance. The topics include the basic principles for deriving organizational objectives hierarchies; developing risk and opportunity information for each objective; understanding risk tolerance and opportunity appetite; composing enterprise risk and opportunity scenario statements; identifying corresponding risk and opportunity leading indicators, including leading indicators for unknown and underappreciated (UU) risks; correlating strategic success likelihoods with leading indicator values; rating the likelihood of success for the various goals and objectives; and identifying/evaluating various options for mitigating risk, availing opportunity, and setting up internal controls. More complete guidance on setting up an internal control structure that is integrated with EROM will be provided in Chapter 10.

3.1 ORGANIZATIONAL OBJECTIVES HIERARCHIES

3.1.1 Objectives Hierarchies for Each Management Unit

Although the particulars of the management structures of TRIO enterprises tend to vary from one organization to another, the process of developing objectives hierarchies for each management unit tends to be uniform. It consists of identifying the unit's top objectives, which tend to be mandated by the entities that the management unit supports, and for each top objective, devising a set of underlying performance objectives whose success leads to the success of the top objective. The top objectives generally have a longer-term focus, and the supporting performance objectives a shorter-term focus.

Strategic planning at the executive level generally produces a set of strategic objectives, and under the strategic objectives a set of top programmatic objectives and a set of top institutional and technical objectives (see Figure 3.1). The strategic objectives typically cover a 10-year time frame or greater, and the top programmatic objectives typically cover a 5- to

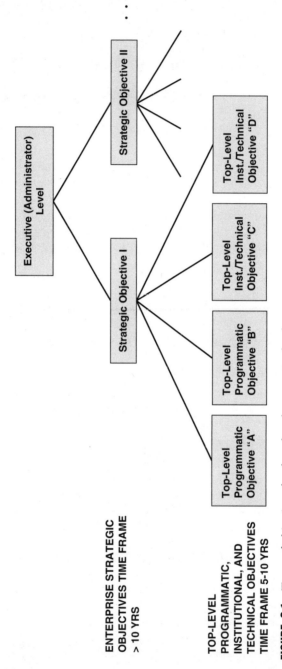

FIGURE 3.1 Types of objectives developed at the executive level

10-year time frame, although these boundaries are flexible. Similarly, the top institutional and technical objectives typically cover a 5- to 10-year time frame and support the top programmatic objectives.

The managerial units at the programmatic level typically consist of a set of program directorates, each of which is responsible for one or more of the top programmatic objectives that flow down from the executive level. Underneath each top programmatic objective is a set of nearer-term objectives, which for convenience are divided into different time frames (see Figure 3.2). At some TRIO enterprises, these nearer-term objectives are referred to as performance goals, which have a one- to five-year time frame, and annual performance goals, which have a one-year or less time frame. For federal agencies, the performance goals with especially high priority are referred to as agency priority goals (APGs), or sometimes as agency priority initiatives (APIs). In this book we refer to the performance goals and annual performance goals as mid-term objectives and short-term objectives, respectively, to keep the nomenclature more-or-less generically applicable across all TRIO enterprises.

The managerial units at the institutional/technical level at TRIO enterprises typically consist of a set of technical centers. Each technical center generally serves two purposes: (1) developing and maintaining the institutional and technical capabilities needed to satisfy those strategic objectives that pertain to infrastructure and technical capability, and (2) taking technical (often including technical management) responsibility for ensuring that the programmatic objectives are successfully satisfied.[1] Similar to the objective breakdown for the program directorates, the objectives for the technical centers start from top objectives passed down from the executive level and continue down to mid-term and short-term objectives. This breakdown is shown in Figure 3.3.

3.1.2 Objectives Hierarchy for the Enterprise as a Whole

Once the objectives hierarchies have been determined for each management unit of the enterprise, it should be possible to combine them into a single enterprise-wide objectives hierarchy that consists of an amalgam of the various management unit hierarchies. A conceptualization of such a composite enterprise-wide objectives hierarchy is shown in Figure 3.4. The dashed arrows between units in this figure are intended to be representative of the interfaces that would exist between different management units and their respective objectives. It is these interfaces that dictate how the status of objectives within the various management units affects the status of the strategic objectives at the top of the enterprise.

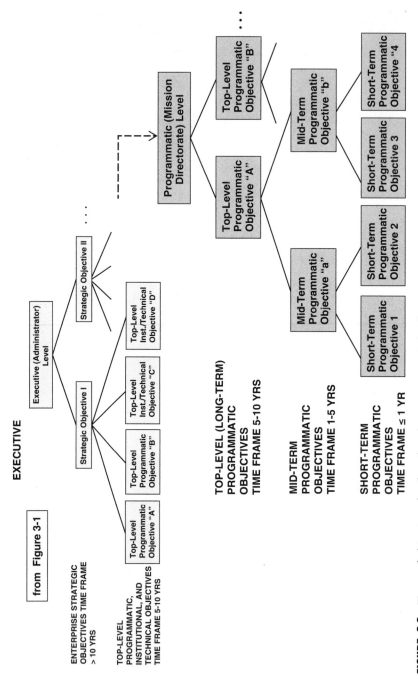

FIGURE 3.2 Types of objectives developed at the programmatic level

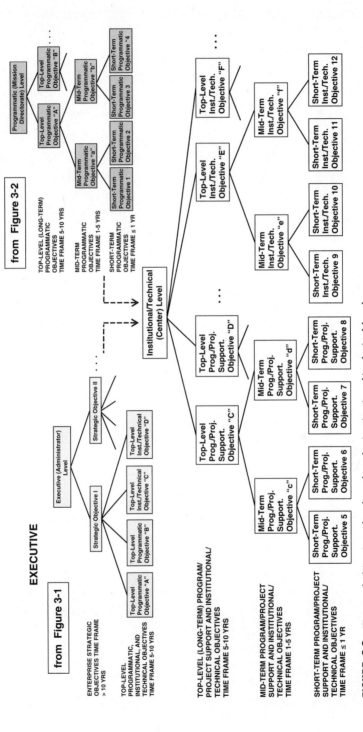

FIGURE 3.3 Types of objectives developed at the institutional/technical level

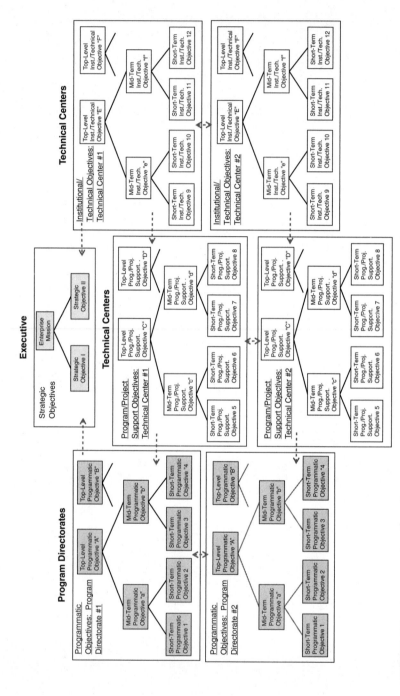

FIGURE 3.4 Conceptualization of an enterprise-wide objectives hierarchy

The interfaces shown by dashed arrows in Figure 3.4 are in reality a simplification of the complex interactions that tend to exist between the various management units and their objectives. These interactions are better displayed by other means such as tables and templates.[2]

3.2 POPULATING THE ORGANIZATIONAL OBJECTIVES HIERARCHIES WITH RISK AND OPPORTUNITY INFORMATION

A principal product that EROM provides to support both organizational planning and organizational performance evaluation is an assessment, including a ranking, or rating, of each objective in the objectives hierarchy in terms of its *cumulative risk* and *cumulative opportunity*. The cumulative risk, or aggregate risk, for an objective is basically the likelihood of not being able to achieve the objective based on following the current plan. The cumulative opportunity for an objective is the likelihood that it will be possible to improve the plan based on future developments so as to be able to achieve the objective. Refer to Section 1.2.4 for a definition of these terms.

This ranking evolves as a result of completing the processes that were outlined in Sections 2.3.1 and 2.3.2 and depicted in Figures 2.6 and 2.7. The processes involve the following steps, the results of which are illustrated in Figure 3.5:

1. Identify the individual risks and opportunities that affect each objective.
2. Identify associated leading indicators that can be used to gauge the significance of the risk/opportunity and trend its status over time.
3. Establish trigger values for the leading indicators based on the risk tolerances and opportunity appetites that the stakeholders (which may include both external funding authorities and internal decision makers) have relative to the affected objective(s).
4. Determine the current status of each leading indicator, accounting for both the current values of the indicators and their current trends.

Two other steps are depicted in Figure 3.5, the intricacies of which may not be immediately obvious to the reader:

5. Roll up the statuses of the risk and opportunity leading indicators for each objective to infer aggregate risk and opportunity status rankings (or ratings) for the objective.
6. Roll up the risk and opportunity status rankings for all objectives in the hierarchy to infer risk and opportunity status rankings that include influences from other objectives.

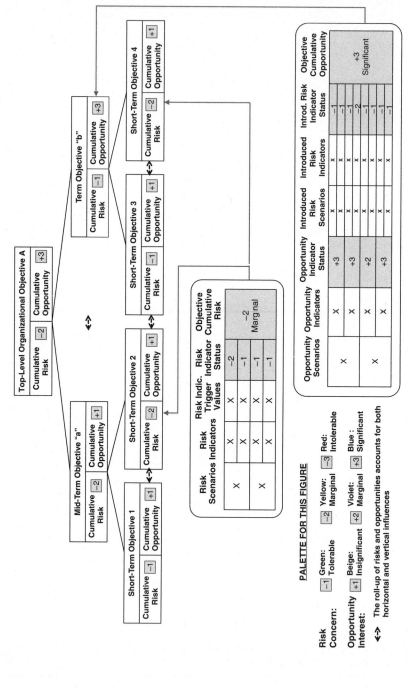

FIGURE 3.5 Associating risk and opportunity information with objectives in the organizational objectives hierarchy

The processes involved in performing these roll-up steps will become more apparent as the explanation of the processes unfolds in later sections.

As called out in Figure 3.5, the same steps are performed with the same form of results being obtained whether the processes are applied during organizational planning or during organizational performance evaluation. During organizational planning, details of architecture and design are generally not yet available, and so the risks and opportunities are based on historical experience. During organizational performance evaluation, the architectures and designs are in a mature enough state to base the risks and opportunities on actual architectures and designs.

In Figure 3.5, the information provided for the individual opportunities may be seen to include not only opportunity scenarios but also introduced risk scenarios. Introduced risks are a byproduct of opportunities in the sense that the fulfillment of an opportunity requires an action that is not currently in the plan and that may introduce one or more associated risks. For example, availing an opportunity created by the emergence of a new technology may introduce risks associated with first-of-a-kind uncertainties and development costs.[3]

3.3 ESTABLISHING RISK TOLERANCES AND OPPORTUNITY APPETITES

As discussed in Section 1.2.3 and depicted conceptually in Figure 1.2, a preliminary step needed before establishing trigger values for leading indicators or rolling up individual risks and opportunities to cumulative values is to establish the risk and opportunity posture for the stakeholders. The risk and opportunity posture is specified through an elicitation of their risk tolerance and opportunity appetite for each objective on the objectives hierarchy.

Risk tolerances and opportunity appetites for the top organizational objectives generally evolve from a roll-up of the tolerances and appetites specified by the stakeholders at the lower levels, taking into account other considerations such as the time frame for response.

3.3.1 Risk and Opportunity Parity Statements

The risk tolerances and opportunity appetites elicited from the stakeholders may be expressed in the form of risk and opportunity parity statements. These statements define boundaries between tolerable and intolerable risks, and between significant and insignificant opportunities.

Each risk and opportunity parity statement reflects a common level of pain or gain from the stakeholders' perspective. This enables comparisons between risk and opportunity to be meaningful because:

- The amount of risk perceived by the stakeholders (i.e., their level of pain) is the same for each parity statement.
- The amount of opportunity perceived by the stakeholders (i.e., their level of gain) is the same for each opportunity parity statement.
- For each pairing of risk and opportunity parity statements, the amount of risk (pain) is balanced by the amount of opportunity (gain).

Risk tolerance and opportunity appetite statements that are elicited from the stakeholders can take various forms. For example, they may involve probabilities of failure or success in satisfying a particular objective, or they may involve changes in the achievable values of key performance parameters that affect a particular objective. To illustrate this point, consider the following hypothetical risk and opportunity parity statements.

EXAMPLES OF RISK AND OPPORTUNITY PARITY STATEMENTS

[*Example Risk Tolerance Statement* 1]: A risk scenario is considered to reach the risk tolerance boundary if the likelihood of failure to achieve Mission X by date Y increases from its targeted value of 10 percent to 20 percent.

[*Example Risk Tolerance Statement* 2]: A risk scenario is considered to reach the risk tolerance boundary if the targeted date of Y for achieving Mission X increases to $Y + \Delta Y$.

[*Example Risk Tolerance Statement* 3]: A risk scenario is considered to reach the risk tolerance boundary if the total cost of achieving Mission X increases by 10 percent.

[*Example Opportunity Appetite Statement* 1]: An opportunity scenario is considered to reach the opportunity appetite boundary if the total cost of achieving Mission X decreases by 20 percent.

[*Example Opportunity Appetite Statement* 2]: An opportunity scenario is considered to reach the opportunity appetite boundary if the system for achieving Mission X will also be capable of being used to achieve a totally different mission, Mission X'.

The implication of parity suggests that these five statements involve equal pain or gain. For example, the stakeholders are willing to accept a doubling of the mission failure probability or a slippage of ΔY years in the mission achievement date in exchange for having the flexibility to use the same system to accomplish a different mission.

In summary, strategic decisions between disparate choices can be made if the baselines for risk and opportunity, as defined by the boundaries, are commensurate in terms pain and gain.

3.3.2 Response Boundaries and Watch Boundaries

To provide greater flexibility to the stakeholders, two separate risk tolerance and opportunity appetite boundaries (i.e., two levels of pain and gain) are elicited to differentiate risks and opportunities that need to be responded to from those that need only to be watched. The two boundaries are illustrated in Figure 3.6, where they are referred to as *response boundaries* and *watch boundaries*:

- Exceedance of a *response boundary* suggests that an action is imminently needed (e.g., mitigation of the risk or exploitation of the

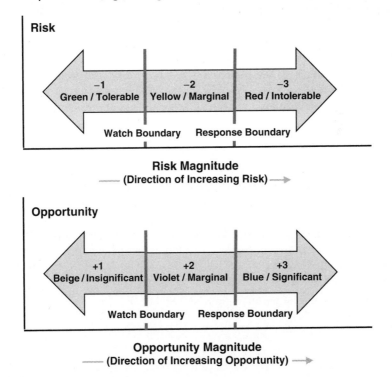

FIGURE 3.6 Risk and opportunity response and watch boundaries

opportunity). A risk that exceeds the risk response boundary is *intolerable* and an opportunity that exceeds the opportunity response boundary is *significant*.

■ Exceedance of a *watch boundary* without exceeding a *response boundary* suggests that an action should be considered but is not imminently needed. Risks and opportunities that exceed the watch boundary but do not exceed the response boundary are referred to as *marginal*.[4] While marginal risks/opportunities fall below the threshold of needing a response, they should be trended and reported at formal reviews.

■ A risk that does not exceed the risk watch boundary is *tolerable* and an opportunity that does not exceed the opportunity watch boundary is *insignificant*.

3.4   IDENTIFYING RISK AND OPPORTUNITY SCENARIOS AND LEADING INDICATORS

Once the stakeholders' risk and opportunity posture has been established by eliciting risk tolerance and opportunity appetite boundaries, the EROM analysis team proceeds to develop a set of risk and opportunity scenarios and associated leading indicators for each entity in the objectives hierarchy. Note that some risks and opportunities and their associated leading indicators may appear under more than one objective.

At lower levels of the objectives hierarchy, risk and opportunity scenarios and leading indicators tend to be specified by direct assignment using historical experience, expert judgment, and what-if analysis. At higher levels, scenarios and indicators that are identified by the EROM analysis team may also be augmented by additional scenarios and indicators that are obtained by roll-up from lower levels. This process recognizes the fact that the success of strategic goals and objectives may be affected not only by scenarios and leading indicators that enter at that level, but also by scenarios and leading indicators that enter at the levels of mid-term and short-term objectives and propagate upward.

An example of an opportunity scenario that is specified directly at a higher level and a risk scenario that is rolled up from lower levels is provided in the following box.

EXAMPLE OF AN OPPORTUNITY SCENARIO THAT IS SPECIFIED DIRECTLY AT A HIGHER LEVEL AND A RISK SCENARIO THAT IS ROLLED UP FROM LOWER LEVELS (STRATEGIC DEFENSE APPLICATION)

Opportunity for 10-Year Strategic Objective a: There is a possibility that new technology in the area of kinetic interceptors may become available within a 10-year time frame, making it possible to achieve a more highly reliable intercept system over the next decade.

Risk for 5-Year Performance Goal X: If milestone slippages that have occurred during the past year in Program X are not corrected, there is a possibility that System X will not be ready for use in 5 years.

Risk for 5-Year Performance Goal Y: If milestone slippages that have occurred during the past year in Program Y are not corrected, there is a possibility that System Y will not be ready for use in 5 years.

Roll-up Risk for 10-Year Strategic Objective a: If Systems X and Y are not ready in 5 years, it may not be possible to achieve an adequately reliable kinetic intercept system over the next decade.

3.4.1   Risk and Opportunity Taxonomies

A taxonomy is a tree structure of classifications that begins with a single, all-encompassing classification at the root of the tree, and partitions this classification into a number of subclassifications at the nodes below the root. This process is repeated iteratively at each node, proceeding from the general to the specific until a desired level of category specificity is reached.

Taxonomies can be used to group enterprise risk and opportunity scenarios into categories that reflect, first, the types of goals and objectives that they affect, and second, the types of events that could create risk and opportunity for each goal or objective. Risk and opportunity taxonomies provide the following benefits:

- They assist in the identification of risk and opportunity scenarios that otherwise might be missed (e.g., by facilitating the brainstorming process), and in the identification and understanding of the cross-cutting nature of some of these scenarios.
- They help identify leading indicators that can be used to rank the likelihood (at least qualitatively) that a postulated event that either threatens or benefits a goal or objective will occur.
- They facilitate the process of identifying planning alternatives and internal controls to effectively mitigate the risks or exploit the opportunities.
- They assist in properly allocating resources among the entities or organizational units of the TRIO enterprise (e.g., to mitigate a risk or exploit an opportunity).

Figure 3.7 illustrates an example three-level enterprise risk and opportunity taxonomy that is applicable to TRIO enterprises. For each categorical unit in the bottom level of the taxonomy, it also provides an example individual risk (R) or opportunity (O) scenario summary description. In addition to categories that derive from the TRIO enterprise's mission and manner of conducting business, TRIO enterprises are responsible for meeting outcomes and milestones that are directly mandated by other entities (e.g., through Congressional amendments signed into law by the president).

As noted in Figure 3.7, each bottom-level subcategory can be further decomposed into one or more goals or objectives that apply to that categorical unit. For example, new technology pursuits pertaining to mission performance is comprised of different individual technology pursuits, each of which represents a goal or objective of the enterprise. Thus, the taxonomy in Figure 3.7 may be construed as having an unseen bottom-level corresponding to the goals and objectives that are affected.

3.4.2 Risk and Opportunity Scenario Statements

According to NASA (2011), risk scenario statements should contain three to four elements, as follows:

1. A condition or set of conditions encapsulating the current key fact-based situation or environment that is causing concern, doubt, anxiety, or uneasiness.
2. A departure event or set of departure events describing a possible change from the baseline plan.

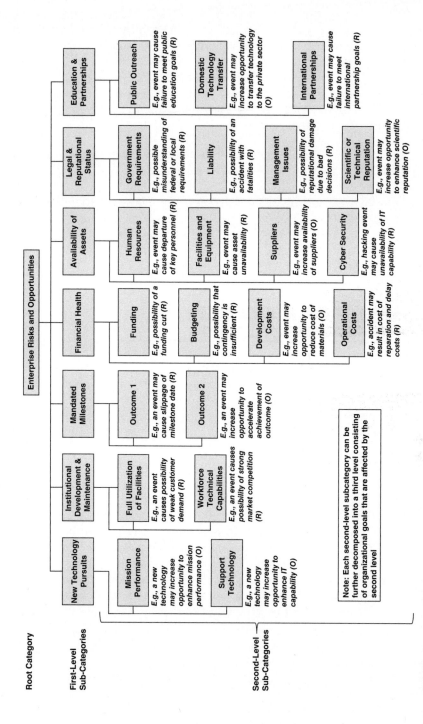

Root Category

First-Level Sub-Categories

Second-Level Sub-Categories

Enterprise Risks and Opportunities

New Technology Pursuits

Institutional Development & Maintenance

Mandated Milestones

Financial Health

Availability of Assets

Legal & Reputational Status

Education & Partnerships

Mission Performance
E.g., a new technology may increase opportunity to enhance mission performance (O)

Support Technology
E.g., a new technology may increase opportunity to enhance IT capability (O)

Full Utilization of Facilities
E.g., an event causes possibility of weak customer demand (R)

Workforce Technical Capabilities
E.g., an event causes possibility of strong market competition (R)

Outcome 1
E.g., an event may cause slippage of milestone date (R)

Outcome 2
E.g., an event may increase opportunity to accelerate achievement of outcome (O)

Funding
E.g., possibility of a funding cut (R)

Budgeting
E.g., possibility that contingency is insufficient (R)

Development Costs
E.g., event may increase opportunity to reduce cost of materials (O)

Operational Costs
E.g., accident may result in cost of reparation and delay costs (R)

Human Resources
E.g., event may cause departure of key personnel (R)

Facilities and Equipment
E.g., event may cause asset unavailability (R)

Suppliers
E.g., event may increase availability of suppliers (O)

Cyber Security
E.g., hacking event may cause unavailability of IT capability (R)

Government Requirements
E.g., possible misunderstanding of federal or local requirements (R)

Liability
E.g., possibility of an accident with fatalities (R)

Management Issues
E.g., possibility of reputational damage due to bad decisions (R)

Scientific or Technical Reputation
E.g., event may increase opportunity to enhance scientific reputation (O)

Public Outreach
E.g., event may cause failure to meet public education goals (R)

Domestic Technology Transfer
E.g., event may increase opportunity to transfer technology to the private sector (O)

International Partnerships
E.g., event may cause failure to meet international partnership goals (R)

Note: Each second-level subcategory can be further decomposed into a third level consisting of organizational goals that are affected by the second level

FIGURE 3.7 Example taxonomy for enterprise risks and opportunities

69

3. (Optional) An organizational entity or set of entities representing the primary resources that are affected by the risk scenario. (*Note*: The resources most affected by the risk scenario may be at the enterprise level or at a lower level in the organization.)

4. A consequence or set of consequences describing the foreseeable, credible negative impacts on the organization's ability to meet its expected performance.

To facilitate strategic planning, it is useful to add the following element to the four cited above:

5. The objective(s) in the organizational objectives hierarchy affected by the risk scenario.

The examples in the following box provide enterprise risk scenarios that conform with this format.

EXAMPLES OF RISK SCENARIO STATEMENTS (STRATEGIC DEFENSE APPLICATION)

1. Category: Mandated performance goals:

    Given that [*condition*] the schedule for System X is much more stringent than was the schedule for previous systems, there is a possibility that [*departure from plan*] integration testing for the kinetic intercept system will be delayed by as much as 6 months resulting in [*entity*] the kinetic intercept program [*consequence*] being unable to reach deployment capability within mandated schedule and funding, adversely affecting [*mid-term objective*] the kinetic intercept system becoming operational by Year Y.

2. Category: Financial:

    Given that [*condition*] economic indicators suggest the possibility of a recession, there is a possibility that [*departure from plan*] funding to the kinetic intercept agency will be cut by Congress resulting in [*entity*] the budgeting organization [*consequence*] having insufficient financial resources to work with, adversely affecting [*strategic objective*] attainment of a kinetic intercept capability.

3. Category: Availability of assets/loss of assets:

    Given that [*condition*] the workforce is aging, there is a possibility that [*departure from plan*] there will be a larger number of retirements next year than anticipated resulting in [*entity*] the hiring and technical organizations [*consequence*] being unable to meet their staffing goals, adversely affecting [*strategic objective*] maintenance of a qualified workforce.

4. Category: Legal and reputational:

    Given that [*condition*] an audit of ethics training has indicated shortcomings in the contents and attendance of the training, there is a possibility that [*departure from plan*] there will be a serious ethical infraction resulting in [*entity*] the TRIO enterprise [*consequence*] losing public confidence, adversely affecting [*long-term objective*] the long-term viability of the TRIO enterprise.

Opportunity scenario statements should contain analogous information:

1. A condition or set of conditions encapsulating the current key fact-based situation or environment that is promoting the possibility of an opportunity
2. An enabling event or potential advance, or a set of enabling events or potential advances, that could happen to promote the possibility to a reality
3. (Optional) An organizational entity or set of entities representing the primary resources that are affected by the opportunity scenario
4. An action that must be taken to realize the opportunity
5. A benefit or set of benefits describing the foreseeable, credible possible impacts on the organization's ability to perform its mission
6. The objective(s) in the organizational objectives hierarchy affected by the opportunity scenario

As discussed in Section 1.2.1, the inclusion of an action, which is not needed for the definition of a risk scenario, is intrinsic to the definition of an opportunity scenario. Example opportunity scenario statements following this format are presented in the following box.

EXAMPLES OF OPPORTUNITY SCENARIO STATEMENTS (SPACE EXPLORATION APPLICATION)

1. Category: New technology development and application:

    Given that [*condition*] new technology in the area of electric propulsion shows promise, there is a possibility that [*enabling event or potential advance*] the technology will become available for use within 5 years so that if [*entity*] the propulsion organization [*action*] implements the new technology for Mission X, it may be able to [*benefit*] achieve its thrust requirements with a 50 percent weight savings, thereby contributing to [*strategic objectives*] development and realization of creative new technologies and more distant exploration of the solar system.

2. Category: Education and partnerships:

   Given that [*condition*] enrollment in NASA's public education STEM programs has been higher than expected, there is a possibility that [*enabling event or potential advance*] enrollment will double in the next two years, so that if [*entity*] the public education organization [*action*] correspondingly doubles the number of STEM courses offered, it may be able to [*benefit*] meet the administration's STEM requirements sooner than expected, thereby contributing to [*strategic objective*] the advancement of the nation's STEM education.

3.4.3   Risk and Opportunity Scenario Narratives

While the risk or opportunity scenario statement provides a concise description of the individual risk or opportunity, this information is not necessarily sufficient to capture all the information that the identifying person has to convey, nor is it necessarily sufficient to describe the concern in enough detail that risk and opportunity management personnel can understand it and respond effectively to it, particularly after the passage of time. In order for enough context to be recorded so that the individual risk or opportunity can stand on its own and be understood by someone not otherwise familiar with the issue, a narrative description field should be provided. The narrative description should include the following (NASA 2011):

- Key circumstances surrounding the risk or opportunity scenario
- Contributing factors
- Uncertainties
- The range of possible consequences
- Related issues such as what, where, when, how, and why

The narrative description is also a place where the identifying person can suggest or recommend potential risk and opportunity responses that he/she feels are most appropriate. It is usually the case that the identifier is a person with significant subject matter expertise in the affected asset, and it is important to capture that expertise, not only concerning the nature of the issue but also its remedy. When a risk or opportunity response is recommended, the identifier should also record the rationale for the recommendation, preferably including an assessment of the expected risk shifting (e.g., from a safety risk to a cost risk) that would result.

3.4.4   Risk and Opportunity Leading Indicators

Risk and opportunity leading indicators are used to infer the likelihood that each objective in the organizational objectives hierarchy will be successfully achieved within the assigned time frame. During the organizational planning process, they are used to help decide from among various candidate objectives on the basis of their projected likelihood of success. During the performance evaluation process, they are used to assess how the likelihoods of success based on current conditions stand with respect to the initial projections.

As stated in the COSO document on key risk indicators (COSO 2010), most organizations monitor numerous key *performance* indicators (KPIs) that shed insights about risk events that have already affected the organization. Leading indicators, on the other hand, "help to better monitor potential future shifts in risk conditions or new emerging risks" so that management is "able to more proactively identify potential impacts on the organization's portfolio of risks."

It should be noted, however, that indicators of past performance (i.e., lagging indicators) can also be indicators of possible future performance. For example, the occurrence of missed milestones in the past may indicate a potential for missed milestones in the future. Therefore, the set of leading indicators normally includes past performance as well as present conditions that are not related to past performance.

Risk and opportunity leading indicators should possess the following characteristics:

- *Quantifiability:* There should be one or more quantifiable measures by which to assess the status of the leading indicator.
- *Correlatability:* There should be a direct correlation between the value of a leading indicator and the likelihood of success of one or more of the objectives in the organizational objective hierarchy.
- *Actionability:* In the event that the value of a leading indicator leads to concern about a risk or optimism about an opportunity, there should be means for reducing the risk or exploiting the opportunity. It is not necessary for all leading indicators to be actionable (as some are caused by external forces that are beyond the control of the organization). Rather, it is only necessary that for each nontrivial risk or opportunity, there are some leading indicators that can be controlled to help contain the risk or grow the opportunity.

Risk and opportunity leading indicators may have different levels of complexity. For example, a simple indicator might be a ratio that management tracks to infer the status of an evolving risk or opportunity. A more elaborate indicator might involve the aggregation of several individual indicators into a multidimensional score about emerging events that may lead to new risks or opportunities. In addition, leading indicators might emerge from internal sources (such as missed project milestones) or from external sources (such as the state of the national economy).

Leading indicators may also be grouped according to the type of risk or opportunity to which they relate. Table 3.1 provides examples showing how various leading indicators may be grouped into categories of risk and opportunity.

3.4.5 Leading Indicators of Unknown and Underappreciated (UU) Risks

As mentioned in Section 1.2.7, the factors that contribute to UU risks can be considered to be leading indicators, and they, too, should be included in the roll-up of risks and opportunities from lower to higher levels in the objectives hierarchy. The following design, organizational, and programmatic factors are among the principal leading indicators of UU risks (NASA 2015; Benjamin et al. 2015):

- *Amount of complexity, particularly involving the interfaces between different elements of the system.* Technical systems more prone to UU failure are complex, tightly coupled systems that make the chain of events leading to a disaster incomprehensible to operators.
- *Amount of scaling beyond the domain of knowledge.* UU risks may occur either from incrementally scaling up a design to achieve higher performance or incrementally scaling down a design to save on cost or time, without providing adequate validation.
- *Use of fundamentally new technology or fundamentally new application of an existing technology.* The use of new technology in place of heritage technology may lead to an increase in UU risks when other factors within this list are not well handled.
- *Degree to which organizational priorities are focused toward safety and reliability.* UU risks occur more frequently when top management is not committed to safety as an organizational goal, when there is no or little margin in the availability of qualified personnel, and when organizational learning is not sufficiently valued.
- *Degree to which the management style is hierarchical.* Two-way flows of information are essential in technological systems to maximize the

TABLE 3.1 Typical Risk and Opportunity Scenario Types and Associated Leading Indicators

Category	Example Risks	Example Opportunities	Example Internal (INT) and External (EXT) Leading Indicators
New technology development and application	Degradation of mission performance or of institutional capability or cost increases due to unknowns	Enhancement of mission performance or of institutional capability or cost reductions because of technology improvements	INT: Initiation of and results from internal state-of-the-art assessments
			INT: Technology Readiness Level (TRL) rate of progress
			INT: Number of patents applied for
			EXT: Technology trends in areas pertinent to the organization's missions
Mandated performance goals	Failure to meet mandated or targeted milestone dates	Exceedance of expectations in meeting mandated or targeted milestone dates	INT: Schedule compared to other programs/projects*
			INT: Number of missed intermediate milestones & slippage amount*
			INT: Unresolved action items & uncorrected problems*
			EXT: Changes in prioritization of agency outcomes
Financial	Funding cut	Funding increase	EXT: Economic indicators
			EXT: Congressional makeup
			EXT: Changes in national priorities
	Insufficient contingency	More-than-sufficient contingency	INT: Contingency relative to other programs/projects*
			INT: Rate of spending compared to other programs/projects*
			INT: Unresolved assignment of roles and responsibilities
	Increased cost of materials/purchased services	Decreased cost of materials/purchased services	EXT: Price trends
			EXT: Threats of foreign conflicts or political changes (e.g., affecting rare material costs)
			EXT: Supplier financial problems

(continued)

TABLE 3.1 (*Continued*)

Category	Example Risks	Example Opportunities	Example Internal (INT) and External (EXT) Leading Indicators
	Increased cost of operations	Decreased cost of operations	INT: Monthly cost reports*
			INT: Low scores on self-assessments and audits*
	Milestone slippage costs	Savings due to milestone acceleration	INT: Earned value reports*
			EXT: Government shutdown
	Accident costs		INT: Precursors, anomalies, mishap reports*
Availability of assets/loss of assets	Loss of key personnel	Gain of key personnel	INT: Age of workforce
			INT: Workplace morale (e.g., from surveys)
			EXT: Changes in competitive labor market
			EXT: Demographic changes
	Loss or unavailability of facilities or equipment	Increased availability of facilities or equipment	INT: Number of unplanned maintenance actions*
			INT: Age of equipment
			EXT: Terrorism trends
			EXT: Changes in OSHA regulations
	Loss or unavailability of suppliers	Increased availability of suppliers	EXT: Market factors (demand versus supply)
			EXT: Supplier financial or legal problems
	Loss or unavailability of IT capability	Increased availability of IT assets	INT: Number of unaddressed vulnerabilities
			EXT: Hacking trends
			EXT: New viruses
Legal and reputational	Failure to meet federal or local requirements	Exceedance of federal or local requirements	INT: Quality of ethics program
			INT: Quality of recordkeeping (e.g., for OSHA requirements)*
			EXT: New regulations
	Increase in financial liability given an accident	Decrease in financial liability given an accident	INT: Increased use of hazardous or toxic materials*
			INT: Accident precursors*
			EXT: Trends in court decisions regarding liability

TABLE 3.1 (*Continued*)

Category	Example Risks	Example Opportunities	Example Internal (INT) and External (EXT) Leading Indicators
	Reputational damage due to mgmt. failures	Reputational enhancement due to mgmt. successes	INT: Findings of independent reviews
			INT: Seeking and resolution of internal dissenting opinions*
	Degradation of scientific reputation	Enhancement or maintenance of scientific reputation	INT: Number of technical papers published
			INT: Number of patents granted
			EXT: Number of citations in technical papers
			EXT: Number of nominations or awards received
Education and partnerships	Failure to meet public educ. goals	Exceedance of public educ. goals	INT: Missed or made milestones
			INT: Low or high enrollment in educational programs
	Failure to meet technology transfer goals	Exceedance of technology transfer goals	INT: Missed or made milestones
			INT: Number of technology transfer agreements
			EXT: Lack or surplus of interest or progress from potential commercial partners
			EXT: Trends regarding the sharing of sensitive information and materials
	Failure to meet international partnership goals	Exceedance of international partnership goals	INT: Missed or made milestones that the organization is responsible for*
			EXT: Lack or surplus of interest or progress from potential international partners
			EXT: New regulations regarding sensitive information
			EXT: Competition from a foreign country

*Asterisked leading indicators are measured at program/project level or center level and are aggregated to obtain leading indicators that apply to the agency as a whole.

sharing of information among all personnel regardless of position in the organizational hierarchy.

■ *Degree of oversight when responsibilities are distributed among various entities.* Interfaces between different elements of the system provided by different suppliers require stringent oversight by the managing agency.

■ *Amount of pressure to meet schedule and budget constraints.* In particular, time pressure beyond the level of comfort is a fundamental reason for high human error rates.

■ *Likelihood of major or game-changing external events that affect the TRIO enterprise's direction, such as changes in the federal administration or geopolitical upheavals.* Such events impact the stability of long-term strategic planning and of external imposed constraints and requirements.

NASA (2015) and Benjamin et al. (2015) provide useful guidelines for determining how various combinations of the above leading indicators tend to affect the relative magnitude of UU risks compared to the magnitude of known risks. Table 3.2 is reproduced (with minor modifications to simplify the presentation of data), and provides a summary of guidelines for estimating the ratio of the system failure probability from UU risks to the system failure probability from known risks when a system is initially put into operation (Benjamin et al. 2015). These estimates are intended only to be representative and not in any way precise, because additional factors not included in the general list may be important for specific applications. In the context of EROM, Table 3.2 provides indications of various combinations of the leading indicators of UU risks that need to be watched and possibly responded to.

3.5 SPECIFYING LEADING INDICATOR TRIGGER VALUES AND EVALUATING CUMULATIVE RISKS AND OPPORTUNITIES

Leading indicator trigger values are used to signal when a risk is reaching a risk-tolerance boundary or when an opportunity is reaching an opportunity appetite boundary. Reaching the trigger values for risk leading indicators implies that the likelihood of not being able to satisfy an objective in the organizational objectives hierarchy is becoming a concern. Reaching the trigger values for opportunity leading indicators implies either that there is a potential for significantly increasing the likelihood of being able to satisfy an objective or that there is an emerging opportunity to achieve

TABLE 3.2   Published Guidelines for Roughly Estimating the Ratio of the System Failure Probability from UU Risks to the System Failure Probability from Known Risks at Time of Initial Operation (Benjamin et al. 2015)

Ratio	Applicable Conditions	Sources
0	Systems that can take credit for at least 125 actual cycles of operation of the same or equivalent systems with positive indication that the risk has leveled off to a mature system value	Results for Shuttle, Atlas, Delta, Molniya/Soyuz after125 flights
~1	New systems that are developed and operated under at most mild time pressure, with reliability and safety having a higher priority than cost and schedule, with an inclusive management structure, and with a design philosophy that does not involve significantly new technology or new integration of an existing technology or scaling of an existing technology beyond the domain of knowledge or tight functional coupling	Results for Delta, first 75 flights
~2	New systems that are developed or operated under at least moderate time pressure, with cost and schedule having at least an equal priority with reliability and safety, and with a tendency for the management structure to be hierarchical, but with a design philosophy that does involve significantly new technology or new integration of an existing technology or scaling of an existing technology beyond the domain of knowledge or tight functional coupling	Results for Atlas, first 75 flights*
~2	New systems that are developed or operated under significant time pressure, and with a design philosophy that involves either new technology or new integration of an existing technology or scaling of an existing technology beyond the domain of knowledge or tight coupling, but with reliability and safety having a higher priority than cost and schedule, and with an inclusive management structure	Results for Shuttle retrospectively, first 75 flights, if post-Columbia return-to-flight improvements had been in place*
~4	New systems that are developed or operated under significant time pressure, with cost and/or schedule having at least an equal priority with reliability and safety, with a tendency for the management structure to be hierarchical, and with a design philosophy that involves either new technology or new integration of an existing technology or scaling of an existing technology beyond the domain of knowledge or tight coupling	Results for Shuttle, first 75 flights. Anecdotally nuclear reactor experience and human reliability experience*
Up to 9	New systems that are developed or operated under extreme time pressure, with cost and/or schedule having significantly higher priority than reliability and safety, with a highly hierarchical management structure, and involving either new technology or new integration of an existing technology or scaling of an existing technology well beyond the domain of knowledge	Results for Molniya/Soyuz first 75 flights. Factors of this magnitude and larger are also suggested in Guarro (2014).

*Ratios of 1 to 4 are also consistent with historical reliability growth estimates cited in Table I of MIL-HDBK-189A for commercial and military systems.

new goals and objectives that were formerly considered unreachable or inconceivable.

Leading indicator trigger values are specified for each risk and opportunity scenario for each objective in the organizational objectives hierarchy. Once specified, it is possible to compare the actual values of the leading indicators to their trigger values to provide a measure of the overall risk and opportunity for each objective in the hierarchy.

3.5.1   Leading Indicator Trigger Values

Similar to the way that risk tolerance and opportunity appetite were characterized by two boundaries, a response boundary and a watch boundary, it is useful to define two triggers for risk and opportunity leading indicators, a response trigger and a watch trigger. The EROM analysis team elicits values of the leading indicator triggers from appropriate technical authorities and subject matter experts.

Leading indicator triggers may be positively or negatively correlated with risk or opportunity. For example, *remaining cost reserve* is defined in the opposite direction from expenditure to date. As cost expenditure increases, the risk of overrun increases (a positive correlation), but as remaining cost reserve increases, the risk of overrun decreases (a negative correlation). This opposite duality is captured by the mirror-image effects of positive and negative correlations shown in Figure 3.8.

Leading indicator triggers are intended to be quantitative surrogates for the often qualitative risk tolerance and opportunity appetite boundaries. Their accuracy as surrogates depends upon the skill of the technical authorities, subject matter experts, and EROM analysis team in defining leading indicators and specifying their trigger values.

3.5.2   Cumulative Risks and Opportunities

The cumulative risk and cumulative opportunity for each objective in the organizational objectives hierarchy is derived from the current status of the associated leading indicators relative to their trigger values, where *current status* refers to both the current value and the current trend. The term *cumulative* in this context refers to the accumulation of the various leading indicators that apply to the objective being evaluated.

Figure 3.5, presented earlier, conceptually illustrates the general process for determining the cumulative risks and opportunities for a set of objectives in an organizational objectives hierarchy.[5]

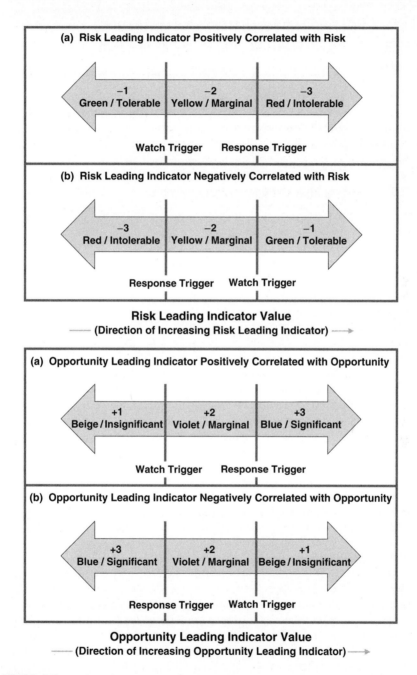

FIGURE 3.8 Risk and opportunity leading indicator triggers

3.6   IDENTIFYING AND EVALUATING RISK MITIGATION, OPPORTUNITY EXPLOITATION, AND INTERNAL CONTROL OPTIONS

If a cumulative risk is intolerable and/or a cumulative opportunity is significant, it may become desirable to consider means for mitigating the risk and/or exploiting the opportunity, along with the associated setting of internal controls. This section discusses processes for identifying and evaluating such options.

3.6.1   Deducing Risk and Opportunity Drivers

Risk drivers are defined as "those elements found within the aggregate performance risk models that contribute most to the performance risks because of uncertainties in their characterization.... When varied over their range of uncertainty, [they] cause the performance risk to change from tolerable to intolerable (or marginal)" (NASA 2011).

In the context of EROM, a risk driver can be thought of as a significant source of risk contributing to the overall cumulative risk of not satisfying a top organizational objective. A risk driver can be a departure event in a risk scenario statement, an underlying cause of a departure event, a leading indicator, a particular assumption used in evaluating the significance of an individual risk, an assumption made in evaluating a cumulative risk, an essential internal control, or any combination of such elements that cause the cumulative risk to change from tolerable (green) to marginal (yellow) or intolerable (red) or from marginal (yellow) to intolerable (red). For example, the following elements in the analysis of risk are potential risk drivers:

- Congress may cut funding for a large, key program next year (a departure event).
- Human error may cause a catastrophic accident to occur during a mission (an underlying cause of the departure event *catastrophic accident*).
- The schedule reserve for a key task in a key program is uncomfortably low and trending lower (a leading indicator of the risk of not completing the key task on time).
- If needed, personnel can be diverted from Task A to Task B (an assumption used to evaluate the significance of the risk of not completing Task B on time).
- All pertinent information needed to evaluate the organization's strategic performance is being transmitted in an unbiased fashion to the technical

authorities (an assumption used to justify assurance that the organization is meeting its strategic objectives).

- There is a process and document trail to ensure that all significant risks and opportunities are elevated to responsible individuals with management authority to act upon them (an internal control).

If no one element individually is sufficient to change the color of the cumulative risk, a combination of them may constitute a risk driver.

Risk drivers focus risk management attention on those potentially controllable situations that present the greatest opportunity for risk reduction. Often, risk drivers affect more than one individual risk and cut across more than one organizational unit.

Similarly, opportunity drivers are generally departure events in an opportunity scenario statement or leading indicators of opportunity. For example, the following elements in the analysis of opportunity are potential opportunity drivers:

- Congress may increase funding for a large, key program next year (a departure event).
- The schedule reserve for a key task in a key program is higher than expected and trending higher (a leading indicator of an opportunity to reduce program cost by reallocating personnel so as to finish the program ahead of schedule).

Risk and opportunity drivers can be identified by applying the risk and opportunity roll-up process (illustrated schematically in Figure 3.5) to determine whether the color of the cumulative risks and opportunities for the top organizational objectives change as various sources of risk and opportunity are eliminated. For example, Figure 3.9, when compared with Figure 3.5, shows schematically how the removal of Risk Driver 1 propagates up through the objectives hierarchy to change the ranking of the cumulative risk for the top objective from marginal to tolerable, and how the removal of Opportunity Driver 1 changes the ranking of the cumulative opportunity for the top objective from significant to marginal.

3.6.2 Deducing Risk and Opportunity Scenario Drivers

TRIO organizations are typically required to identify their top risk scenarios, report on the likelihood of their occurrence and severity of their impact, and explain how they are being responded to. OMB Circulars A-11 and A-123 lay out requirements to this effect for government agencies, as described in Section 2.5.

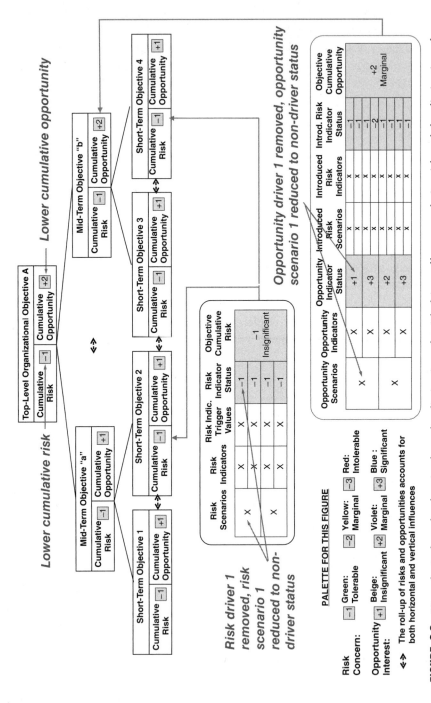

FIGURE 3.9 Hypothetical results showing how the elimination of a risk driver affects cumulative risk and the elimination of an opportunity driver affects cumulative opportunity

Risk and opportunity scenario drivers are a higher-order representation of risk and opportunity drivers. The elements that constitute risk and opportunity drivers (i.e., key departure events, underlying causes, assumptions, existing controls, etc.) are embedded within risk and opportunity scenarios, either as part of the conditions, departure events, and consequences that comprise a risk or opportunity scenario statement or as part of the narrative that accompanies one. Therefore, just as a risk or opportunity driver is defined in Section 3.6.1 as an element or set of elements that cause the cumulative risk or opportunity for a top objective to change color, a risk or opportunity scenario driver can be defined as a scenario or set of scenarios that lead to the same result.

Also, just as risk or opportunity drivers can be identified by applying the risk or opportunity roll-up process while selectively eliminating one or more sources of risk or opportunity until the color of a top objective changes, risk or opportunity scenario drivers can be identified in the same way by selectively eliminating one or more risk or opportunity scenarios. Figure 3.9 provides an indication of how risk and opportunity drivers interact with risk and opportunity scenario drivers.

3.6.3 Evaluating Risk and Opportunity Scenario Likelihoods and Impacts

As discussed in Sections 2.5.3 and 2.5.4 and illustrated in Table 2.3, OMB Circular A-123 stipulates that risk profiles prepared by an agency of the government should include an assessment of both the likelihood and the impact of each risk scenario.

The guidance in the OMB circular for assessment of likelihood as high, medium, or low is based on whether the risk scenario is reasonably expected to occur, more likely to occur than not, or more unlikely to occur or not. For many risks, such as those associated with fraud, malpractice leading to inefficiency, or slippages in cost or schedule that are not mission critical, it makes sense to define likelihood in these terms. But for pioneering TRIO enterprises whose risks (and opportunities) are more mission-critical and possibly even life-critical, a more stringent definition of likelihood is needed. It is more useful to define likelihood for such enterprises in terms of risk tolerance and opportunity appetite. The likelihood of a risk or opportunity should be objective-dependent, and should be considered to be high if it is comparable to or greater than the decision maker's risk tolerance for that objective. For example, if a decision maker is willing to tolerate a likelihood of 10^{-2} (1 in 100) for loss of a critical mission, the likelihood of a risk scenario that could lead to failure to execute that critical mission would be considered high if it is comparable to or greater than 10^{-2}. Conversely, it would be considered low if it is significantly less than 10^{-2}.

Risk tolerance and opportunity appetite are measurable in terms of the decision maker's watch and response boundaries. As stated in Section 3.3.2, exceedance of a response boundary (such as 10^{-2} for the failure likelihood of critical mission) suggests that an action is imminently needed, whereas exceedance of a watch boundary (say, 10^{-3} for the failure likelihood) without exceeding the response boundary suggests that an action should be considered but is not imminently needed. Watch boundaries specify the boundary between "tolerable" and "marginal" for risks, and between "insignificant" and "marginal" for opportunities.

Table 3.3 provides an example of how risk and opportunity scenario likelihoods could be defined for the critical objectives that are undertaken by a pioneering TRIO enterprise. In this example, the scale is divided into three ranks, as suggested in Table 3.3. If greater resolution is needed, the number of ranks may be expanded from three to five by adding "very high" and "very low" to the other ranks in the table and defining associated criteria in terms of distance above or below the watch and response boundaries.

In addition to likelihoods, the guidance in the OMB circular for assessment of impact as high, medium, or low is based on the degree of impairment of the entity's ability to achieve one or more of its objectives should the risk scenario occur. It is clear from the OMB guidance (and from the general principles in this book) that the determination of the "impact" of a risk or opportunity scenario for a TRIO enterprise cannot be made without considering the effect of the risk or opportunity scenario on the cumulative risk or opportunity of the objective. The cumulative effect on the objective is determined during the risk and opportunity roll-up processes and is reflected in the determination of risk and opportunity drivers, as discussed in Section 3.6.1, and scenario drivers, as discussed in Section 3.6.2.

It is easiest and perhaps most reasonable to assess impact on a scenario-by-scenario basis by determining whether the scenario appears in a scenario driver for any top-level objective and examining the color of the cumulative risk/opportunity for that objective. If any risk scenario drivers for a given objective contain a particular individual risk scenario

TABLE 3.3 Example Likelihood Scale for a Risk or Opportunity Relative to a Critical Organizational Objective

Rank	Criteria
High	Likelihood of occurrence of departure event(s) exceeds the decision maker's risk/opportunity response boundary
Medium	Likelihood of occurrence of departure event(s) is between the decision maker's risk/opportunity watch and response boundaries
Low	Likelihood of occurrence of departure event(s) is lower than the decision maker's risk/opportunity watch boundary

TABLE 3.4 Example Impact Scale for a Risk or Opportunity Relative to a Critical Organizational Objective

Rank	Criteria
High	Scenario appears in a scenario driver and the cumulative risk/opportunity for the objective is red/blue (intolerable/significant)
Medium	Scenario appears in a scenario driver and the cumulative risk/opportunity for the objective is yellow/violet (marginal)
Low	Scenario does not appear in a scenario driver

and the cumulative risk is red (intolerable), the risk scenario may be considered to have high impact. If the cumulative risk is yellow (marginal), the risk scenario may be considered to have medium impact. Similarly, if any opportunity scenario drivers for a given objective contain a particular individual opportunity scenario and the cumulative opportunity is blue (significant), the opportunity scenario may be considered to have high impact, and if the cumulative opportunity is violet (marginal), it may be considered to have medium impact.

Table 3.4 provides a demonstration of this process for determining risk and opportunity scenario impacts. Again, if greater resolution is needed, the number of ranks may be expanded from three to five by adding "very high" and "very low" to the other ranks in the table and defining their criteria in an analogous manner.

3.6.4 Identifying Options for Risk Response, Opportunity Action, and Internal Control

When there is a need to reduce the cumulative risk or a desire to take advantage of the cumulative opportunity for one or more top objectives, there are several types of options to be considered:

- Responses to mitigate the cumulative risk
- Actions to seize the cumulative opportunity
- Institution of internal controls to provide effective management oversight and protect operative assumptions

The formulation of risk responses and opportunity actions can take many forms, including changes in the design of a system that is in development, retrofits to existing systems, changes in manufacturing processes, changes in operating procedures, changes in management, formation of partnerships, proactive actions to inform and influence governing agencies, improved public relations, and cost sharing arrangements, to name a few. What these various formulations have in common is that they are based on certain assumptions, and their effectiveness depends on the accuracy of those assumptions. For example, design changes to a system are based on assumptions about the environments that the system will be exposed to, and whether those environments will stay within the parameters that are called out in the design specifications. One of the main function of internal controls, therefore, pertains to the protection of the accuracy of the assumptions.

Leveson (2015) emphasizes the use of internal controls to protect operative assumptions within the domain of safety performance. The types of assumptions of interest to Leveson include the following:

- Assumptions about the system hazards and the paths to (causes of) hazards
- Assumptions about the effectiveness of the controls, that is, the shaping and hedging actions, used to reduce or manage hazards
- Assumptions about how the system will be operated and the environment (context) in which it will operate, for example, assumptions that the controls will be operating as assumed by the designers
- Assumptions about the development environment and processes
- Assumptions about the organizational and societal control structure during operations (i.e., that it is working as designed), the design was adequate to ensure the system requirements are enforced, and the system controllers are fulfilling their responsibilities and operating as designed
- Assumptions about vulnerability or severity in risk assessment that may change over time and thus require a redesign of the risk management and leading indicators system itself

These types of assumptions, with minor modification, apply not only to the safety domain considered by Leveson but as well to virtually all other risk domains (technical, cost, schedule, institutional, acquisition, financial viability, liability, etc.) at all levels of the organization (enterprise, program directorate, technical directorate, etc.). In the context of an enterprise, internal controls should ensure:

- Either that such assumptions remain valid over time in all risk and opportunity domains for all organizational levels
- Or, if the conditions should change, that the operative assumptions are changed accordingly and the new assumptions are monitored and controlled.

The identification of risk mitigation responses, opportunity exploitation actions, and internal controls is directed at finding viable ways to act upon the risk and opportunity drivers and/or scenario drivers discussed in the preceding subsection. The purpose is to reduce risks or act on opportunities when the cumulative risks and opportunities demand that such influence be exercised. There is, however, an obvious limitation on the ability of an agency or business to influence risk and opportunity drivers, in that not all drivers are actionable. When a driver is not actionable, the fallback is to identify other risk and opportunity drivers that are actionable and that can exert an influence on the cumulative risk or opportunity. For example, it is not within the province of a government agency to influence whom the voters choose to elect to federal office, but it is within their province to track public sentiment and plan for alternative scenarios.[6]

3.6.5 Evaluating Options for Risk Response, Opportunity Action, and Internal Control

Options for risk response, opportunity action, and internal control can be evaluated by assessing how the cumulative risks and opportunities for the top organizational objectives would change as a result of incorporating the responses, actions, and controls into the organizational structure and its operation. The process for performing this assessment includes the need to consider not only the positive effects that such options might have on some parts of a system or operation but also the possible unintended negative effects on other parts of the system or operation.

The process for performing this evaluation follows the framework that was developed in Sections 3.4 and 3.5. Risk and opportunity scenarios are redeveloped, taking into account the proposed response, action, and internal control option. In the case of opportunity actions, new risk scenarios introduced by the proposed actions and associated internal controls are included in the accounting. The existing leading indicators are modified and new ones added to reflect the content of the redeveloped risk and opportunity scenarios. Leading indicator trigger values are specified consistent with the modified leading indicators. Finally, the cumulative risks and opportunities are reevaluated based on a roll-up of the new risk and opportunity information.

Figure 3.10 presents a flowchart depicting the development of a risk response, opportunity action, and internal control plan as an iterative process. The plan is initially proposed if the evaluation of the cumulative risks and opportunities of the various objectives indicates that one or more risks is intolerable or marginal and/or one or more opportunities is significant or marginal. The iteration of the plan continues until there is an optimal or near-optimal balance between the cumulative risks, the cumulative opportunities, and the cost of implementing the plan. Optimality is considered to be reached when the following conditions all apply:

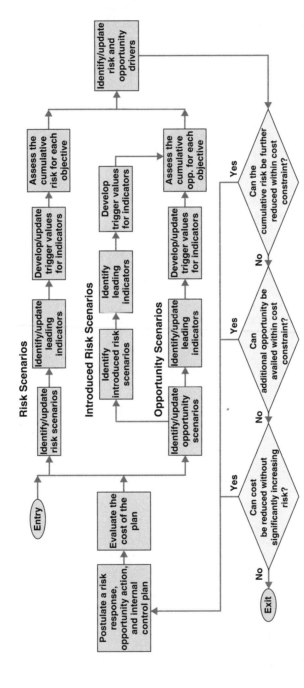

FIGURE 3.10 Iterative process for identifying and evaluating a risk response, opportunity action, and internal control plan that balances cumulative risk, cumulative opportunity, and cost

- The cumulative risks and opportunities for the top objectives are in balance (a condition that evolves from using the risk and opportunity drivers to guide the development of the plan at each iteration).
- The cumulative risks cannot be reduced further without violating cost constraints imposed on the organization.
- The cumulative opportunities cannot be availed further without violating the cost constraints.
- The cost of implementing the plan cannot be reduced further without negatively changing the status of one or more of the cumulative risks.

3.6.6 Brief Comparison of this Approach with the COSO Internal Control Framework and the GAO Green Book

The preceding two subsections have presented the position that internal controls should derive principally from the organization's strategic objectives and from considerations of the risk and opportunity drivers that affect the organization's ability to meet those objectives. The drivers are determined from the factors that most significantly affect aggregate risks and opportunities rather than just from individual risks and opportunities. The identification and evaluation of internal controls focus largely on protection of the assumptions that need to be maintained for the aggregate risks and opportunities to be effectively and efficiently controlled within the decision maker's risk tolerance and opportunity appetite.

This position differs philosophically somewhat from the approach taken in the COSO framework for internal controls (COSO 2013), which presents internal controls as being a part of ERM but ERM not necessarily being a part of internal controls. The following statements quoted from Appendix G of COSO (2013) explain the position advocated by COSO:

- "This *Internal Control—Integrated Framework* specifies three categories of objectives: operations, reporting, and compliance.... The *Enterprise Risk Management—Integrated Framework* adds a fourth category of objectives, strategic objectives, which operate at a higher level than the others.... Enterprise risk management is applied in setting strategies, as well as in working toward achievement of objectives in the other three categories."
- "The *Enterprise Risk Management Framework* introduces the concepts of risk appetite and risk tolerance.... The concept of risk tolerance is included in the *Framework* as a pre-condition to internal control, but not as a part of internal control."
- "A concept not contemplated in the *Internal Control—Integrated Framework* is a portfolio view of risk. Enterprise risk management

requires that in addition to focusing on risk in considering the achievement of entity objectives on an individual basis, it is necessary to consider composite risks from a portfolio perspective. Internal control does not require that the entity develop such a view."

- "*The Internal Control—Integrated Framework* focuses on identifying risks and does not include the concept of identifying opportunities as the decision to pursue opportunities is part of the broader strategy-setting process."

- "While both frameworks call for assessment of risk, the *Enterprise Risk Management—Integrated Framework* suggests viewing risk assessment through a sharper lens. Risks are considered on an inherent and a residual basis, preferably addressed in the same unit of measure established for the objectives to which the risks relate. Time horizons should be consistent with an entity's strategies and objectives and, where possible, observable data. The *Enterprise Risk Management—Integrated Framework* also calls attention to interrelated risks, describing how a single event may create multiple risks."

- "The *Internal Control—Integrated Framework* presents a more current view of technology and its impact on managing the entity."

- "The *Enterprise Risk Management—Integrated Framework* takes a broader view of information and communication, highlighting data derived from past, present, and potential future events,...consistent with the entity's need to identify events and assess and respond to risks and remain within its risk appetite. The *Internal Control—Integrated Framework* focuses more narrowly on data quality and relevant information needed for internal control."

The main point is that whereas the COSO ERM Framework considers all types of risk, including strategic risks, the COSO internal control framework looks only at day-to-day operational, reporting, and compliance risks. The COSO view of internal controls is aligned with its emphasis on enterprises whose principal objectives are financial. In the COSO framework, internal controls are viewed as an input to ERM but not as an output from it. In this book, EROM and internal controls are considered in a totally integrated fashion, so that strategic risks are intrinsically considered in the identification and evaluation of internal controls.

At the same time, the COSO formulation allows for entities to treat ERM and internal controls in a fully integrated manner at their discretion: "While it [ERM] is not intended to and does not replace the internal control framework, but rather incorporates the internal control framework within it, companies may decide to look to this enterprise risk management framework both to satisfy their internal control needs and to move toward a fuller risk management process" (COSO 2004).

The GAO Green Book (GAO 2014a), and by extension the updated version of OMB Circular A-123, takes an intermediate view of the integration of internal controls and ERM. The following statements quoted from the Green Book explain the position advanced by GAO:

- (OV2.10): "A direct relationship exists among an entity's objectives, the five components of internal control, and the organizational structure of an entity. Objectives are what an entity wants to achieve. The five components of internal control are what are required of the entity to achieve the objectives."
- (OV2.16): "Management, with oversight by an oversight body, sets objectives to meet the entity's mission, strategic plan, and goals and requirements of applicable laws and regulations."
- (OV2.18): "Management groups objectives into one or more of the three categories of objectives:
  - Operations Objectives—Effectiveness and efficiency of operations
  - Reporting Objectives—Reliability of reporting for internal and external use
  - Compliance Objectives—Compliance with applicable laws and regulations"
- (OV2.19): "Operations objectives relate to program operations that achieve an entity's mission. An entity's mission may be defined in a strategic plan. Such plans set the goals and objectives for an entity along with the effective and efficient operations necessary to fulfill those objectives. Effective operations produce the intended results from operational processes, while efficient operations do so in a manner that minimizes the waste of resources."

A significant difference between the Green Book and the COSO formulation is that the Green Book defines operational objectives to include strategic objectives, whereas the COSO formulation does not. Thus, ERM and internal controls are more fully integrated in the Green Book philosophy. However, the Green Book still tends to emphasize the control of day-to-day operations and issues such as fraud and financial transparency as the most critical objectives of internal controls.

OMB Circular-A-123 (OMB 2016b) takes the position that agencies formulating an internal controls framework that is integrated with ERM should initially, at a minimum, concentrate on the day-to-day operational, reporting, and compliance objectives defined by COSO (2013), but should within a reasonable amount of time, as part of their maturity model development, extend the framework to include the integration of internal controls with strategic objectives.

NOTES

1. As indicated in Table 2.1, the technical centers also serve in an additional role as Technical Authority, but this role does not entail an associated decomposition of objectives and is therefore not included in the discussion that follows.
2. The use of templates to account for inter-unit interactions in the roll-up of risks and opportunities to strategic level will be demonstrated in Chapter 4.
3. The nature of introduced risks will be explored more fully in Sections 4.4 and 4.5.
4. The term *watch* is used advisedly in this context. In practice, tolerable risks may be accepted, but continue to be watched to ensure they remain tolerable.
5. A more detailed illustration of the roll-up process will be provided in Sections 4.6.2 and 4.6.3 in connection with a particular example.
6. The identification of meaningful responses, actions, and internal controls will be discussed further in Section 4.7.3.

REFERENCES

Benjamin, A., Dezfuli, H., and Everett, C. 2015. "Developing Probabilistic Safety Performance Margins for Unknown and Underappreciated Risks." *Journal of Reliability Engineering and System Safety*. Available online from ScienceDirect.

Committee of Sponsoring Organizations of the Treadway Commission (COSO). 2004. Enterprise Risk Management—Integrated Framework: Application Techniques.

Committee of Sponsoring Organizations of the Treadway Commission (COSO), 2010. *Developing Key Risk Indicators to Strengthen Enterprise Risk Management.* http://www.coso.org/documents/COSOKRIPaperFull-FINALforWeb PostingDec110_000.pdf

Committee of Sponsoring Organizations of the Treadway Commission (COSO). 2013. Internal Control—Integrated Framework (Framework and Appendices).

Guarro, S. June 2014. "Quantitative Launch and Space Transport Vehicle Reliability and Safety Requirements: Useful or Problematic?" *Proc. PSAM-12 Int. Conference on Probabilistic Safety Assessment and Management*, Honolulu, HI.

GAO-14-704G. 2014a. The Green Book, Standards for Internal Control in the Federal Government. Washington, DC: Government Accountability Accounting Office. (September).

Leveson, N. April 2015. "A Systems Approach to Risk Management through Leading Safety Indicators." *Journal of Reliability Engineering and System Safety* 136: 17–34.

National Aeronautics and Space Administration (NASA). 2011. NASA/SP-2011-3422. *NASA Risk Management Handbook*. Washington, DC: National Aeronautics and Space Administration. http://www.hq.nasa.gov/office/codeq/doctree/NHBK_2011_3422.pdf

National Aeronautics and Space Administration (NASA). 2015. NASA/SP-2014-612. *NASA System Safety Handbook, Volume 2: System Safety Concepts, Guidelines, and Implementation Examples*. Washington, DC: National Aeronautics and Space Administration. http://www.hq.nasa.gov/office/codeq/doctree/NASASP2014612.pdf

Office of Management and Budget (OMB). 2016b. OMB Circular A-123. "Management's Responsibility for Enterprise Risk Management and Internal Control." (July) https://www.whitehouse.gov/sites/default/files/omb/memoranda/2016/m-16-17.pdf

The Development and Utilization of EROM Templates for Performance Evaluation and Strategic Planning

4.1   OVERVIEW

As discussed earlier (e.g., Section 1.1.4), the literature on ERM/EROM contains a significant amount of guidance on the organizational aspects of the topic and the fundamental framework to be used. However, it provides very few details on how to conduct the analyses that are needed in order to reap the benefits. Chapter 4 attempts to fill that gap by describing and demonstrating how comprehensive EROM analyses can be conducted using templates. In Sections 4.1 through 4.8, the templates will be introduced by pursuing an example that examines EROM's role in evaluating organizational performance for its ongoing programs, projects, activities, and initiatives, and in identifying and evaluating actions and controls to reduce risk and/or seize opportunity. In Section 4.9, the example will be modified to show how the same templates with different inputs can be applied to examine EROM's role in organizational planning, where the organization is interested in examining its likelihood of success in meeting its top objectives for various candidate sets of programs, projects, and so forth that are in the conceptual stage.

The use of templates is a practical, efficient, and broad-based approach for implementing the framework for EROM that is discussed in Chapters 2 and 3. To illustrate how templates can be applied effectively, a real-world example relevant to NASA will be pursued. The example will treat EROM from various vantage points: first by considering EROM implementation from the perspective of each of the major management levels in the organization (i.e., the executive, programmatic, and institutional/technical levels), and then from the perspective of the enterprise as a whole (i.e., integrated across the major management units).

The templates developed for this demonstration pertain principally to TRIO enterprises that conduct risky technical or scientific ventures and whose interest is mainly in achieving technical gain and knowledge advancement rather than financial gain for its stakeholders.[1] Following are the types of results that will be generated by the templates used in this demonstration:

High-Level Results (Suitable as a Synopsis for Management)
- A hierarchical list of objectives to be satisfied across the enterprise and the way that they interface with various levels of the organization (executive; programmatic; institutional/technical)
- A substantiated ranking (or rating) of the level of risk of not being able to achieve each objective
- A substantiated ranking of the level of opportunity available for improving the ability to achieve each objective
- A list of risk and opportunity drivers for each objective, leading to suggestions for responses such as mitigations and internal controls

Low-Level Results (Suitable for Explaining the Details behind the High-Level Results)
- Identification of the complex interfaces between each objective, and the rationale for how the likelihood of success for each objective affects the likelihood of success for other objectives
- A list of the significant individual risks and opportunity scenarios for each objective, and the rationale for why these scenarios are considered significant
- A list of the key risk and opportunity indicators and the rationale for how these indicators relate to the likelihood of success of each objective
- Specification of trigger values for each indicator, and the rationale for why these particular values signal the need for increased watchfulness or for a direct response
- A roll-up of the significant individual risks and opportunities from the bottom level of the objectives hierarchy (near-term objectives) to the top level (long-term or strategic objectives), along with the rationale for choices made during the roll-up
- Sensitivity results showing how the cumulative risk and opportunity for each objective are affected by various combinations of risk and opportunity scenarios and their constituent parts
- Risk and opportunity driver charts showing the time criticality for initiating response
- Assessment of the likelihoods and impacts of the risk and opportunity scenarios

4.2   DEMONSTRATION EXAMPLE: THE NASA NEXT-GENERATION SPACE TELESCOPE AS OF 2014

The example application involves the development, deployment, and operation of the next-generation space telescope. The demonstration is closely patterned after the James Webb Space Telescope (JWST) project at NASA, but the overall intent of the demonstration is to focus the reader's attention on the structure and form of the templates and how they may be used to facilitate strategic planning and performance evaluation in a general sense. To lend authenticity and promote recognition of the kinds of risks and opportunities that have to be dealt with, data pertinent to both the JWST and the Hubble Space Telescope (HST) are used throughout the example. The data for the JWST project reflects its status as of the end of 2014.

Timely completion of the JWST development and launching of the telescope is an agency priority goal (APG): "By October 2018, NASA will launch the James Webb Space Telescope, the premier space-based observatory. To enable this launch date, NASA will complete the James Webb Space Telescope primary mirror backplane and backplane support structures and deliver them to the Goddard Space Flight Center for integration with the mirror segments by September 30, 2015" (NASA 2014c, p. 24). The principal source of information is Report GAO-15-100 on the JWST project issued by the US Government Accountability Office in December 2014 to Congressional committees (GAO 2014b). Among other things, the report addresses the degree to which technical challenges have impacted the JWST project's ability to stay on schedule and budget, and the extent to which budget and cost estimates reflect information about project risks. The following bits of information obtained from this and other sources are mentioned here not to criticize the project or its management but rather to provide a basis for analyzing risks and opportunities in this demonstration using published information:[2]

Information Pertinent to JWST Schedule and Cost
- JWST is one of the most complex projects in NASA's history (GAO 2014b).
- In addition to the design, the scale of JWST's integration and test effort is more complex than most NASA projects (GAO 2014b).
- The cryocooler subsystem is particularly complex and challenging because of the relatively great distance between the cooling components and the need to overcome multiple sources of unwanted heat (GAO 2014b).
- The cryocooler subcontractor has experienced prior schedule delays and continued performance challenges (Leone 2014).

- The cryocooler element deferred seven earlier milestones until fiscal year 2015 as a result of manufacturing and development delays (GAO 2014b).
- The schedule reserve for development of the cryocooler subsystem diminished in 2014 from 5 months to 0 months (GAO 2014b).
- The schedule reserve for the development of other subsystems has also diminished in the past year, but not as much as that for the cryocooler subsystem (GAO 2014b).
- The project entered fiscal year 2015 with approximately 40 percent of its cost reserves already committed, leaving fewer dollars available to mitigate other threats to the project schedule (GAO 2014b).
- The White House and Congress have sparred about canceling existing operating programs (e.g., SOFIA, Spitzer) to help fund JWST, although no such cancellations have yet occurred (Foust 2014).

Information Pertinent to JWST Technical Requirements, Performance, and Design

- Successful attainment of high-resolution data requires a highly controlled environment, including minimum vibration, minimum stray light, particularly in the mid-infrared range, and minimum departures from a cold and stable temperature environment (GAO 2014b; also NASA 2016b).
- Although the subcontractor has built test cryogenic compressor units that perform to NASA's specifications when connected to the spacecraft platform by bolts, it has not yet been able to get a brazed unit to perform to specification, and brazing is a design requirement for NASA systems (Leone 2014).
- The cold head assembly for the cryocooler has not been vacuum-tested in its flight-ready configuration to verify leak-tight operation with replacement valves that were recently installed in the assembly (Leone 2014).
- The JWST is considered unserviceable, since it will be located far from Earth at the second LaGrange point approximately 1 million miles from Earth (NASA 2016b).
- Although nominally unserviceable, the JWST is designed to have a grapple arm for docking, implying that the option to conduct service missions has not been completely relinquished (NASA 2016b).

In addition to information pertaining to the JWST project, historical experience obtained from the operation of the HST in low earth orbit is relevant to this demonstration because of the similarity of the missions. Of particular interest are the following bits of information obtained from various sources:

Relevant Information Pertaining to HST

- The HST has undergone several successful servicing missions enabled by its proximity to Earth, but initially there was uncertainty as to whether a successful servicing mission could be accomplished (HubbleSite.org 2016).
- Several serious operational difficulties for the Hubble required servicing missions to perform retrofits and/or corrective actions, including the famous mirror fabrication error, which greatly degraded the quality of the image (Harwood 2009).
- Other operational difficulties that required a servicing mission included replacement of solar panels to correct a jitter problem caused by excessive flexing due to orbital cycling of solar input, and replacement of several gyros that were adversely affected by the launch environment (Harwood 2009).
- New opportunities were also availed through servicing missions, including incorporation of new, more sensitive instruments and addition of the Advanced Camera for Surveys, which was used to explore dark energy and other cosmological findings revealed by the HST (NASA 2009).

4.3   EXAMPLE OBJECTIVES HIERARCHIES

We first specify objectives separately for each organizational management unit and then integrate them together into a single objectives hierarchy that spans over the organization. The management units for this example are grouped into the following three NASA organizational levels: executive (E), mission directorate or programmatic (P), and center (C).[3]

4.3.1   Objectives Hierarchies for Different Management Levels

Executive-level objectives are the strategic objectives of the enterprise, derived in this case from the NASA Strategic Plan, and are considered to have a time frame of more than 10 years. Two strategic objectives are considered in this example, as shown in Figure 4.1.

Programmatic-level objectives are concerned with design, development, fabrication, fielding, and operation of systems that support the various strategic objectives that relate to NASA's mission. Four programmatic-level objectives are included in this example, as shown in Figure 4.2, differentiated according to the time frames over which they apply.

Center-level objectives fall into two different categories: program/project support and development of the institutional capability. Two of each category are considered in this example, as shown in Figure 4.3.

Executive-Level Objectives: Strategic Focus

> 10 Years

Discover how the universe works, explore how it began and evolved, and search for life on planets around other stars

> 10 Years

Attract and advance a highly skilled, competent, and diverse workforce, cultivate an innovative work environment, and provide the facilities, tools, and services needed to conduct NASA's missions

FIGURE 4.1   Executive-level objectives for the example demonstration

Programmatic-Level Objectives: Program/Project Management Focus

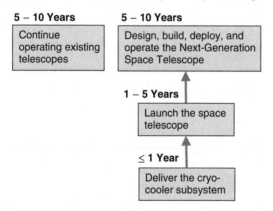

5 – 10 Years

Continue operating existing telescopes

5 – 10 Years

Design, build, deploy, and operate the Next-Generation Space Telescope

1 – 5 Years

Launch the space telescope

≤ 1 Year

Deliver the cryo-cooler subsystem

FIGURE 4.2   Programmatic-level objectives for the example demonstration

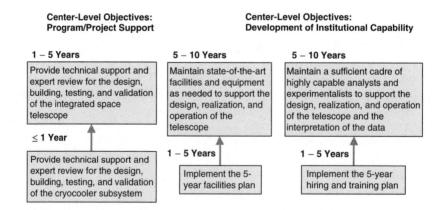

Center-Level Objectives:
Program/Project Support

Center-Level Objectives:
Development of Institutional Capability

1 – 5 Years

Provide technical support and expert review for the design, building, testing, and validation of the integrated space telescope

≤ 1 Year

Provide technical support and expert review for the design, building, testing, and validation of the cryocooler subsystem

5 – 10 Years

Maintain state-of-the-art facilities and equipment as needed to support the design, realization, and operation of the telescope

1 – 5 Years

Implement the 5-year facilities plan

5 – 10 Years

Maintain a sufficient cadre of highly capable analysts and experimentalists to support the design, realization, and operation of the telescope and the interpretation of the data

1 – 5 Years

Implement the 5-year hiring and training plan

FIGURE 4.3   Center-level objectives for the example demonstration

Like programmatic-level objectives, they are differentiated according to the time frames over which they apply.

4.3.2 Integrated Objectives Hierarchies for the Enterprise as a Whole

Figure 4.4 illustrates for the example demonstration how the objectives hierarchies at executive, programmatic, and center levels are integrated into a single objectives hierarchy that maintains the relationships between objectives within each level and introduces the principal interfaces that exist across levels. In general, the programmatic-level objectives support one or more executive-level objectives, whereas the center-level objectives may support both the programmatic-level objectives and one or more executive-level objectives. For example, the objective numbered C (5–10) #6 and titled "Maintain a Sufficient Cadre of Highly Capable Analysts" directly supports both objective P (5–10) #4 titled "Design, Build, Deploy, and Operate the Next Generation Space Telescope," and objective E (>10) #2 titled "Attract and Advance a Highly Skilled Workforce, Cultivate an Innovative Work Environment, and Provide the Facilities, Tools, and Services Needed to Conduct NASA's Missions."[4]

4.4 RISKS, OPPORTUNITIES, AND LEADING INDICATORS

In the demonstration, as in the methodology development presented earlier (e.g., Section 1.2.4), we speak of two levels of risk and opportunity: (1) individual and (2) cumulative or aggregate. Individual risks and opportunities are introduced by means of scenario statements. Each objective in the hierarchy may have several risk and opportunity scenarios associated with it. Each objective also has cumulative risk and opportunity, which represents the roll-up of both of the following:

1. The individual risk and opportunity scenarios that feed into it
2. The cumulative risks and opportunities of the interfacing objectives that feed into it (i.e., its daughter objectives)

In preparation for demonstrating each step that is needed to complete the space telescope example, it is important to keep an eye on the principal outcomes that are sought. These include:

- Identification, evaluation, and ranking of individual known risks
- Identification, evaluation, and ranking of individual known opportunities

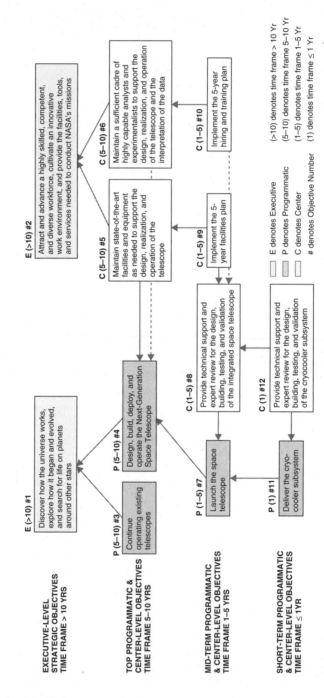

FIGURE 4.4 Integrated objectives hierarchy showing primary interfaces between objectives

- Evaluation and ranking of cumulative known risks
- Evaluation and ranking of cumulative known opportunities
- Evaluation and ranking of cumulative UU risks
- Identification of risk and opportunity drivers and suggestions for responses, including actions and internal controls

For conceptual purposes, a high-level schematic of the form of the anticipated results for cumulative risks and opportunities is shown in Table 4.1. The pursuit of the example in the following sections leads to results such as these.

4.4.1 Known Risk and Opportunity Scenarios

Based on the information pertinent to JWST and HST presented in Section 4.2, a total of eight individual risks and one individual opportunity are postulated for this demonstration. Two of the individual risks are assigned to strategic objective E(>10) #1, as shown in Figure 4.5, and one of those is also assigned to objective E(>10) #2 because it directly affects both objectives. Also shown are suggested leading indicators that apply to each risk.

In Figure 4.6, another three risks, with associated leading indicators, are assigned, respectively, to programmatic objectives at the top level, the mid-term level, and the short-term level, and in Figure 4.7, two risks, with associated leading indicators, are assigned to mid-term mission support objectives C (1–5) #9 and C (1–5) #10 in the institutional category. Finally, in Figure 4.8, a single opportunity, with associated leading indicators, is identified for strategic objective E (>10) #1, along with three introduced risks, with their own associated leading indicators, that would be of concern if the opportunity were acted on.

4.4.2 Cross-Cutting Risks and Opportunities

Risk and opportunity scenarios identified during the practice of EROM may be cross-cutting in several ways:

- Organizationally cross-cutting scenarios affect multiple organizational units within an enterprise. All the risks and opportunities in Figures 4.5 through 4.8 are cross-cutting in this sense.
- Programmatically cross-cutting scenarios affect multiple programs and/or projects within the enterprise. One of the two risks in Figure 4.5 (the one placed higher in the chart) and both risks in Figure 4.7 are programmatically cross-cutting.

TABLE 4.1 A View of the Form of the Outcome for Cumulative Risks and Opportunities

Objective Index	Objective Description	Risk to Objective Level of Concern (−1, −2, −3)	Opportunity Level of Interest (+1, +2, +3)	Drivers	Suggested Responses and Internal Controls	UU Risk to Objective Level of Concern (−1, −2, −3)	UU Drivers	Suggested Responses and Internal Controls
C (1) #12	Provide tech. support and expert review for design, building, testing, validation of the cryocooler subsystem	TBD	TBD	TBD	TBD	TBD	TBD	TBD
P (1) #11	Deliver the cryocooler subsystem	TBD	TBD	TBD	TBD	TBD	TBD	TBD
C (1–5) #10	Implement the 5-year hiring and training plan	TBD	TBD	TBD	TBD	TBD	TBD	TBD
C (1–5) #9	Implement the 5-year facilities plan	TBD	TBD	TBD	TBD	TBD	TBD	TBD
C (1–5) #8	Provide technical support and expert review for the design, building, testing, validation of the integrated space telescope	TBD	TBD	TBD	TBD	TBD	TBD	TBD
P (1–5) #7	Launch the space telescope	TBD	TBD	TBD	TBD	TBD	TBD	TBD
C (5–10) #6	Maintain a sufficient cadre of highly capable analysts and experimentalists to support design, realization, and operation of telescope and interpretation of data	TBD	TBD	TBD	TBD	TBD	TBD	TBD
C (5–10) #5	Maintain state-of-the-art facilities and equipment to support design, realization, and operation of the telescope	TBD	TBD	TBD	TBD	TBD	TBD	TBD

P (5–10) #4 Design, build, deploy, and operate the Next-Generation Space Telescope	TBD	TBD	TBD	TBD	TBD	TBD	TBD	TBD
P (5–10) #3 Continue operating existing telescopes	TBD	TBD	TBD	TBD	TBD	TBD	TBD	TBD
E (>10) #2 Attract/advance a highly skilled workforce, cultivate an innovative work environment, and provide the facilities, tools, and services needed to conduct NASA's missions	TBD	TBD		TBD		TBD	TBD	TBD
E (>10) #1 Discover how the universe works, explore how it began and evolved, and search for life on planets around other stars	TBD	TBD	TBD	TBD	TBD	TBD	TBD	TBD

Palette for TBD Shaded Cells:

Green Risk: Tolerable −1	Yellow Risk: Marginal −2	Red Risk: Intolerable −3	Beige Oppor.: Insignificant +1	Violet Oppor.: Marginal +2	Blue Oppor.: Significant +3

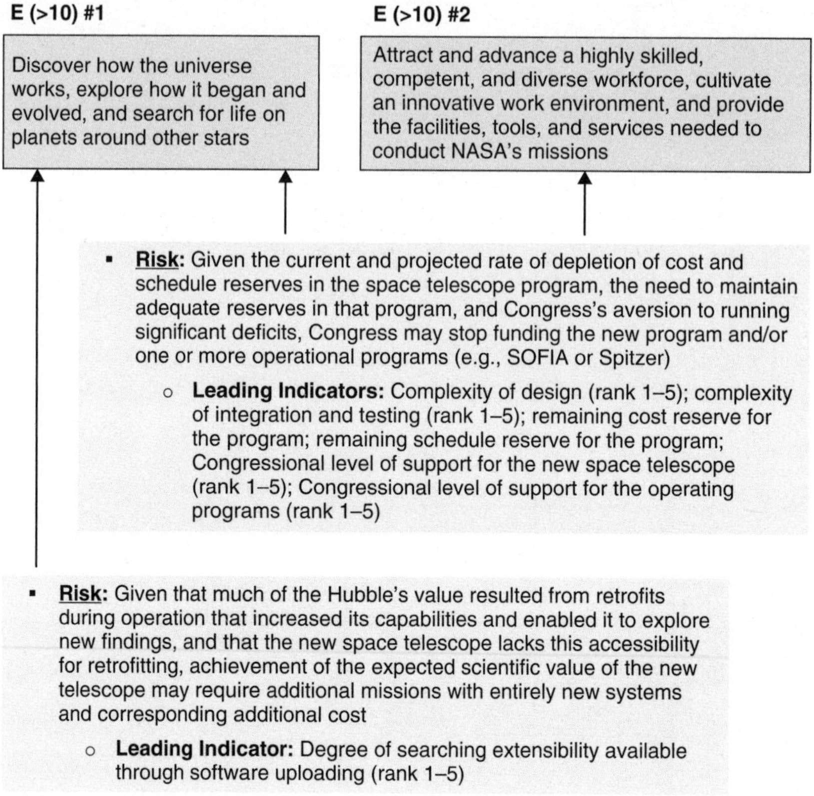

E (>10) #1

Discover how the universe works, explore how it began and evolved, and search for life on planets around other stars

E (>10) #2

Attract and advance a highly skilled, competent, and diverse workforce, cultivate an innovative work environment, and provide the facilities, tools, and services needed to conduct NASA's missions

- **Risk:** Given the current and projected rate of depletion of cost and schedule reserves in the space telescope program, the need to maintain adequate reserves in that program, and Congress's aversion to running significant deficits, Congress may stop funding the new program and/or one or more operational programs (e.g., SOFIA or Spitzer)
    - o **Leading Indicators:** Complexity of design (rank 1–5); complexity of integration and testing (rank 1–5); remaining cost reserve for the program; remaining schedule reserve for the program; Congressional level of support for the new space telescope (rank 1–5); Congressional level of support for the operating programs (rank 1–5)

- **Risk:** Given that much of the Hubble's value resulted from retrofits during operation that increased its capabilities and enabled it to explore new findings, and that the new space telescope lacks this accessibility for retrofitting, achievement of the expected scientific value of the new telescope may require additional missions with entirely new systems and corresponding additional cost
    - o **Leading Indicator:** Degree of searching extensibility available through software uploading (rank 1–5)

FIGURE 4.5 Individual risks and associated leading indicators for executive-level objectives

- Strategically cross-cutting scenarios directly affect multiple high-level objectives in the objectives hierarchy. The risk in Figure 4.5 identified in the previous bullet as being programmatically cross-cutting is also strategically cross-cutting.
- Pan-agency cross-cutting scenarios affect more than one agency. Such risks occur when agencies are involved in a cooperative effort.

Furthermore, it may be observed in Figures 4.5 through 4.8 that certain leading indicators may affect multiple risk scenarios and/or multiple objectives. For example, the indicator "complexity of design" affects a risk scenario and two objectives in Figure 4.5, as well as two risks and two objectives in Figure 4.6. This may be thought of as a "cross-cutting" leading indicator.

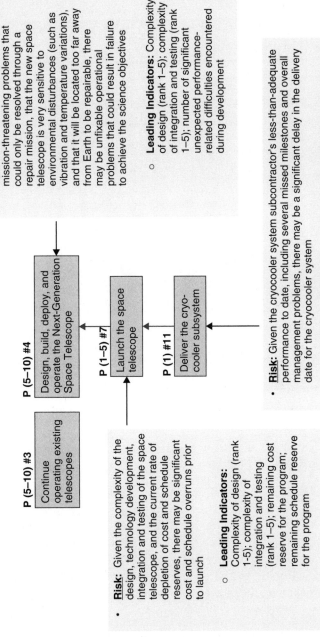

P (5–10) #3

Continue operating existing telescopes

P (5–10) #4

Design, build, deploy, and operate the Next-Generation Space Telescope

P (1–5) #7

Launch the space telescope

P (1) #11

Deliver the cryocooler subsystem

- **Risk:** Given that the Hubble had mission-threatening problems that could only be resolved through a repair mission, that the new space telescope is very sensitive to environmental disturbances (such as vibration and temperature variations), and that it will be located too far away from Earth to be repairable, there may be unfixable operational problems that could result in failure to achieve the science objectives

  ○ **Leading Indicators:** Complexity of design (rank 1–5); complexity of integration and testing (rank 1–5); number of significant unexpected performance-related difficulties encountered during development

- **Risk:** Given the complexity of the design, technology development, integration and testing of the space telescope, and the current rate of depletion of cost and schedule reserves, there may be significant cost and schedule overruns prior to launch

  ○ **Leading Indicators:** Complexity of design (rank 1–5); complexity of integration and testing (rank 1–5); remaining cost reserve for the program; remaining schedule reserve for the program

- **Risk:** Given the cryocooler system subcontractor's less-than-adequate performance to date, including several missed milestones and overall management problems, there may be a significant delay in the delivery date for the cryocooler system

  ○ **Leading Indicators:** Remaining schedule reserve for cryocooler development; remaining cost reserve that can be allocated to cryocooler development; severity of unresolved technical issues for cryocooler development (scale 1–5); GAO evaluation of cryocooler development problems (scale 1–5)

FIGURE 4.6 Individual risks and associated leading indicators for program-level objectives

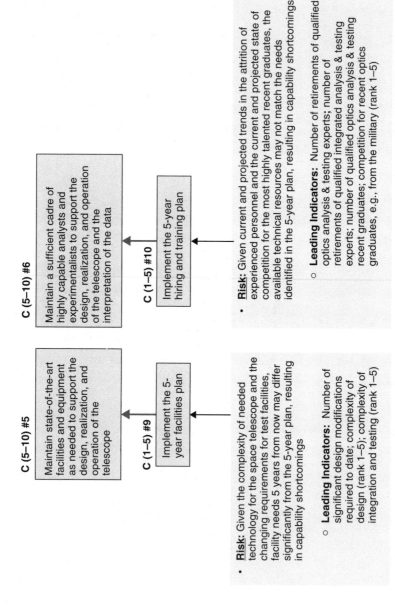

C (5–10) #5

Maintain state-of-the-art facilities and equipment as needed to support the design, realization, and operation of the telescope

C (5–10) #6

Maintain a sufficient cadre of highly capable analysts and experimentalists to support the design, realization, and operation of the telescope and the interpretation of the data

C (1–5) #9

Implement the 5-year facilities plan

C (1–5) #10

Implement the 5-year hiring and training plan

- **Risk:** Given the complexity of needed technology for the space telescope and the changing requirements for test facilities, facility needs 5 years from now may differ significantly from the 5-year plan, resulting in capability shortcomings

  o **Leading Indicators:** Number of significant design modifications required to date; complexity of design (rank 1–5); complexity of integration and testing (rank 1–5)

- **Risk:** Given current and projected trends in the attrition of experienced personnel and the current and projected state of competition for the most highly talented recent graduates, the available technical resources may not match the needs identified in the 5-year plan, resulting in capability shortcomings

  o **Leading Indicators:** Number of retirements of qualified optics analysis & testing experts; number of retirements of qualified integrated analysis & testing experts; number of qualified optics analysis & testing recent graduates; competition for recent optics graduates, e.g., from the military (rank 1–5)

FIGURE 4.7 Individual risks and associated leading indicators for center-level objectives

E (>10) #1

Discover how the universe works, explore how it began and evolved, and search for life on planets around other stars

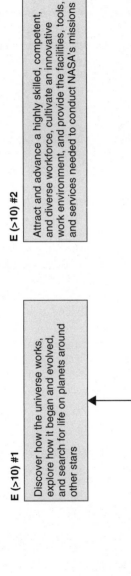

E (>10) #2

Attract and advance a highly skilled, competent, and diverse workforce, cultivate an innovative work environment, and provide the facilities, tools, and services needed to conduct NASA's missions

- **Opportunity:** Given the rate of technology advancement and the fact that the space telescope has a grapple arm, it is possible that significant new technology advancements (such as a camera with improved resolution) could be delivered and installed on the telescope through retrofitting either by astronauts or robotically

  o **Leading Indicators:** Technology readiness level for improved resolution infrared cameras; readiness level for SLS/Orion including docking capability

- **First Introduced Risk:** If the retrofit requires astronaut participation, the likelihood of loss of crew for a lunar mission

  o **Leading Indicator:** Predicted probability of loss of crew for SLS/Orion for a lunar mission

- **Second Introduced Risk:** If the retrofit can be performed robotically, the likelihood of loss of mission may be unacceptable

  o **Leading Indicator:** Predicted probability of loss of mission for SLS

- **Third Introduced Risk:** The cost of the retrofit mission, whether crewed or robotic, may be unacceptable

  o **Leading Indicator:** Predicted cost for a similar rendezvous mission

FIGURE 4.8 Individual opportunities, introduced risks, and associated leading indicators for executive-level objectives

The EROM methodology is designed to promote consideration of cross-cutting risks, opportunities, and leading indicators by allowing for them to be entered into the accounting wherever is appropriate. Multiple listings of the same scenario or indicator under different entities, programs, or objectives is not a problem so long as they are treated consistently each time they are encountered. The use of taxonomies, as described in Section 3.4.1, can facilitate the identification of cross-cutting risk and opportunity scenarios and cross-cutting leading indicators.

4.4.3   Unknown and Underappreciated Risks

The process of identifying risk and opportunity scenarios is, of course, aimed at known risks and opportunities. In addition to known scenarios, however, the potential for unknown and/or underappreciated (UU) risks must be considered when determining the overall likelihood of success or failure (i.e., the cumulative risk of not being able to satisfy the top objectives).

It may be noted that several of the leading indicators listed in Figure 4.5 through 4.7 pertain either directly or indirectly to sources of UU risk. For example, "complexity of design" and "complexity of integration and testing" are direct exemplars of the first UU factor cited in Section 3.4.5: "amount of complexity, particularly involving the interfaces between different elements of the system." In addition, the following leading indicator cited in Figure 4.6: "severity of unresolved technical issues for cryocooler development," is an indirect exemplar of the third UU factor in Section 3.4.5: "use of fundamentally new technology or fundamentally new application of an existing technology." If the assessment in this example had been performed prior to 2010, the sixth UU factor in Section 3.4.5 might also have been cited as a leading indicator of future risks about former management deficiencies pertaining to subcooler development: "degree of oversight when responsibilities are distributed among various entities" (NASA 2016b; HubbleSite.org 2016).

Beside these indicators, there are also other leading indicators (see Section 3.4.5) that tend to be correlated with the occurrence of UU challenges. Two of the most important are:

- Pressures to meet extremely tight schedules and/or budgets, particularly in combination with a complex set of tasks
- Deficiencies of management such as failure to maintain adequate oversight of distributed suppliers and failure to respect and promote open communication

In addition to the ranking of cumulative known risks and opportunities for each objective, therefore, the principal outcome of the demonstration will also include a ranking of the cumulative level of concern for UU risks based on the leading indicators that pertain to UU risks, along with a list of the key attributes of the UU indicators that drive that cumulative ranking.[5]

4.5　EXAMPLE TEMPLATES FOR RISK AND OPPORTUNITY IDENTIFICATION AND EVALUATION

Sections 4.5, 4.6, and 4.7 present a series of templates intended to demonstrate how the information presented in the preceding sections can be used first to evaluate the aggregate risk and aggregate opportunity associated with each objective in the integrated hierarchy of objectives, and then to identify and evaluate options for risk mitigation, opportunity action, and internal control. The principal purpose of the templates is to ensure that all relevant information is brought to bear in a fashion that is rational, comprehensive, and transparent.

4.5.1　Risk and Opportunity Identification Template

Table 4.2 presents the Risk and Opportunity Identification Template, which collects the information about known risks and opportunities presented in Section 4.4. It does this by tabulating the identified individual risk, opportunity, and introduced risk scenarios, the leading indicators for each scenario, and the objective to which each scenario is assigned.

4.5.2　Leading Indicator Evaluation Template

Table 4.3 presents the Leading Indicator Evaluation Template, which is used to assign watch and response trigger values to each leading indicator, record the current value of the indicator, and provide an indication of the trend. As explained earlier, leading indicator trigger values are used to signal when a risk is reaching a risk tolerance boundary or when an opportunity is reaching an opportunity appetite boundary. Reaching the trigger values for risk leading indicators implies that the likelihood of not being able to satisfy an element of the strategic objectives hierarchy is becoming a concern. Reaching the trigger values for opportunity leading indicators implies either that there is a potential for significantly increasing the likelihood of being able to satisfy an element of the strategic objectives hierarchy or that there is an emerging opportunity to achieve new goals and objectives that were formerly considered unreachable or inconceivable. Exceedance of a *watch trigger* suggests that an action should be considered but is not imminently needed.

TABLE 4.2 Risk and Opportunity Identification Template

Italic typeface denotes repeated instances of risks, opportunities, or leading indicators

Obj. No.	Objective Description	Scen. Type	Scen. No.	Scenario Statement	Leading Indicator Number	Leading Indicator Description
P (1) #11	Deliver the cryocooler subsystem	Risk	1	Given the cryocooler system subcontractor's less-than-adequate performance to date, including several missed milestones and overall management problems, there may be a significant delay in the delivery date for the cryocooler system	1	Remaining schedule reserve for cryocooler development
					2	Remaining cost reserve for the program that can be allocated to cryo devel.
					3	Severity of unresolved technical issues for cryo development (scale 1–5)
					4	GAO evaluation of cryocooler development problems (scale 1–5)
C (1–5) #10	Implement the 5-year hiring and training plan	Risk	2	Given current and projected trends in the attrition of experienced personnel and the current and projected state of competition for the most highly talented recent graduates, the available technical resources may not match the needs identified in the 5-year plan, resulting in capability shortcomings	5	Number of retirements of qualified optics analysis & testing experts
					6	Number of retirements of qualified integated analysis & testing experts
					7	Number of qualified optics analysis & testing recent graduates
					8	Competition for recent optics graduates, e.g., from the military (rank 1–5)
C (1–5) #9	Implement the 5-year facilities plan	Risk	3	Given the complexity of needed technology for the space telescope and the changing requirements for test facilities, facility needs 5 years from now may differ significantly from the 5-year plan, resulting in capability shortcomings	9	Number of significant design modifications required to date
					10	Complexity of design (rank 1–5)
					11	Complexity of integration and testing (rank 1–5)

114

P (1–5) #7	Launch the space telescope	Risk	4	Given the complexity of the design, technology development, integration and testing of the space telescope and the current rate of depletion of cost and schedule reserves, there may be significant cost and schedule overruns prior to launch	10	*Complexity of design (rank 1–5)*
					11	*Complexity of integration and testing (rank 1–5)*
					12	Remaining cost reserve for the program
					13	Remaining schedule reserve for the program
P (5–10) #4	Design, build, deploy, and operate the Next-Generation Space Telescope	Risk	5	Given that the Hubble had mission-threatening problems that could only be resolved through a repair mission, that the new space telescope is very sensitive to environmental disturbances, and that it will be located too far away from Earth to be repairable, there may be unfixable operational problems that could result in failure to achieve the science objectives	10	*Complexity of design (rank 1–5)*
					11	*Complexity of integration and testing (rank 1–5)*
					14	Number of significant unexpected performance-related difficulties encountered during development
E (>10) #2	Attract a highly skilled workforce, cultivate an innovative work environment, and provide needed facilities, tools, and services	Risk	6	Given the current and projected rate of depletion of cost and schedule reserves in the space telescope program, the need to maintain adequate reserves in that program, and Congress's aversion to running significant deficits, Congress may stop funding the new program and/or one or more operational programs (e.g., SOFIA or Spitzer)	12	*Cost reserve for the program*
					13	*Schedule reserve for the program*
					15	Congressional level of support for the new space telescope (rank 1–5)
					16	Congressional level of support for the operating programs (rank 1–5)

(continued)

TABLE 4.2 (*Continued*)

Italic typeface denotes repeated instances of risks, opportunities, or leading indicators

Obj. No.	Objective Description	Scen. Type	Scen. No.	Scenario Statement	Leading Indicator Number	Leading Indicator Description
E (>10) #1	Discover how the universe works, explore how it began and evolved, and search for life on planets around other stars	*Risk*	6	*Same as above*	*10–13, 15,16*	*Same as above*
		Risk	7	Given that much of the Hubble's value resulted from retrofits during operation that increased its capabilities and enabled it to explore new findings, and that the new space telescope lacks this accessibility for retrofitting, achievement of the expected scientific value of the new telescope may require additional missions with entirely new systems and corresponding additional cost	17	Degree of searching extensibility available through software uploading (rank 1–5)
E (>10) #1	Discover how the universe works, explore how it began and evolved, and search for life on planets around other stars	Opp.	8	Given the rate of tech. advancement and the fact that the space telescope has a grapple arm, it is possible that significant new technology advancements (such as a camera with improved resolution) could be delivered and installed on the telescope through retrofitting either by astronauts or robotically	18	Technology readiness level for improved resolution infrared cameras
					19	Readiness level for SLS/Orion, including docking capability
		Intr. Risk	9	If the retrofit requires astronaut participation, the likelihood of loss of crew may be unacceptable	20	Predicted P(LOC) for SLS/Orion for a lunar mission
		Intr. Risk	10	If the retrofit can be performed robotically, the likelihood of loss of mission may be unacceptable	21	Predicted P(LOM) for SLS
		Intr. Risk	11	The cost of the retrofit mission, whether crewed or robotic, may be unacceptable	22	Predicted cost for a rendezvous mission

TABLE 4.3 Leading Indicator Evaluation Template

Italic typeface denotes repeated instances of leading indicators

Obj. No.	Leading Indicator Number	Leading Indicator Description	Risk, Opp., or Intr.	Scen. No.	Lead. Ind. Watch Value	Ration-ale or Source	Lead. Ind. Resp. Value	Ration-ale or Source	Lead. Ind. Current Value	Ration-ale or Source	Lead. Ind. 1-Yr. Projected Value	Ration-ale or Source	Lead. Ind. Level of Concern or Interest
P (1) #11	1	Remaining schedule reserve for cryocooler development	Risk	1	XX	XX	XX	XX	XX	XX	XX to XX	XX	TBD
	2	Remaining cost reserve that can be allocated to cryo devel.	Risk	1	XX	XX	XX	XX	XX	XX	XX to XX	XX	TBD
	3	Severity of unresolved technical issues for cryo devel.	Risk	1	XX	XX	XX	XX	XX	XX	XX to XX	XX	TBD
	4	GAO evaluation of cryocooler development problems	Risk	1	XX	XX	XX	XX	XX	XX	XX to XX	XX	TBD
C (1–5) #10	5	No. of retirements of qualif. optics anal. & testing experts	Risk	2	XX	XX	XX	XX	XX	XX	XX to XX	XX	TBD
	6	No. of retirements of qualif. integr. anal. & testing experts	Risk	2	XX	XX	XX	XX	XX	XX	XX to XX	XX	TBD
	7	No. of qualified optics analysis & testing recent graduates	Risk	2	XX	XX	XX	XX	XX	XX	XX to XX	XX	TBD
	8	Competition for recent optics grads, e.g., from the military	Risk	2	XX	XX	XX	XX	XX	XX	XX to XX	XX	TBD

(continued)

TABLE 4.3 (*Continued*)

Italic typeface denotes repeated instances of leading indicators

Obj No.	Leading Indicator Number	Leading Indicator Description	Risk, Opp., or Intr. Risk	Scen. No.	Lead. Ind. Watch Value	Rationale or Source	Lead. Ind. Resp. Value	Rationale or Source	Lead. Ind. Current Value	Rationale or Source	Lead. Ind. 1-Yr. Projected Value	Rationale or Source	Lead. Ind. Level of Concern or Interest
C (1–5) #9	9	No. of significant design modifications required to date	Risk	3	XX	XX	XX	XX	XX	XX	XX to XX	XX	TBD
	10	Complexity of design (rank 1–5)	Risk	3	XX	XX	XX	XX	XX	XX	XX to XX	XX	TBD
	11	Complexity of integration and testing (rank 1–5)	Risk	3	XX	XX	XX	XX	XX	XX	XX to XX	XX	TBD
P (1–5) #7	*10*	*Complexity of design (rank 1–5)*	Risk	4	XX	XX	XX	XX	XX	XX	XX to XX	XX	TBD
	11	*Complexity of integration and testing (rank 1–5)*	Risk	4	XX	XX	XX	XX	XX	XX	XX to XX	XX	TBD
	12	Remaining cost reserve for the program	Risk	4	XX	XX	XX	XX	XX	XX	XX to XX	XX	TBD
	13	Remaining schedule reserve for the program	Risk	4	XX	XX	XX	XX	XX	XX	XX to XX	XX	TBD
P (5–10) #4	*10*	*Complexity of design (rank 1–5)*	Risk	5	XX	XX	XX	XX	XX	XX	XX to XX	XX	TBD
	11	*Complexity of integration and testing (rank 1–5)*	Risk	5	XX	XX	XX	XX	XX	XX	XX to XX	XX	TBD
	14	No. significant unexpected perf. difficulties during devel.	Risk	5	XX	XX	XX	XX	XX	XX	XX to XX	XX	TBD

E (>10) #2	12	Cost reserve for the program	Risk	6	XX	XX	XX	XX	XX	XX to XX	XX	TBD
	13	Schedule reserve for the program	Risk	6	XX	XX	XX	XX	XX	XX to XX	XX	TBD
	15	Congressional level of support for the new space telescope	Risk	6	XX	XX	XX	XX	XX	XX to XX	XX	TBD
	16	Congressional level of support for the operational progs.	Risk	6	XX	XX	XX	XX	XX	XX to XX	XX	TBD
E (>10) #1	10	Complexity of design (rank 1–5)	Risk	6	XX	XX	XX	XX	XX	XX to XX	XX	TBD
	11	Complexity of integration and testing (rank 1–5)	Risk	6	XX	XX	XX	XX	XX	XX to XX	XX	TBD
	12	Cost reserve for the program	Risk	6	XX	XX	XX	XX	XX	XX to XX	XX	TBD
	13	Schedule reserve for the program	Risk	6	XX	XX	XX	XX	XX	XX to XX	XX	TBD
	15	Congressional level of support for the new space telescope	Risk	6	XX	XX	XX	XX	XX	XX to XX	XX	TBD
	16	Congressional level of support for the operational progs.	Risk	6	XX	XX	XX	XX	XX	XX to XX	XX	TBD
	17	Degree of searching extensibility avail. thru S/W uploading	Risk	7								TBD

(continued)

TABLE 4.3 *(Continued)*

Italic typeface denotes repeated instances of leading indicators

Obj No.	Leading Indicator Number	Leading Indicator Description	Risk, Opp., or Intr. Risk	Scen. No.	Lead. Ind. Watch Value	Ration-ale or Source	Lead. Ind. Resp. Value	Ration-ale or Source	Lead. Ind. Current Value	Ration-ale or Source	Lead. Ind. 1-Yr. Projected Value	Ration-ale or Source	Lead. Ind. Level of Concern or Interest
E (>10) #1	18	Tech. readiness level for improved resolution IR cameras	Opp.	8	XX	XX	XX	XX	XX	XX	XX to XX	XX	TBD
	19	Readiness level for SLS/ Orion, including docking capability	Opp.	8	XX	XX	XX	XX	XX	XX	XX to XX	XX	TBD
	20	Predicted P(LOC) for SLS/ Orion lunar mission	Intr. R.	9	XX	XX	XX	XX	XX	XX	XX to XX	XX	TBD
	21	Predicted P(LOM) for SLS	Intr. R.	10	XX	XX	XX	XX	XX	XX	XX to XX	XX	TBD
	22	Predicted cost for a rendezvous mission	Intr. R.	11	XX	XX	XX	XX	XX	XX	XX to XX	XX	TBD

Palette for TBD Shaded Cells:

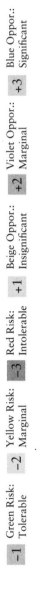

-1 Green Risk: Tolerable   -2 Yellow Risk: Marginal   -3 Red Risk: Intolerable   +1 Beige Oppor.: Insignificant   +2 Violet Oppor.: Marginal   +3 Blue Oppor.: Significant

Exceedance of a *response trigger* suggests that an action may be imminently needed (e.g., mitigation of the risk or exploitation of the opportunity).

The level of concern for a given leading indicator is determined by where the current value of the leading indicator and/or a projected future value lie with respect to the watch and response trigger values. In Table 4.3, the projected future value one year from the present (referred to earlier as the "trend") is shown as a range to account for uncertainty. For conceptual purposes, it may be helpful for some people to think of the uncertainty range as being more-or-less a 90 percent confidence interval for the future value of the leading indicator. However, if confidence levels are used in this context, they should be thought of as qualitative degrees of belief and not statistical quantities.

Table 4.4 illustrates how the Leading Indicator Evaluation Template might be completed for short-term programmatic objective P (1) #11, titled "Deliver the cryocooler subsystem." The entries are based principally on information about the JWST that was previously itemized in Section 4.2—that is, publicly available material. The use of this information is summarized in the columns labeled "Rationale." In short, the template records the following information:

- The 100 percent reduction during the past year in the schedule margin for development of the cryocooler (leading indicator 1) has caused concern about the cryocooler delivery date and the schedule of the program as a whole.
- The 40 percent reduction during the past year in the cost margin for the program as a whole (leading indicator 2) has caused concern about the amount of resources that can be reallocated to the cryocooler.
- The fact that several significant technical issues have not yet been completely resolved (leading indicator 3) has caused further concern.
- A somewhat negative progress report written by the GAO (leading indicator 4) about management problems concerning the cryocooler development has again caused concern.
- A trending analysis by JPL implying that the schedule margin will not be further degraded (one-year projected value for leading indicator 1) has alleviated some concern, particularly since the analysis indicates that the schedule for integrating the cryocooler with the spacecraft and beginning the integrated testing should remain intact.
- The warning signs discussed by the GAO, however, suggest there is a large amount of uncertainty in JPL's estimate, leading to additional concern.

TABLE 4.4 Example Entries for Leading Indicator Evaluation Template for Objective P(1) #11: Deliver the Cryocooler Subsystem

Objec. No.	Leading Indicator Number	Leading Indicator Description	Risk, Opp., or Ind. Risk	Scen. No.	Lead. Ind. Watch Value	Rationale or Source	Lead. Ind. Resp. Value	Rationale or Source	Lead. Ind. Current Value	Rationale or Source	Lead. Ind. 1-Yr. Projected Value	Projected Rationale or Source	Leading Indicator Level of Concern
P (1) #11	1	Remaining schedule reserve for cryocooler development	Risk	1	50% of plan	Historically correlated with moderate likelihood of overrun	10% of plan	Historically correlated with high likelihood of overrun	0% of plan	As reported by GAO	0% to 30% of plan	The schedule reserve for cryo development diminished from 5 months to 0 months in the past year, but there is enough schedule reserve in other tasks to divert manpower to the cryocooler development task so as to regain its positive reserve	−3 Red: Intolerable

122

P (1) #11	2	Remaining cost reserve for the program that can be allocated to cryocooler development	Risk	1	50% of plan	Historically correlated with moderate likelihood of overrun	10% of plan	Historically correlated with high likelihood of overrun	10% of plan	As reported by GAO, 60% of last year's program cost reserve remains. Assuming that 50% of the initial cost reserve has to be available for other contingencies, there is a remaining reserve of 10% that can be allocated to cryo devel.	30% to 50% of plan	More cost reserves will become available in 2016, according to the GAO. Also, JPL's analysis of subcontractor performance trends projects that cryocooler development will not be delayed by more than 7 months, making it likely that integrated testing will begin on time (February 2016).	−2 Yellow: Marginal

(continued)

TABLE 4.4 (*Continued*)

Objec. No.	Leading Indicator Number	Leading Indicator Description	Risk, Opp., or Ind. Risk	Scen. No.	Lead. Ind. Watch Value	Rationale or Source	Lead. Ind. Resp. Value	Rationale or Source	Lead. Ind. Current Value	Rationale or Source	Lead Ind. 1-Yr. Projected Value	Rationale or Source	Leading Indicator Level of Concern
P (1) #11	3	Severity of unresolved technical issues for cryocooler development (scale 1–5)	Risk	1	2	Any nontrivial unresolved technical issue requires watching	3	Technical issues of moderate severity require a response	3	Unresolved issues include (1) failure of compressor to perform to specification when brazed to spacecraft; (2) validation of replacement valves in cold-head assembly during vacuum testing; (3) cryocooler generated vibration possibly exceeding permissible levels	1 to 3	Resolution of these technical issues has to be verified by as-flown testing of prototype assemblies, which will occur during 2015. Successful results are expected but, as with any test, success is not guaranteed beforehand.	−2 Yellow: Marginal

P (1) #11	4	GAO evaluation of cryocooler development problems (scale 1–5, 1 = very low confidence, 5 = very high confidence)	Risk	1	4	When confidence is high but not very high, watchfulness is needed	2	When confidence is low, a response is needed	3	GAO report: "During the past year, delays have occurred on every element and major subsystem schedule—especially with the cryocooler—leaving all at risk of negatively impacting the overall project schedule reserve if further delays occur."	3 to 5	JPL's analysis of subcontractor performance trends, cited above, suggests that GAO's concerns may be resolved within the next year.	–2 Yellow: Marginal

4.6 EXAMPLE TEMPLATES FOR RISK AND OPPORTUNITY ROLL-UP

4.6.1 Objectives Interface and Influence Template

While the principal interfaces between the objectives were displayed in Figure 4.4, a number of secondary interfaces could also be postulated. For this demonstration, three secondary interfaces between the top level of the programmatic and mission support objectives and the executive level strategic objectives are also considered, as shown in Figure 4.9.

Two of the secondary objectives account for the fact that the success of the exploratory programs and projects (objectives P (5–10) #3 and P (5–10) #4) influence the success of attracting a highly skilled workforce and providing the needed facilities (objective E (>10) #2) by defining the technical qualifications that are needed within the workforce, by providing an incentive for qualified technical people to work at NASA, and by providing the driving function for the facilities to be developed. The third recognizes the fact that maintaining a sufficient cadre of highly capable analysts (objective C (5–10) #6) is necessary in order to successfully interpret the data obtained from the telescopes during their operation and to set the direction for additional observations.

The objectives interface and influence template encodes this sort of information in tabular form, as shown in Table 4.5.

4.6.2 Known Risk Roll-Up Template

The aggregate risk of not successfully meeting an objective can be evaluated by rolling up the individual risk scenarios in either of two alternative ways. The first alternative is illustrated in Figure 4.10, with reference to one of the top objectives in Figure 4.4, and consists of the following steps:

1. Identify the objective of interest from the objectives hierarchy (Figure 4.4).
2. Identify the risk scenarios associated with the objective from the Risk and Opportunity Identification Template (Table 4.2).
3. Identify the risk leading indicators associated with each risk scenario from the Risk and Opportunity Identification Template (Table 4.2), and evaluate the leading indicator levels of concern using the Leading Indicator Evaluation Template (Table 4.3).
4. Roll up the leading indicator levels of concern for each risk scenario to obtain a corresponding level of concern for each risk scenario using a transparent and documented roll-up rationale.

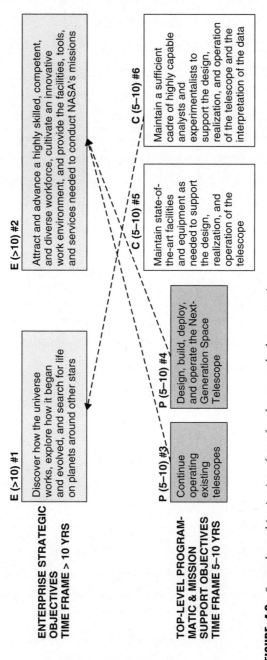

FIGURE 4.9 Secondary objective interfaces for the example demonstration

TABLE 4.5 Objectives Interface and Influence Template
Asterisk denotes secondary interfaces

Obj. No.	Objective Description	Num. Infl. Objs.	Influencing Obj. No.	Influencing Objective Description	Basis for Influence
C (1) #12	Provide technical support and expert review for the design, building, testing, and validation of the cryocooler subsystem	0			
P (1) #11	Deliver the cryocooler system	1	C (1) #12	Provide technical support and expert review for the design, building, testing, and validation of the cryocooler subsystem	Necessary milestone before delivery
C (1–5) #10	Implement the 5-year hiring and training plan	0			
C (1–5) #9	Implement the 5-year facilities plan	0			
C (1–5) #8	Provide technical support and expert review for the design, building, testing, validation of the integrated space telescope	3	C (1) #12	Provide technical support and expert review for the design, building, testing, and validation of the cryocooler subsystem	Necessary milestone before integration
			C (1–5) #10	Implement the 5-year hiring and training plan	Necessary capability to achieve objective
			C (1–5) #9	Implement the 5-year facilities plan	Necessary capability to achieve objective
P (1–5) #7	Launch the space telescope	2	P (1) #11	Deliver the cryo system	Necessary milestone before launch readiness
			C (1–5) #8	Provide technical support and expert review for the design, building, testing, validation of the integrated space telescope	Necessary milestone before launch readiness

C (5–10) #6	Maintain a sufficient cadre of highly capable analysts and experimentalists to support the design, realization, and operation of the telescope and the interpretation of the data	1	C (1–5) #10	Implement the 5-year hiring and training plan	Necessary capability to achieve objective
C (5–10) #5	Maintain state-of-the-art facilities and equipment as needed to support the design, realization, and operation of the telescope	1	C (1–5) #9	Implement the 5-year facilities plan	Necessary capability to achieve objective
P (5–10) #4	Design, build, deploy, and operate the Next-Generation Space Telescope	3	P (1–5) #7	Launch the space telescope	Necessary milestone before operation
			C (5–10) #6	Maintain a sufficient cadre of highly capable analysts and experimentalists to support the design, realization, and operation of the telescope and the interpretation of the data	Supports telescope design, development, deployment, and operation
			C (5–10) 5	Maintain state-of-the-art facilities and equipment as needed to support the design, realization, and operation of the telescope	Supports telescope design, development, deployment, and operation
P (5–10) #3	Continue operating existing telescopes	0			

(continued)

TABLE 4.5 (*Continued*)

Asterisk denotes secondary interfaces

Obj. No.	Objective Description	Num. Infl. Objs.	Influencing Obj. No.	Influencing Objective Description	Basis for Influence
E (>10) #2	Attract and advance a highly skilled, competent, and diverse workforce, cultivate an innovative work environment, and provide the facilities, tools, and services needed to conduct NASA's missions	4	C (5–10) #6	Maintain a sufficient cadre of highly capable analysts and experimentalists to support the design, realization, and operation of the telescope and the interpretation of the data	Supports maintenance of technical capabilities
			C (5–10) #5	Maintain state-of-the-art facilities and equipment as needed to support the design, realization, and operation of the telescope	Supports maintenance of technical capabilities
			P (5–10) #4	* Design, build, deploy, and operate the Next-Generation Space Telescope	* Program success promotes public interest and supports NASA's mission
			P (5–10) #3	* Continue operating existing telescopes	* Program success promotes public interest
E (>10) #1	Discover how the universe works, explore how it began and evolved, and search for life on planets around other stars	3	C (5–10) 6	* Maintain a sufficient cadre of highly capable analysts and experimentalists to support the design, realization, and operation of the telescope and the interpretation of the data	* Necessary capability to ensure optimal science gain
			P (5–10) 4	Design, build, deploy, and operate the next space telescope	Program success promotes discovery of universe
			P (5–10) 3	Continue operating existing telescopes	Program success promotes discovery of universe

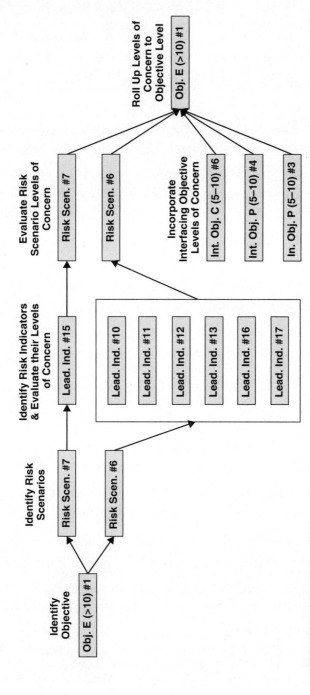

FIGURE 4.10 Schematic of roll-up method alternative 1 for Objective E (>10) #1

5. Roll up the levels of concern for the risk scenarios, obtained from the previous bullet, with the levels of concern obtained for the interfacing objectives, using the Objectives Interface and Influence Template (Table 4.5) to identify the interfacing objectives. (The order of the roll-up is such that the levels of concern for the interfacing objectives will have been determined prior to the present roll-up.)

The rolled-up level of concern at the end of the process is defined as the aggregate, or cumulative, risk of not meeting the objective, and the transparent and documented rationale for the roll-up process defines the justification for the aggregate risk.

The second alternative for rolling up levels of concern to obtain the aggregate risk of an objective is illustrated in Figure 4.11. The difference between it and the first alternative is that it cuts out one of the steps. Specifically, the aggregate risk of the objective is determined by rolling up the levels of concern for the leading indicators directly (together with the levels of concern for the interfacing objectives), without first performing a roll-up from the leading indicators to the risk scenarios. The rationale is that the leading indicators are de facto surrogates for the risk scenarios, and so it is as reasonable to infer the aggregate risk of not meeting an objective from the levels of concern associated with the leading indicators as it is to infer the aggregate risk from the levels of concern of the risk scenarios. Thereafter, it is possible to determine levels of concern for each risk scenario by performing an after-the-fact roll-up from leading indicators to individual risk scenarios in order to assess the importance of each risk scenario.

Using the second alternative, the aggregate risk of not being successful in delivering the cryocooler subsystem in a timely manner (Objective P (1) #11) is reflective of a roll-up of the levels of concern for Leading Indicators 1 through 4 and the aggregate risk of not being able to provide the needed technical support for this task (Objective C (1) #12), as shown in Figure 4.12.

The associated roll-up is performed on the Known Risk Roll-Up Template, Table 4.6. A similar template for opportunity roll-up will be discussed in the next subsection.

For each objective, starting from the bottom and working up to the top, the Known Risk Roll-Up Template lists all the risk indicators and interfacing objectives that feed into it. As mentioned, these inputs are obtained from prior templates. The following paragraphs discuss the additional information that is contained in the template, starting from the sixth column.

Composite Indicator The column labeled "Composite Indicator" provides a means for accounting for the fact that the trigger values for some of the indicators may depend on the values of other indicators. Such codependencies may be important. (For example, trigger values for cost and schedule

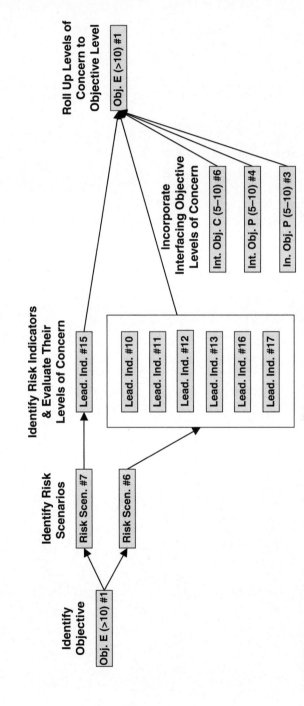

FIGURE 4.11 Schematic of roll-up method alternative 2 for Objective E (>10) #1

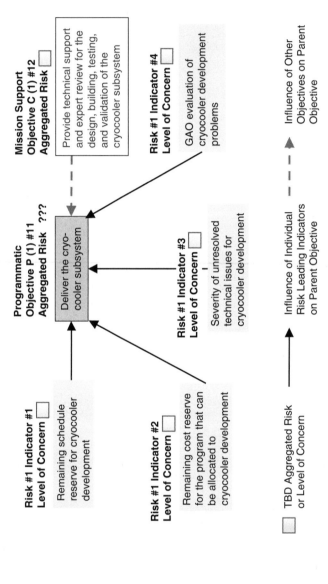

FIGURE 4.12 Schematic of risk roll-up for Objective P (1) #11 in the example demonstration

TABLE 4.6 Known Risk Roll-Up Template

Italic typeface denotes repeated instances of leading indicators   Asterisk denotes secondary interfaces

Objec. No.	Objective Description	Type of Scen.	Lead. Ind. No. or Influencing Objec. No.	Description of Leading Indicator or Influencing Objective	Composite Indicator	Lead. Ind. Concern or Objec. Aggr. Risk	Aggregate Risk of Objective	Roll-up Rationale
C (1) #12	Provide tech. support and expert review for design, building, testing, and validation of the cryocooler subsystem	None	None	None	None	None	None	No risks entered
P (1) #11	Deliver the cryocooler subsystem	Risk	1	Remaining schedule reserve for cryocooler development	None	TBD	TBD	TBD
			2	Remaining cost reserve for the program allocatable to cryo devel.	None	TBD		
			3	Severity of unresolved tech issues for cryo devel. (scale 1–5)	None	TBD		
			4	GAO evaluation of cryocooler development problems (scale 1–5)	None	TBD		
			C (1) #12	Provide tech support & expert review for design,... of cryo subsys.	None	None		
C (1–5) #10	Implement the 5-year hiring and training plan	Risk	5	No. of retirements of qualified optics analysis & testing experts	None	TBD	TBD	TBD
			6	No. of retirements of qualified integated analysis & testing experts	None	TBD		

(continued)

TABLE 4.6 (Continued)

Italic typeface denotes repeated instances of leading indicators   Asterisk denotes secondary interfaces

Objec. No.	Objective Description	Type of Scen.	Lead. Ind. No. or Influencing Objec. No.	Description of Leading Indicator or Influencing Objective	Composite Indicator	Lead. Ind. Concern or Objec. Aggr. Risk	Aggregate Risk of Objective	Roll-up Rationale
			7	No. of qualified optics analysis & testing recent graduates	None	TBD		
			8	Competition for recent optics graduates, e.g., from the military	None	TBD		
C (1–5) #9	Implement the 5-year facilities plan	Risk	9	Number of significant design modifications required to date	None	TBD	TBD	TBD
			10	Complexity of design	None	TBD		
			11	Complexity of integration and testing	None	TBD		
C (1–5) #8	Provide technical support and expert review for the design, building, testing, and validation of the integrated space telescope	Risk	C (1) #12	Provide tech support & expert review for design, ... of cryo subsys	None	None	TBD	TBD
			C (1–5) #10	Implement the 5-year hiring and training plan	None	TBD		
			C (1–5) #9	Implement the 5-year facilities plan	None	TBD		
P (1–5) #7	Launch the space telescope	Risk	10	*Complexity of design (rank 1–5)*	None	TBD	TBD	TBD
			11	*Complexity of integration and testing (rank 1–5)*	None	TBD		
			12	Cost reserve for the program	None	TBD		
			13	Schedule reserve for the program	None	TBD		

	Risk	Measure	Description				
		P (1) #11	Deliver the cryo system	None	TBD		
		C (1–5) #8	Provide tech. support & expert review for design, ... of integr. scope	None	TBD	TBD	TBD
Maintain a sufficient cadre ...to support ... operation of telescope and interpretation of data	Risk	C (1–5) #10	Implement the 5-year hiring and training plan	None	TBD	TBD	TBD
C (5–10) #6		C (1–5) #9	Implement the 5-year facilities plan	None	TBD	TBD	TBD
Maintain state-of-the-art facilities and equipment ...to support the design, realization, and operation of the telescope	Risk	10	*Complexity of design (rank 1–5)*	None	TBD	TBD	TBD
C (5–10) #5		11	*Complexity of integration and testing (rank 1–5)*	None	TBD		
Design, build, deploy, and operate the Next-Generation Space Telescope	Risk	14	No. of significant unexpected performance-related difficulties encountered during development	None	TBD		
P (5–10) #4		P (1–5) #7	Launch the space telescope	None	TBD		
		C (5–10) #6	Maintain a sufficient cadre ...to support ... operationoftelescope and interpretation of data	None	TBD		
		C (5–10) #5	Maintain state-of-the-art facilities & equipment to support design, realization, operation of the telescope	None	TBD		

(continued)

TABLE 4.6 (Continued)

Italic typeface denotes repeated instances of leading indicators   Asterisk denotes secondary interfaces

Objec. No.	Objective Description	Type of Scen.	Lead. Ind. No. or Influencing Objec. No.	Description of Leading Indicator or Influencing Objective	Composite Indicator	Lead. Ind. Concern or Objec. Aggr. Risk	Aggregate Risk of Objective	Roll-up Rationale
P (5–10) #3	Continue operating existing telescopes	Risk	None	None	None	TBD	TBD	TBD
E (>10) #2	Attract a highly skilled workforce, cultivate an innovative work environment, and provide needed facilities, tools, and services	Risk	12	Cost reserve for the program	None	TBD	TBD	TBD
			13	Schedule reserve for the program	None	TBD		
			15	Congressional level of support for new space telescope (rank 1–5)	None	TBD		
			16	Congressional level of support for existing programs (rank 1–5)	None	TBD		
			17	Degree of searching extensibility available through S/W uploading	None	TBD		
			C (5–10) #6	Maintain a sufficient cadre …to support … operation of telescope and interpretation of data	None	TBD		
			C (5–10) #5	Maintain state-of-the-art facilities & equipment to support design, realization, & operation of the telescope	None	TBD		
			P (5–10) #4	* Design, build, deploy, & operate the next-generation telescope	None	TBD		
			P (5–10) #3	Continue operating existing telescopes	None	TBD		

E (>10) #1	Risk		None	TBD	TBD	TBD
Discover how the universe works, explore how it began and evolved, and search for life on planets around other stars	10	Complexity of design (rank 1–5)	None	TBD	TBD	TBD
	11	Complexity of integration and testing (rank 1–5)	None	TBD		
	12	Cost reserve for the program	None	TBD		
	13	Schedule reserve for the program	None	TBD		
	15	Congressional level of support for new space telescope (rank 1–5)	None	TBD		
	16	Congressional level of support for existing programs (rank 1–5)	None	TBD		
	C (5–10) #6	* Maintain a sufficient cadre ... to support ... operation of telescope and interpretation of data	None	TBD		
	P (5–10) #4	Design, build, deploy, and operate the next-generation telescope	None	TBD		
	P (5–10) #3	Continue operating existing telescopes	None	TBD		

Palette for TBD Shaded Cells:

Green Risk: –1 Tolerable   Yellow Risk: –2 Marginal   Red Risk: –3 Intolerable

margins will normally depend on the amount of work remaining to be accomplished, as indicated by the number and complexity of unresolved issues.) For simplicity, we initially assume that we do not need to specify codependencies between indicators to execute the demonstration, but we will return to the subject later.[6]

Leading Indicator Level of Concern/Influencing Objective Level of Risk   As mentioned, the roll-up process accounts for two types of risk input: (1) the level of concern for the leading indicators that are associated with the objective, and (2) the aggregate risk for the interfacing objectives that feed into it. The level of concern for leading indicators has already been recorded in the Leading Indicator Evaluation Template (Table 4.3) and is transcribed from that template into the Known Risk Roll-Up Template. The aggregate risk for influencing objectives, on the other hand, is obtained from the portion of the roll-up process that has already been performed and entered earlier into the Known Risk Roll-Up Template. For example, the aggregate risk for Objective C(1) #12, which feeds into P(1) #11, has been entered higher up in Table 4.6.

Aggregate Risk of Objective and Roll-Up Rationale   The roll-up of levels of concern for leading indicators and aggregate risks for influencing objectives is conducted according to the rationale provided in the last column of the Risk Roll-Up Template. The process is objective but not quantitative. It is most easily demonstrated by considering the roll-up rationale that might be employed for Objective P(1) #11: Deliver the cryocooler subsystem. Table 4.7 provides this demonstration. As before with the example for the Leading Indicator Evaluation Template (Table 4.4), the rationale is based on publicly available information about the JWST that was previously itemized in Section 4.2. In short, the template records the following information:

- The cryocooler development schedule can be accelerated by diverting additional budget and manpower to this task from other tasks whose reserves are not at risk.
- JPL's analysis of subcontractor performance trends projects that development will not be delayed by more than seven months to November 2015, making it likely that integrated testing will begin on time during February 2016.
- Therefore, the overall risk of not meeting the objective of delivering the cryocooler subsystem is marginal, even though the year's schedule reserve for cryocooler development has been depleted.

For comparison, Table 4.8 illustrates how Table 4.7 would be reconstructed to reflect the alternative 1 roll-up method, which includes

TABLE 4.7 Example Entries for Known Risk Roll-Up Template for Objective P(1) #11: Deliver the Cryocooler Subsystem

Objec. No.	Objective Description	Type of Scen.	Lead. Ind. No. or Infl. Obj. No.	Description of Leading Indicator or Influencing Objective	Composite Indicator	Lead. Ind. Concern or Objec. Aggr. Risk	Aggregate Risk of Objective	Roll-up Rationale
C (1) #12	Provide tech. support and expert review for design, building, testing, and validation of the cryo subsystem	None	None	None	None	−1 Green Tolerable	−1 Green Tolerable	No risks entered
P (1) #11	Deliver the cryocooler subsystem	Risk	1	Remaining schedule reserve for cryocooler development	None	−3 Red Intolerable	−2 Yellow Marginal	Although the remaining schedule reserve for the cryocooler development is red (surpassing the response trigger), the overall risk of not meeting the objective of delivering the cryocooler subsystem is yellow (marginal) because: 1. According to the current track and control plan, the cryocooler development schedule can be accelerated if needed by diverting additional budget and manpower to this task from other tasks whose reserves are not at risk (note that the divertible remaining cost reserve from other tasks is yellow, not red) 2. JPL's analysis of subcontractor performance trends projects that development will not be delayed by more than 7 months, making it likely that integrated testing will begin on time (February 2016)
			2	Remaining cost reserve for the program that can be allocated to cryocooler development	None	−2 Yellow Marginal		
			3	Severity of unresolved technical issues for cryocooler development (scale 1–5)	None	−2 Yellow Marginal		
			4	GAO evaluation of cryocooler development problems (scale 1–5, 1 = very low confidence, 5 = very high confidence)	None	−2 Yellow Marginal		
			C (1) #12	Provide technical support and expert review for design, building, testing, and validation of cryocooler subsystem	None	−1 Green Tolerable		

TABLE 4.8 Example Entries for Risk Roll-Up Template for Objective P(1) #11 Including an Intermediate Roll-Up to Risk Scenario Level

Objec. No.	Objective Descrip.	Type of Scen.	Risk No. or Influencing Objec. No.	Risk or Influencing Objec. Descrip.	Lead. Ind. No.	Description of Leading Indicator	Composite Indicator	Leading Indicator Level of Concern	Roll-up to Risk Scen. Level of Concern	Rationale for Roll-up to Risk Scenario Level	Aggregated Risk of Objective	Rationale for Roll-up to Objective Level
C (1) #12	Provide tech. support and expert review for design, building, testing, and validation of the cryo subsystem								−1 Green Tolerable	No risks entered	−1 Green Tolerable	No roll-up at the lowest level
P (1) #11	Deliver the cryocooler subsystem	Risk	1	There may be a significant delay in the delivery date for the cryocooler system	1	Remaining schedule reserve for cryocooler development	None	−3 Red Intolerable	−2 Yellow Marginal	Although the remaining schedule reserve for the cryo. development is red, the overall risk of not meeting the objective of delivering the cryo. subsystem is yellow (marginal) because: 1. The cryo. development schedule can be accelerated by diverting additional budget and manpower to this task from other tasks 2. JPL's analysis of subcontractor performance trends projects that development will not be delayed by more than 7 months	−2 Yellow Marginal	There are no compensating factors in rolling up Risk 1 with the risk of not not meeting Objective C (1) #12.
					2	Remaining cost reserve for the program that can be allocated to cryocooler development	None	−2 Yellow Marginal				
					3	Severity of unresolved technical issues for cryocooler development (scale 1–5)	None	−2 Yellow Marginal				

142

Risk	C (1) #12	Org. may fail to provide adequate technical support and expert review for design, building, testing, and validation of cryo subsystem	4	GAO evaluation of cryocooler development problems (scale 1–5, 1 = very low confidence, 5 = very high confidence)	None	–2 Yellow Marginal	–2 Yellow Marginal	Carried down from Objective C (1) #12

an intermediate roll-up of leading indicators to risk scenario level in accordance with the schematic representation in Figure 4.10.

4.6.3 Opportunity Roll-Up Template

The Opportunity Roll-Up Template, Table 4.9, is comparable to the Known Risk Roll-Up Template, Table 4.6, with the exception that the opportunity scenarios generally have accompanying introduced risks. For the example being considered, the opportunity scenario (as entered into the Risk and Opportunity Identification Template, Table 4.2) is that it may be possible for significant new technology advancements (such as a camera with improved resolution) to be delivered and installed on the telescope through retrofitting either by astronauts or robotically, since the JWST spacecraft is designed with a grapple arm. This could be the case even though the JWST is described by NASA as unserviceable, given that the incentive for trying such a rendezvous mission is strong enough to justify the risks. In this case, the introduced risks are that the likelihood of loss of crew (LOC) or loss of mission (LOM), depending on whether the mission is crewed or robotic, may be unacceptably high, and/or that the cost of the retrofit mission may likewise be too high. The leading indicators for the opportunity are the technology readiness level for improved-resolution infrared cameras and the readiness level for the Space Launch System (SLS), including *Orion* if the mission is crewed. The leading indicator for the introduced risk pertaining to the probability of LOC or LOM is the most current predictive estimate of P(LOC) or P(LOM) obtained from a probabilistic risk assessment (PRA) for an analogous SLS/*Orion* mission involving lunar orbit. The leading indicator for the introduced risk pertaining to cost is likewise the most current cost estimate for the analogous mission.

Since the only opportunity scenario for this example is introduced at the top level of the objectives hierarchy (i.e., at Objective E(>10) #1), there are no roll-ups for opportunity from lower-level objectives to higher level objectives. Rather, the roll-up in this example concerns only the relevant leading indicators for opportunity and introduced risk at the level of Objective E(>10) #1 (which is entered at the bottom of Table 4.9). Before performing this roll-up, the significance of the opportunity leading indicators and the tolerability of the introduced risk leading indicators are transferred from the Leading Indicator Evaluation Template (Table 4.3) to the column labeled "Leading Indicator Significance" in Table 4.9. The roll-up for the aggregate opportunity in the next-to-last column of Table 4.9 is based on the perceived balance between the opportunity and the introduced risks as informed by the values of the respective leading indicators. The rationale for the perception of balance is recorded in the last column of Table 4.9.

TABLE 4.9 Opportunity Roll-Up Template

Objec. No.	Objective Description	Type of Scen.	Lead. Ind. No. or Influencing Objec. No.	Description of Leading Indicator or Influencing Objective	Composite Indicator	Lead. Ind. Significance or Objec. Aggr. Opp.	Aggregate Opp. of Objective	Roll-Up Rationale
C (1) #12	Provide tech. support and expert review for design, building, testing, and validation of the cryo subsystem	None	None	None	None	None	None	No opps. entered
P (1) #11	Deliver the cryocooler subsystem	None	None	None	None	None	None	No opps. entered
C (1–5) #10	Implement the 5-year hiring and training plan	None	None	None	None	None	None	No opps. entered
C (1–5) #9	Implement the 5-year facilities plan	None	None	None	None	None	None	No opps. entered
C (1–5) #8	Provide tech. support and expert review for the design, building, testing, and validation of the integrated space telescope	None	None	None	None	None	None	No opps. entered
P (1–5) #7	Launch the space telescope	None	None	None	None	None	None	No opps. entered
C (5–10) #6	Maintain a sufficient cadre … to support … operation of telescope and interpretation of data	None	None	None	None	None	None	No opps. entered
C (5–10) #5	Maintain state-of-the-art facilities and equipment to support design, realization, operation of the telescope	None	None	None	None	None	None	No opps. entered
P (5–10) #3	Continue operating existing telescopes	None	None	None	None	None	None	No opps. entered

(*continued*)

TABLE 4.9 (*Continued*)

Objec. No.	Objective Description	Type of Scen.	Lead. Ind. No. or Influencing Objec. No.	Description of Leading Indicator or Influencing Objective	Composite Indicator	Lead. Ind. Significance or Objec. Aggr. Opp.	Aggregate Opp. of Objective	Roll-Up Rationale
E (>10) #2	Attract/advance a highly skilled, competent, and diverse workforce, cultivate an innovative work environment, and provide the facilities, tools, and services needed to conduct NASA's missions	None	None	None	None	None	None	No opps. entered
E (>10) #1	Discover how the universe works, explore how it began and evolved, and search for life on planets around other stars	Oppor.	18	Tech. readiness level for improved resolution IR cameras	None	TBD (+)	TBD (+)	TBD
			19	Readiness level for SLS/ Orion, including docking capability	None	TBD (+)		
		Intr. Risk	20	Predicted P(LOC) for SLS/ Orion	None	TBD (−)		
			21	Predicted P(LOM) for SLS	None	TBD (−)		
			22	Predicted cost for a rendezvous mission	None	TBD (−)		

Palette for TBD Shaded Cells:

Red Risk: Intolerable	-3	Violet Oppor.: Marginal	Blue Oppor.: Significant
Yellow Risk: Marginal	-2	Beige Oppor.: Insignificant	+2
Green Risk: Tolerable	-1		+1	+3

An example opportunity roll-up is shown in Table 4.10. In this example, the likelihood of being able to conduct a service mission to install a significantly improved IR camera is considered high based on anticipated technology developments, and so the opportunity leading indicators are colored blue (significant opportunity). Less happily, the present-day cost of a rendezvous mission is considered intolerable by today's standards, and hence the leading indicator for the introduced risk associated with cost is red (intolerable). However, the cost may be perceived to be more tolerable once the system is operational because of the following rationale:

- Public enthusiasm for the program will likely increase substantially, as it did for Hubble, once the telescope is operational and its scientific value is fully appreciated.
- Issues about the feasibility of performing a rendezvous will likely abate once the SLS/*Orion* system becomes operational and is shown to be reliable and safe.
- The economic recovery will likely increase the willingness of the country to spend more on space.

Since it is considered likely that the perceived cost of the rendezvous will become more tolerable over time, the aggregate opportunity considering leading indicators for both opportunity and introduced risks is ranked as marginal rather than insignificant.

4.6.4 Composite Indicator Identification and Evaluation Template

In the examples shown so far, all of the leading indicators have been considered to be standalone indicators, even though the templates have included the possibility for introducing composite indicators. Considering them to be independent in setting trigger values is acceptable as long as the rationale for aggregating them accounts for the more complex relationships that may exist between them. Thus, ameliorating factors were introduced in the rationale column in Table 4.7 to justify an aggregated risk that was yellow (marginal) rather than red (intolerable), and in Table 4.10 to justify an aggregated opportunity that was violet (marginal) rather than beige (insignificant), even though one of the indicators in each case was red.

Using a composite indicator recognizes the fact that the trigger values of some of the indicators may depend on the values of other indicators. For example, in the example for the Leading Indicator Evaluation Template in Table 4.4, leading indicators 1, 2, and 3 have just such a codependency that would justify the use of a composite indicator. That is, the amount of

TABLE 4.10 Example Entries for Opportunity Roll-Up for Objective E(>10) #1: Discover How the Universe Works, Explore How It Began/Evolved, Search for Life on Planets Around Other Stars

Objec. No.	Objective Description	Type of Scen.	Lead. Ind. No. or Influencing Objec. No.	Description of Leading Indicator or Influencing Objective	Composite Indicator	Lead. Ind. Significance or Objec. Aggr. Opp.	Aggregate Opp. of Objective	Roll-Up Rationale
E (>10) #1	Discover how the universe works, explore how it began and evolved, and search for life on planets around other stars	Oppor.	18	Tech. readiness level for improved resolution IR cameras	None	+3 Blue Significant	+2 Violet Marginal	Although the estimated cost of a rendezvous is intolerable based on current funding for the program, it may become more tolerable once the system is operational because:
			19	Readiness level for SLS/Orion, including docking capability	None	+3 Blue Significant		1. Public enthusiasm for the program will likely increase substantially, as it did for Hubble, once the telescope is operational and its scientific value is fully appreciated
		Intr. Risk	20	Predicted P(LOC) for SLS/Orion	None	−2 Yellow Marginal		2. Issues about the feasibility of performing a rendezvous will likely abate once the SLS/Orion system becomes operational and is shown to be reliable and safe
			21	Predicted P(LOM) for SLS	None	−1 Green Tolerable		3. The economic recovery will likely increase the willingness of the country to spend more on space
			22	Predicted cost for a rendezvous mission	None	−3 Red Intolerable		

schedule margin needed for cryocooler development (Indicator 1) depends on both the amount of cost margin from other tasks that can be diverted to the cryocooler development task (Indicator 2) and the severity of the technical issues that remain to be resolved (Indicator 3). Note that a composite indicator does not necessarily collapse all the individual indicators for a risk or opportunity scenario. For example, Leading Indicator 4, which concerns GAO's evaluation of the cryocooler development progress, remains as a separate indicator for the risk of not delivering the cryocooler subsystem when required.

The following box provides an example of how one might define a composite indicator to recognize the dependencies between leading indicators 1, 2, and 3.

EXAMPLE REPRESENTATION OF A COMPOSITE INDICATOR

To define a composite indicator, the individual indicators comprising it must first be defined in precise quantitative terms. Suppose, for example, that leading indicators 1 through 3 are defined exactly as follows:

Ind(1) = the fraction of the original planned schedule margin for the cryocooler development task that remains unused; has a possible value of 0 to 1.

Ind(2) = the fraction that remains unused of the original planned cost margin allocable to the cryocooler development task from the program as a whole; has a possible value of 0 to 1.

Ind(3) = the severity ranking of all unresolved technical issues for cryocooler development; has possible values of 1, 2, 3, 4, and 5.

Suppose Composite Indicator A is introduced at this point and is defined as follows:

CInd(A) = $-4 \times$ Ind(1) $- 4 \times$ Ind(2) $+$ Ind(3) $+ 7$; has a possible value of 0 (best case) to 12 (worst case).

This example composite indicator has the feature that a change in any one of the three indicators from its worst value to its best value has the same numerical effect on CInd(A) as a change in any other of the three indicators from its worst value to its best value. For example, changing Ind(1) from 1 to 0 causes CInd(A) to change by a total of 4 in the positive direction, as does changing Ind(2) from 1 to 0 or changing Ind(3) from 1 to 5. As a further illustration, the compound indicator has a value of 6 for any of the following conditions:

- Schedule margin = 0% of plan, cost margin = 50% of plan; technical issue ranking = 1
- Schedule margin = 25% of plan, cost margin = 25% of plan; technical issue ranking = 1
- Schedule margin = 0% of plan, cost margin = 100% of plan; technical issue ranking = 3
- Schedule margin = 50% of plan, cost margin = 50% of plan; technical issue ranking = 3
- Schedule margin = 50% of plan, cost margin = 100% of plan; technical issue ranking = 5
- Schedule margin = 75% of plan, cost margin = 75% of plan; technical issue ranking = 5

In other words, all of these combinations produce the same level of concern.

The Composite Indicator Identification and Evaluation Template for this example is shown in Table 4.11. The third column in that table indicates that the following combination is a *watch peg point*:

- Schedule margin = 50% of plan, cost margin = 50% of plan; technical issue ranking = 2

and the fourth column indicates that the following combination is a *response peg point*:

- Schedule margin = 10% of plan, cost margin = 10% of plan; technical issue ranking = 3

> These peg points set the watch and response triggers for the composite index as follows:
>
> - Composite indicator watch trigger $= -4 \times (0.5) - 4 \times (0.5) + 2 + 7 = 5.0$
> - Composite indicator response trigger $= -4 \times (0.1) - 4 \times (0.1) + 3 + 7 = 9.2$
>
> These values appear in the 10th and 11th columns of Table 4.11.

Table 4.12 illustrates how the Known Risk Roll-Up Template example in Table 4.7 would change as a result of using this composite indicator. Note that the Roll-Up result remains the same but there is no longer a red (intolerable) risk indicator feeding into it.

4.6.5   UU Risk Roll-Up Template

In addition to the leading indicators for known risks provided in the Risk and Opportunity Identification Template, Table 4.2, and the Leading Indicator Evaluation Template, Table 4.3, there is an additional set of leading indicators that correlate with the relative importance of UU risks. Some of the more important ones were identified in Sections 3.4.5 and 4.4.3.

Just as the known risks were rolled up via the Known Risk Roll-Up Template, Table 4.6, to obtain insight into how known risks are affecting the likelihood of being able to satisfy the top objectives of the organization, it is possible to roll up the leading indicators for UU risks via a UU Risk Roll-Up Template to obtain insight into how UU risk indicators are affecting the likelihood of successful objectives achievement. For this example, we postulate the following two UU leading indicators to be the most significant sources of UU risk:

- Schedule/budget pressure
- Quality of oversight and communication

Both indicators are measured on a scale of 1 to 5 for each objective, with the lower end indicating lowest concern and the upper end indicating highest concern. The steps in the Roll-Up are identical to Section 4.6.2. The example template is shown in Table 4.13.

TABLE 4.11 Composite Indicator Identification and Evaluation Template

Comp. Ind. No.	Lead. Ind. No.	Description of Leading Indicator or Composite Function of Leading Indicators	Watch Peg Point	Resp. Peg Point	Current Value	1-Yr. Projected Value	Composite Function	Rationale for Composite Function	Comp. Ind. Watch Trigger	Comp. Ind. Resp. Trigger	Comp. Ind. Current Value	Comp. Ind. 1-Yr. Projected Value	Comp. Leading Indicator Concern
A	1	Remaining schedule reserve for cryo devel. (fraction of plan)	0.5	0.1	0.0	0.3 best to 0.0 worst	CompInd(A): $= -4 \times$ Ind(1) $- 4 \times$ Ind(2) $+$ Ind(3) $+ 7$	Historically informed correlation between time to complete a task of similar magnitude and complexity, funding required, and severity of unresolved technical issues pertaining to the task (source: XX)	5.0	9.2	9.6	4.8 best to 8.8 worst	−2 Yellow Marginal
	2	Remaining cost reserve for the program that can be allocated to cryo devel. (fraction of plan)	0.5	0.1	0.1	0.5 best to 0.3 worst							
	3	Severity of significant unresolved technical issues pertaining to cryo devel. (scale 1 to 5)	2	3	3	1 best to 3 worst							

TABLE 4.12 Example Entries for Risk Roll-Up Template for Objective P(1) #11 Using a Composite Indicator

Objec. No.	Objective Description	Type of Scen.	Lead. Ind. No. or Infl. Obj. No.	Description of Leading Indicator or Influencing Objective	Composite Indicator	Lead. Ind. Concern or Objec. Aggr. Risk	Aggregate Risk of Objective	Roll-Up Rationale
C (1) #12	Provide tech. support and expert review for design, building, testing, and validation of the cryo subsystem	None	None	None	None	−1 Green Tolerable	−1 Green Tolerable	No risks entered
P (1) #11	Deliver the cryocooler subsystem	Risk	1	Remaining schedule reserve for cryocooler development	$\text{CompInd}(A) := -4 \times \text{Ind}(1) - 4 \times \text{Ind}(2) + \text{Ind}(3) + 7$	−2 Yellow Marginal	−2 Yellow Marginal	Although the remaining schedule reserve for the cryocooler development has been depleted, the overall risk of not meeting the objective of delivering the cryocooler subsystem is yellow (marginal) because: 1. The cryocooler development schedule can be accelerated by diverting additional budget and manpower to this task from other tasks whose reserves are not at risk (note that the divertible remaining cost reserve from other tasks is yellow, not red) 2. JPL's analysis of subcontractor performance trends projects that development will not be delayed by more than 7 months, making it likely that integrated testing will begin on time (February 2016)
			2	Remaining cost reserve for the program that can be allocated to cryocooler development				
			3	Severity of unresolved technical issues for cryocooler development (scale 1–5)				
			4	GAO evaluation of cryocooler development problems (scale 1–5, 1 = very low confidence, 5 = very high confidence)	None	−2 Yellow Marginal		
			C (1) #12	Provide technical support and expert review for design, building, testing, and validation of cryocooler subsystem	None	−1 Green Tolerable		

TABLE 4.13 UU Risk Roll-Up Template

Italic typeface denotes repeated instances of leading indicators   Asterisk denotes secondary interfaces

Objec. No.	Objective Description	Type of Scen.	Lead. Ind. No. or Influencing Objec. No.	Description of Leading Indicator or Influencing Objective	Composite Indicator	Lead. Ind. UU Concern or Objec. Aggr. UU Risk	Aggregate UU Risk of Objective	Roll-Up Rationale
C (1) #12	Provide tech. support and expert review for design, building, testing, and validation of the cryocooler subsystem	UU Risk	UU1	Schedule/budget pressure (scale 1–5)	None	TBD	TBD	TBD
			UU2	Quality of oversight and communication (scale 1–5)	None	TBD		
P (1) #11	Deliver the cryocooler subsystem	UU Risk	*UU1*	*Schedule/budget pressure (scale 1–5)*	None	TBD	TBD	TBD
			UU2	*Quality of oversight and communication (scale 1–5)*	None	TBD		
			C (1) #12	Provide tech support & expert review for design, . . . of cryo subsys.	None	TBD		
C (1–5) #10	Implement the 5-year hiring and training plan	UU Risk	*UU1*	*Schedule/budget pressure (scale 1–5)*	None	TBD	TBD	TBD
			UU2	*Quality of oversight and communication (scale 1–5)*	None	TBD		
C (1–5) #9	Implement the 5-year facilities plan	UU Risk	*UU1*	*Schedule/budget pressure (scale 1–5)*	None	TBD	TBD	TBD
			UU2	*Quality of oversight and communication (scale 1–5)*	None	TBD		

C (1–5) #8	Provide technical support and expert review for the design, building, testing, and validation of the integrated space telescope	UU Risk	UU1	Schedule/budget pressure (scale 1–5)	None	TBD	TBD	TBD
			UU2	Quality of oversight and communication (scale 1–5)	None	TBD		
			C (1) #12	Provide tech support & expert review for design,...of cryo subsys	None	TBD		
			C (1–5) #10	Implement the 5-year hiring and training plan	None	TBD		
			C (1–5) #9	Implement the 5-year facilities plan	None	TBD		
P (1–5) #7	Launch the space telescope	UU Risk	UU1	Schedule/budget pressure (scale 1–5)	None	TBD	TBD	TBD
			UU2	Quality of oversight and communication (scale 1–5)	None	TBD		
			P (1) #11	Deliver the cryo system	None	TBD		
			C (1–5) #8	Provide tech. support & expert review for design,...of integr. scope	None	TBD		
C (5–10) #6	Maintain a sufficient cadre...to support...operation of telescope and interpretation of data	UU Risk	UU1	Schedule/budget pressure (scale 1–5)	None	TBD	TBD	TBD
			UU2	Quality of oversight and communication (scale 1–5)	None	TBD		
			C (1–5) #10	Implement the 5-year hiring and training plan	None	TBD		

(*continued*)

155

TABLE 4.13 (*Continued*)

Italic typeface denotes repeated instances of leading indicators   Asterisk denotes secondary interfaces

Objec. No.	Objective Description	Type of Scen.	Lead. Ind. No. or Influencing Objec. No.	Description of Leading Indicator or Influencing Objective	Composite Indicator	Lead. Ind. UU Concern or Objec. Aggr. UU Risk	Aggregate UU Risk of Objective	Roll-Up Rationale
C (5–10) #5	Maintain state-of-the-art facilities and equipment . . . to support the design, realization, and operation of the telescope	UU Risk	*UU1*	*Schedule/budget pressure (scale 1–5)*	None	TBD	TBD	TBD
			UU2	*Quality of oversight and communication (scale 1–5)*	None	TBD		
			C (1–5) #9	Implement the 5-year facilities plan	None	TBD		
P (5–10) #4	Design, build, deploy, and operate the Next-Generation Space Telescope	UU Risk	*UU1*	*Schedule/budget pressure (scale 1–5)*	None	TBD	TBD	TBD
			UU2	*Quality of oversight and communication (scale 1–5)*	None	TBD		
			P (1–5) #7	Launch the space telescope	None	TBD		
			C (5–10) #6	Maintain a sufficient cadre . . . to support . . . operation of telescope and interpretation of data	None	TBD		
			C (5–10) #5	Maintain state-of-the-art facilities & equipment to support design, realization, operation of the telescope	None	TBD		

P (5–10) #3	Continue operating existing telescopes	UU Risk	UU1	Schedule/budget pressure (scale 1–5)	None	TBD	TBD	TBD
			UU2	Quality of oversight and communication (scale 1–5)	None	TBD		
E (>10) #2	Attract a highly skilled workforce, cultivate an innovative work environment, and provide needed facilities, tools, and services	UU Risk	UU1	Schedule/budget pressure (scale 1–5)	None	TBD	TBD	TBD
			UU2	Quality of oversight and communication (scale 1–5)	None	TBD		
			C (5–10) #6	Maintain a sufficient cadre…to support… operation of telescope and interpretation of data	None	TBD		
			C (5–10) #5	Maintain state-of-the-art facilities & equipment to support design, realization, & operation of the telescope	None	TBD		
			P (5–10) #4	* Design, build, deploy, and operate the next-generation telescope	None	TBD		
			P (5–10) #3	* Continue operating existing telescopes	None	TBD		

(continued)

TABLE 4.13 *(Continued)*

Italic typeface denotes repeated instances of leading indicators　　　　Asterisk denotes secondary interfaces

Objec. No.	Objective Description	Type of Scen.	Lead. Ind. No. or Influencing Objec. No.	Description of Leading Indicator or Influencing Objective	Composite Indicator	Lead. Ind. UU Concern or Objec. Aggr. UU Risk	Aggregate UU Risk of Objective	Roll-Up Rationale
E (>10) #1	Discover how the universe works, explore how it began and evolved, and search for life on planets around other stars	UU Risk	UU1	Schedule/budget pressure (scale 1–5)	None	TBD	TBD	TBD
			UU2	Quality of oversight and communication (scale 1–5)	None	TBD		
			C (5–10) #6	* Maintain a sufficient cadre … to support … operation of telescope and interpretation of data	None	TBD		
			P (5–10) #4	Design, build, deploy, and operate the next-generation telescope	None	TBD		
			P (5–10) #3	Continue operating existing telescopes	None	TBD		

Palette for TBD Shaded Cells:

| −1 | Green Risk: Tolerable | −2 | Yellow Risk: Marginal | −3 | Red Risk: Intolerable |

4.7   EXAMPLE TEMPLATES FOR THE IDENTIFICATION OF RISK AND OPPORTUNITY DRIVERS, RESPONSES, AND INTERNAL CONTROLS

4.7.1   Risk and Opportunity Driver Identification Template

As discussed in Section 3.6.1, a risk driver causes the cumulative risk for one or more top organizational objectives to change color from green to yellow or red or from yellow to red. Risk factors might include any combination of departure events, underlying causes of departure events, leading indicators, unprotected key assumptions, deficiencies in internal controls, or other factors that affect the risk of meeting the objectives. Similarly, an opportunity driver can be any combination of opportunity factors/elements that collectively cause the cumulative opportunity for one or more top organizational objectives to change color. Risk or opportunity drivers, as already defined, constitute a detailed resolution of the principal factors that contribute to the cumulative risk or opportunity. They therefore are suitable for identifying the constituents of risk mitigations, opportunity actions, and internal controls.

As discussed in Section 3.6.2, a risk or opportunity *scenario* driver is any combination of risk or opportunity *scenarios* that cause the cumulative risk or opportunity of one or more top objectives to change color. Risk and opportunity scenario drivers provide a higher-level view of the concerns that need to be addressed, and are therefore suitable for summary presentations.

The Risk and Opportunity Driver Identification Templates facilitate the process of identifying both drivers (henceforth called *constituent drivers* for clarity) and scenario drivers. Table 4.14 illustrates the process schematically for the next-generation space telescope example. A table similar to Table 4.14 is prepared for each strategic/top objective of the organization.

In Table 4.14, two risk scenarios are identified as candidate risk scenario drivers for the objective "Discover how the universe works . . . . " The first is "Failure to deliver the cryocooler subsystem on time," a scenario that most directly affects the lower-level objective of delivering the cryocooler subsystem but also propagates up through the Known Risk Roll-Up Template to the top objective. The second is "Unavailability of expert technical staff for review." This second risk scenario was not included in the earlier development of risks for this example, but is added here to make a point.

As shown in Table 4.14, neither of the risk scenarios causes the color of the cumulative risk for the top objective to change from yellow to green, but the combination of the two scenarios does.

Therefore, the risk scenario driver consists of the combination of the scenarios. The associated risk driver constituents, or principal factors that

TABLE 4.14 Example Risk and Opportunity Driver Identification Template

Objec. Index	Objective Description	Objective Cumulative Level of Concern or Interest	Candidate Scenario Driver Number	Scenario Number(s)	Candidate Scenario Driver Description	Objec. Level of Concern or Interest if Candidate Driver Is Removed	Qualify as Driver?	Timeframe to Complete Response	Driver Constituent Number	Driver Constituent Description	Timeframe to Begin Response
E (>1) #1	Discover how the universe works, explore how it began and evolved, and search for life on planets around other stars	−2 Yellow Marginal Risk	1	1	Failure to complete the cryocooler subsystem on time	Remains −2 Yellow Marginal	No				
			2	2	Unavailability of expert technical staff for review	Remains −2 Yellow Marginal	No				
			3	1 and 2	Failure to deliver the cryocooler subsystem on time and unavailability of expert technical staff for review	Changes to −1 Green Tolerable	Yes	6 Months	1	Cryo delivery schedule reserve	Now
									2	Subcontractor mgmt. issues	Now
									3	Compressor performance for brazed unit	Now
									4	Thermal vac. testing of cold head assy	Now
									5	Cross-project competition for qualified review personnel	Now
		+3 Blue Significant Opportunity	4	3	Commitment to develop new IR camera and demonstrate ability to conduct retrofit mission	Becomes +1 Beige Insignificant	Yes	5 Years	6	TRL for IR camera	1 Year
									7	Readiness of SLS/Orion docking capability	2 Years
									8	Predicted P(LOC) for SLS/Orion	2 Years
									9	Predicted cost for rendezvous mission	2 Years
									10	Congress may cancel or defer other SLS/Orion missions	Now

contribute to the cumulative risk, are shown in the next-to-last column of Table 4.14. They are the factors that are noted in the Known or UU Risk Roll-Up Template as being of particular concern, such that all of them have to be addressed in order for the cumulative risk to be reduced to a tolerable state.

It may be noted that although there are no UU risks included in this example for identifying risk drivers, there is no reason why they should not be included if the UU Roll-Up Template shows that they are a large source of concern.

The lower part of Table 4.14 concerns the identification of opportunity drivers. In this example there is only one opportunity scenario, and it is a driver because the deletion of the scenario causes the color of the cumulative opportunity for the top objective to change from blue (significant) to beige (insignificant). The associated opportunity driver constituents, shown in the next-to-last column, are the factors that are noted in the Opportunity Roll-Up Template as being of particular concern.

Also indicated in the Risk and Opportunity Driver Identification Template is the spare time available to initiate a response to mitigate the risk drivers or an action to avail the opportunity drivers without exceeding the available time frame to complete the response. The combination of the identified driver scenarios, the driver identified constituents, and the time frame available to begin a response for each constituent can be illustrated in a matrix format, as shown in Figures 4.13 and 4.14. This form of display is particularly useful for high-level presentations.

4.7.2   Risk and Opportunity Scenario Likelihood and Impact Evaluation Template

As discussed in Sections 2.5.3 and 2.5.4, the likelihoods and impacts of individual risk and opportunity scenarios need to be assessed separately by virtue of the latest draft of OMB Circular A-123. In Section 3.6.3, a ranking scheme of high, medium, and low was presented for likelihoods based on the decision maker's risk tolerance and opportunity appetite, and for impacts based on the identification of risk and opportunity scenario drivers. Suggested ranking criteria were depicted in Tables 3.3 and 3.4. The Risk and Opportunity Scenario Likelihood and Impact Evaluation Template in Table 4.15 provides a means for actualizing the approach in Sections 2.5.3, 2.5.4, and 3.6.3.

4.7.3   Risk Mitigation, Opportunity Action, and Internal Control Identification Templates

As discussed in Section 3.6.4, the identification of risk mitigations, opportunity actions, and internal controls is directed at finding viable ways to

	Objective E(>10) #1 Discover how the universe works, explore how it began and evolved, and search for life on planets around other stars		Objective E(>10) #2 Attract a highly skilled workforce, cultivate an innovative work environment, and provide needed facilities, tools, and services	
Time Criticality for Initiation of Response or Activity	Risk Scenario Driver	Opportunity Scenario Driver	Risk Scenario Driver	Opportunity Scenario Driver
1 (≤ 1 Yr)	*3a. Possible failure to deliver the cryocooler subsystem on time* *3b. Possible unavailability of tech. experts for review of next-gen telescope project*	*4. Possibility of a retrofit mission to install improved IR camera on next-gen telescope*		
2 (1–3 Yr)				
3 (> 3 Yr)				

FIGURE 4.13 Illustration of risk and opportunity scenario drivers and their time-frame criticalities

| | Objective E(>10) #1 | | Objective E(>10) #2 | |
| Time Criticality for Initiation of Response of Activity | Discover how the universe works, explore how it began and evolved, and search for life on planets around other stars | | Attract a highly skilled workforce, cultivate an innovative work environment, and provide needed facilities, tools, and services | |
	Risk Driver Constituents	Opportunity Driver Constituents	Risk Driver Constituents	Opportunity Driver Constituents
1 (≤ 1 Yr)	1. Cryo delivery sched. reserve 2. Subcontractor mgmt. issues 3. Compressor performance for brazed unit 4. Thermal vac. testing of cold head assy. 5. Cross-project competition for qualified review personnel	6. Technical Readiness Level for new IR camera 10. Congress may cancel or defer other SLS/Orion missions to pay for retrofit mission		
2 (1–3 Yr)		7. Readiness of SLS/Orion docking capability 8. Predicted P(LOC) for SLS/Orion 9. Predicted cost for rendezvous mission		
3 (> 3 Yr)				

FIGURE 4.14 Illustration of risk and opportunity constituent drivers and their time-frame criticalities

TABLE 4.15 Example Entries for Risk and Opportunity Scenario Likelihood and Impact Evaluation Template

Objective 3

Objective 2

Objective 1

Cum. Risk: [−3] Intolerable   Cum. Opp.: [+3] Significant

Scenario Number	Scenario Description	Scenario Likelihood	Scenario Likelihood Rationale	Scenario Drivers Impacted	Scenario Impact	Scenario Impact Rationale
			Risk Scenarios			
1	Failure to complete the cryo subsystem on time	High	XX	1, 2	High	XX
2	Unavailability of expert technical staff for review	Medium	XX	1, 2, 3	High	XX
XX	Congress may defund program	Low	XX	---	Low	XX
			Opportunity Scenarios			
3	Commitment to develop new IR camera and demo ability to conduct retrofit mission	Medium	XX	4, 5	High	XX
XX	Congress may double funding of program	Low	XX	4	High	XX

act on the risk and opportunity drivers that are identified after the risk and opportunity roll-up processes. This identification is performed on the Risk Mitigation and Internal Control Identification Template, demonstrated in Table 4.16 for the next-generation space telescope example, and on the Opportunity Action and Internal Control Identification Template, demonstrated in Table 4.17 for the same example. The former starts from the risk drivers and the latter from the opportunity drivers that were identified in the Risk and Opportunity Driver Identification Template, Table 4.14.

For each risk or opportunity driver, there are one or more proposed mitigations or actions intended to respond to the driver, and for each mitigation or action, there are one or more internal controls intended to provide assurance of success. The internal control is labeled "Assumption" if the intent is to protect an assumption made in defining the mitigation or action, and "Deficiency" if the intent is to address a shortcoming in the present internal controls. These proposed mitigations, actions, and controls are purely hypothetical and intended for illustration purposes only.

4.7.4   High-Level Display Template

The High-Level Display Template, shown in Table 4.18, displays results obtained from the preceding templates in a condensed form. It also includes suggested responses and internal controls that address the risk and opportunity drivers. The entries that are completed in Table 4.18 correspond to those presented in Tables 4.7 and 4.10 and in Tables 4.16 and 4.17.

4.8   UPWARD PROPAGATION OF TEMPLATES FOR FULL-SCOPE EROM APPLICATIONS

4.8.1   Scope of the Problem

The demonstration in the preceding sections was of limited scope, involving only 12 objectives, of which two were strategic objectives with time frames greater than 10 years, four were top programmatic and mission support objectives with time frames of 5 to 10 years, four were mid-term performance objectives with time frames of 1 to 5 years, and two were short-term performance objectives with time frames of less than or equal to 1 year. Comparatively, this represents a very small sampling of all the objectives that NASA has listed in its 2014 Strategic Plan and its 2015 Performance and Management Plan, including 15 strategic objectives and hundreds of medium-term and short-term performance objectives. For an undertaking of this size, the volume of information to be collected, encoded, and integrated is challenging, to say the least.

TABLE 4.16 Example Entries for Risk Mitigation and Internal Control Template for Objective E (>10) #1: Discover How the Universe Works

Top Objec. Index	Top Objec. Descrip.	Risk to Objective (Level of Concern)	Risk to Objec. if Driver Removed	Driver/ Constituent No.	Driver/ Constituent Type	Driver Constituent Description	Proposed Mitigations	Rationale for Proposed Mitigations	Internal Control No.	Type of Control	Deficiency Needing Control or Assumption Needing Watchfulness	Proposed Internal Control
E (>10) #1	Discover how the universe works, explore how it began and evolved, and search for life on planets around other stars	−2 Yellow Marginal Risk	−1 Green Tolerable Risk	3 / 1	Risk	Cryo delivery schedule reserve	Borrow personnel from Task X	Task X has a larger schedule reserve than needed	1	Assumption	Personnel that can be transferred from Task X to cryo task are available and have applicable skills	Monitoring of Task X schedule and cost reserve assigned with responsibility to report status
									2	Assumption	Appropriate person has authority to move personnel between tasks	Responsibility to shift personnel assigned to a manager who has authority over both tasks
							If necessary, approve overtime	Cryo devel. task has adequate cost reserve	3	Assumption	Appropriate person has authority to approve overtime	Process for elevating overtime decision to the proper level
				3 / 2	Risk	Subcontractor management issues	Strengthen subcontractor management team	GAO evaluation	4	Deficiency	Acquirer's expectations not met	Process for acquirer to review qualifications and concur with subcontr. management choices
									5	Deficiency	Provider not motivated to provide best management team	Penalites for underperformance

Objective	Risk legend	Rating	Type	Description	Mitigation	GAO evaluation	#	Category	Finding	Process
E (>10) #1 — Discover how the universe works, explore how it began and evolved, and search for life on planets around other stars	−2 Yellow Marginal Risk; −1 Green Tolerable Risk				Increase oversight of subcontractor	GAO evaluation	6	Deficiency	Spotty and irregular communications	Regularly scheduled meetings and progress reports
							7	Deficiency	Action items not properly tracked and resolved	Process for assigning action items and monitoring progress
		3 / 3	Risk	Compressor performance for brazed unit	Add tests with modified brazing of compressor to platform	Brazing is a design reqt., and present brazing has not yet performed to spec.	8	Assumption	Needed test facility is available for the amount of time required	Process for elevating facility allocation decision to the proper level
		3 / 4	Risk	Thermal vac. testing of cold head assy.	Add thermal vac. testing of cold head assy. using replacement valves	Replacement valves have not been tested	9	Assumption	Needed test facility is available for the amount of time required	Process for elevating facility allocation decision to the proper level
		3 / 5	Risk	Cross-project competition for qualified review personnel	Establish project review priority	Project with highest impact on top objective should have highest review priority	10	Assumption	Appropriate person has authority to assign qualified review personnel to highest priority task	Responsibility to assign personnel to a manager who has authority over competing projects

TABLE 4.17 Example Entries for Opportunity Action and Internal Control Template for Objective E (>10) #1: Discover How the Universe Works

Top Objec. Index	Top Objec. Descrip.	Opportunity (Level of Interest)	Opportunity if Driver Removed	Driver Constituent No.	Driver Constituent Type	Driver Constituent Description	Proposed Actions	Rationale for Proposed Actions	Internal Control No.	Type of Control	Deficiency Needing Control or Assumption Needing Watchfulness	Proposed Internal Control
E (>10) #1	Discover how the universe works, explore how it began and evolved, and search for life on planets around other stars	+3 Blue Significant Opportunity	+1 Beige Insignificant Opportunity	4 / 6	Opp.	Technical Readiness Level for new IR camera	Increase priority of new IR camera R&D	Scientific value as described below	1	Assumption	TRL progress is being tracked and reported	Protocol for tracking and reporting on IR camera TRL progress
				4 / 7	Opp.	Readiness to launch a crewed mission to retrofit the space telescope with a new high-resolution IR camera	Increase priority of SLS/Orion usage for a space telescope retrofit mission	Camera replacement will greatly improve the mission's scientific value such as increasing the likelihood of understanding dark matter and energy	2	Assumption	Early success of space telescope will increase public support for improving its capability when new technology becomes available	Extremely high quality control and qualification testing to ensure that the telescope has no flaws at the time of launch that would degrade its scientific value
									3	Assumption	The economic recovery will increase the willingness of the country to spend more on space	Provisions to factor trends in economic conditions and public sentiment into planning for upgrades to the space telescope

		ID	Type	Description	+3 Blue Significant Opportunity	+1 Beige Insignificant Opportunity			#			
		4 / 8	Intr. Risk	P(LOC) during retrofit mission exceeding P(LOC) threshold			None	None	4	Assumption	A rigorous probabilistic risk assessment of the retrofit mission will be performed	Provisions to ensure that adequate funding will be available to perform a rigorous PRA
									5	Assumption	P(LOC) reserve for unknown and under appreciated (UU) risks will be sufficient to avoid significant P(LOC) underestimation	Protocol for ensuring that P(LOC) reserves are consistent with prior experience pertaining to UU risks
E (>10) #1	Discover how the universe works, explore how it began and evolved, and search for life on planets around other stars	4 / 9	Intr. Risk	Cost of retrofit mission			None	None	6	Assumption	Cost reserve for UU risks will be sufficient to avoid significant cost underestimation	Protocol for ensuring that cost reserves are consistent with prior experience pertaining to UU risks
		4 / 10	Intr. Risk	Increased priority on space telescope retrofit could result in other SLS/Orion applications being canceled/deferred			None	None	7	Assumption	Congress and the public are aware of the benefits of all the SLS/Orion planned projects	Provisions for educating Congress and the public about the benefits of all the SLS/Orion planned projects

TABLE 4.18 High-Level Display Template

Objective Index	Objective Description	Risk to Objective (Level of Concern)	Oppor-tunity (Level of Interest)	Drivers	Suggested Responses and Internal Controls	UU Risk to Objective Level of Concern	UU Drivers	Suggested Responses and Internal Controls
C (1) #12	Provide tech. support and expert review for devel. of the cryo. subsystem	−1 Green Tolerable	+1 Beige Insignificant	None	None	TBD	TBD	TBD
P (1) #11	Deliver the cryocooler subsystem	−2 Yellow Marginal	+1 Beige Insignificant	■ Cryocooler schedule reserve ■ Subcontractor management issues ■ Compressor performance for brazed unit ■ Thermal vac. testing of cold head assy.	■ Redistribution of resources ■ Increased project oversight ■ Brazing mod. testing XX ■ Cold head assy. vac. testing XX	TBD	TBD	TBD
C (1–5) #10	Implement the 5-year hiring and training plan	TBD	+1 Beige Insignif.	TBD	TBD	TBD	TBD	TBD
C (1–5) #9	Implement the 5-year facilities plan	TBD	+1 Beige Insignif.	TBD	TBD	TBD	TBD	TBD
C (1–5) #8	Provide technical support and expert review for the design, building, testing, and validation of the integrated space telescope	TBD	+1 Beige Insignif.	TBD	TBD	TBD	TBD	TBD

P (1–5) #7	Launch the space telescope	TBD	+1 Beige Insignif.	TBD	TBD	TBD	TBD	TBD
C (5–10) #6	Maintain a sufficient cadre of highly capable analysts and experimentalists to support design, realization, and operation of telescope and interpretation of data	TBD	+1 Beige Insignif.	TBD	TBD	TBD	TBD	TBD
C (5–10) #5	Maintain state-of-the-art facilities and equipment to support design, realization, and operation of the telescope	TBD	+1 Beige Insignif.	TBD	TBD	TBD	TBD	TBD
P (5–10) #4	Design, build, deploy, and operate the Next-Generation Space Telescope	TBD	+1 Beige Insignif.	TBD	TBD	TBD	TBD	TBD
P (5–10) #3	Continue operating existing telescopes	TBD	+1 Beige Insignif.	TBD	TBD	TBD	TBD	TBD

(continued)

TABLE 4.18 (*Continued*)

Objective Index	Objective Description	Risk to Objective (Level of Concern)	Opportunity (Level of Interest)	Drivers	Suggested Responses and Internal Controls	UU Risk to Objective Level of Concern	UU Drivers	Suggested Responses and Internal Controls
E (>10) #2	Attract/advance a highly skilled workforce, cultivate an innovative work environment, and provide the facilities, tools, and services needed to conduct NASA's missions	TBD	+1 Beige Insignif.	TBD	TBD	TBD	TBD	TBD
E (>10) #1	Discover how the universe works, explore how it began and evolved, and search for life on planets around other stars	TBD	+2 Violet Marginal	■ Public enthusiasm after results obtained ■ Economic conditions ■ P(LOC) ■ Others TBD for risk to objective	■ Explore cost savings options ■ Others TBD for risk to objective	TBD	TBD	TBD

Palette for TBD Shaded Cells:

Green Risk: Tolerable   −1   Yellow Risk: Marginal   −2   Red Risk: Intolerable   −3

4.8.2 Propagation of Templates

The development and population of templates for a full-scope EROM effort involves collaborative participation of all the organizational units in the enterprise, from the bottom to the top. Each unit should have its own objectives hierarchy, individual risks, individual opportunities, and leading indicators. Each should complete the templates described in this book in a consistent manner, as shown in Figure 4.15, and pass the completed templates on to the next level of authority in the organization. Each higher level in the organization should utilize the templates provided by the organizations subordinate to it to create its own set of templates. Cross-organizational communication (vertically and horizontally) should freely occur during this process so that the templates produced by any one organizational unit are complete and consistent with those produced by other interfacing organizational units.

Obviously, this process requires that all organizational units use the same format in preparing their templates. Using the same format ensures that the information gleaned from the analysis can be passed readily up the chain of authority. It does not mean, however, that the information provided in the templates should be constrained to only risks and opportunities that are already recognized by others. Rather, each organizational unit should be creative in determining the risks and opportunities that influence the likelihood of success in meeting its objectives.

After receiving templates from its subordinate organizational units, the organizational unit at the next level up should determine whether the completed templates it receives are consistent in terms of assumptions made, the interpretation of input information, recognition of important interfaces, and overall conclusions. If there are inconsistencies or misunderstandings in these areas, then the higher-level unit has the obligation of determining why that is the case and how to resolve them.

The highest level of analysis in the EROM analysis scheme is the enterprise-wide level, as illustrated in Figure 4.15. The templates at enterprise-wide level represent a compilation of the templates from all the entities in the organization. Any differences between organizational units in terms of assumptions, interfaces, interpretations, and conclusions should be resolved at the enterprise-wide level. Once completed, the enterprise-wide level templates are passed back down the organizational chain of authority so that the individual organizational units can review them and provide their assent or dissent.

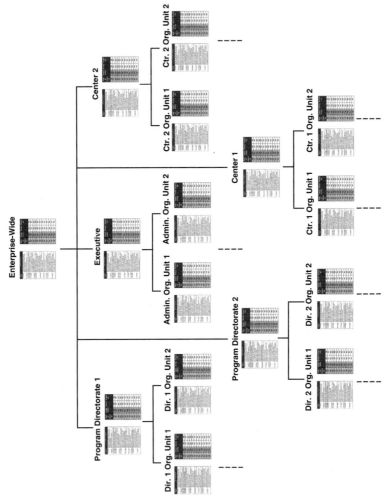

FIGURE 4.15 Schematic showing the upward propagation of templates for full-scope EROM applications

4.8.3 Development of an Integrated EROM Database

The templates prepared by the various units become part of an integrated database. Databases of risks, opportunities, and leading indicators that exist at each unit in the organization are integrated upward first to program directorate, center, and executive levels, and then into an enterprise-wide integrated database. At the extended enterprise level, the integrated database should typically include the information in the risk and opportunity templates, the owner for each risk and opportunity, the organizational entities that are involved, corresponding working groups and management boards, change plans, change history, and status. The development of an enterprise-wide database helps to ensure that cross-cutting risks and opportunities are correctly identified, consistently analyzed, and treated in an integrated manner. It also helps to facilitate the process of rolling up individual risk and opportunity scenarios from lower levels to an aggregate view of the organization's overall likelihood of success in meeting its strategic objectives.

A later section will discuss the challenges of creating and managing a database that integrates risk and opportunity information vertically and horizontally across an extended enterprise consisting of both internal organizational entities and external partners. It will also discuss some best practices for doing so.[7]

4.9 APPLICATION OF THE TEMPLATES TO ORGANIZATIONAL PLANNING AND THE SELECTION FROM AMONG ALTERNATIVE CANDIDATE PORTFOLIOS

The templates developed in the preceding subsections can be applied, with some modification to the inputs, to examine EROM's role in organizational strategic and performance planning. In this application, the organization is interested in examining its likelihood of success in meeting its top objectives for various candidate sets of programs, projects, activities, and initiatives that are in the conceptual stage. There may be no detailed designs and likewise no direct experience in the development, fabrication, testing, deployment, and operation of the systems that would eventually unfold.

The form of the templates for organizational planning can be the same as the form of the templates for the evaluation of organizational performance,

but the entries into the templates would need to be different in the following ways:

- Any risks, opportunities, leading indicators, and associated trigger values would have to be inferred from historical experience with related
  systems and from the judgment of those who are expert in the missions
  to be pursued and the challenges they bring, rather than from real-time
  experience with the actual systems to be used.
- Short-term objectives (e.g., those with time frames of a year or less) in
  most cases would not be applicable since they tend to relate to milestones
  that emanate from a well-defined design.

Consider, for example, what would be included in the entries to the
templates if the JWST project was in a conceptual stage and had not yet
been initiated. The JWST challenges highlighted in the GAO report and
other sources mentioned in Section 4.2 would not yet have been identified. The principal information for identifying risks and opportunities for a
next-generation space telescope would be from the experience gained for the
HST system, which would already have been launched and operating. The
risks in Table 4.2 associated with development and delivery of the cryocooler
subsystem would probably not appear in the Risk and Opportunity Identification Template, because the design of the next-generation telescope would
probably not yet be known in enough detail to identify that the cryocooler
subsystem had to be completely unlike previous cryocooler subsystems. The
potential status of leading indicators associated with shortages in cost and
schedule reserves would have to be inferred without any direct information
from the JWST project, but rather, from HST experience and from the anticipated overall complexity of the next-generation mission.

In accordance with these observations, Table 4.19 shows how the
entries in the Risk and Opportunity Roll-Up Template might appear if the
next-generation telescope was being considered for inclusion in the agency's
portfolio but was not yet past the concept stage. Those entries associated
with the short-term (1-year) objectives relating to the cryocooler subsystem
are no longer present, and the ones associated with cost and schedule
reserves for the system as a whole are based on inference from the HST
project (see highlighted entries in Table 4.19).

The other templates presented in Tables 4.2 through 4.18 would similarly be modified.

TABLE 4.19 Example Risk Roll-Up Template for the Next-Generation Space Telescope as Applied to Alternative Selection during Organizational Planning

Italic denotes repeated instances of leading indicators   Asterisk denotes secondary interfaces   Bold/enlarged denotes Hubble precedent

Objec. No.	Objective Description	Type of Scen.	Lead. Ind. No. or Influencing Objec. No.	Description of Leading Indicator or Influencing Objective	Composite Indicator	Lead. Ind. Concern or Objec. Aggr. Risk	Aggregate Risk of Objective	Roll-Up Rationale
C (1–5) #10	Implement the 5-year hiring and training plan	Risk	5	No. of retirements of qualified optics analysis & testing experts	None	TBD	TBD	TBD
			6	No. of retirements of qualified integrated analysis & testing experts	None	TBD		
			7	No. of qualified optics analysis & testing recent graduates	None	TBD		
			8	Competition for recent optics graduates, e.g., from the military	None	TBD		
C (1–5) #9	Implement the 5-year facilities plan	Risk	**9**	**Number of significant design modifications experienced for HST**	None	TBD	TBD	TBD
			10	Complexity of design	None	TBD		
			11	Complexity of integration and testing	None	TBD		
C (1–5) #8	Provide technical support and expert review for the design, building, testing, and validation of the integrated space telescope	Risk	C (1) #12	Provide tech support & expert review for design,…of cryo subsys	None	None	TBD	TBD
			C (1–5) #10	Implement the 5-year hiring and training plan	None	TBD		
			C (1–5) #9	Implement the 5-year facilities plan	None	TBD		

(continued)

TABLE 4.19 (*Continued*)

Italic denotes repeated instances of leading indicators   Asterisk denotes secondary interfaces   Bold/enlarged denotes Hubble precedent

Objec. No.	Objective Description	Type of Scen.	Lead. Ind. No. or Influencing Objec. No.	Description of Leading Indicator or Influencing Objective	Composite Indicator	Lead. Ind. Concern or Objec. Aggr. Risk	Aggregate Risk of Objective	Roll-Up Rationale
P (1–5) #7	Launch the space telescope	Risk	*10*	*Complexity of design (rank 1–5)*	None	TBD	TBD	TBD
			11	*Complexity of integration and testing (rank 1–5)*	None	TBD		
			12	**Cost reserve needed for HST**	None	TBD		
			13	**Schedule reserve needed for HST**	None	TBD		
			P (1) #11	Deliver the cryo system	None	TBD		
C (5–10) #6	Maintain a sufficient cadre…to support… operation of telescope and interpretation of data	Risk	C (1–5) #10	Implement the 5-year hiring and training plan	None	TBD	TBD	TBD
C (5–10) #5	Maintain state-of-the-art facilities and equipment…to support the design, realization, and operation of the telescope	Risk	C (1–5) #9	Implement the 5-year facilities plan	None	TBD	TBD	TBD
P (5–10) #4	Design, build, deploy, and operate the Next-Generation Space Telescope	Risk	*11*	*Complexity of integration and testing (rank 1–5)*	None	TBD	TBD	TBD
			14	**No. of significant unexpected performance-related difficulties encountered during development of HST**	None	TBD		

Category	Objective	Risk	No.	Metric				
P (5–10) #4	Design, build, deploy, and operate the Next-Generation Space Telescope	Risk	P (1–5) #7	Launch the space telescope	None	TBD		
			C (5–10) #6	Maintain a sufficient cadre…to support…operation of telescope and interpretation of data	None	TBD		
			C (5–10) #5	Maintain state-of-the-art facilities & equipment to support design, realization, operation of the telescope	None	TBD		
P (5–10) #3	Continue operating existing telescopes	Risk	None	None	None	TBD	TBD	TBD
E (>10) #2	Attract a highly skilled workforce, cultivate an innovative work environment, and provide needed facilities, tools, and services	Risk	12	*Cost reserve needed for HST*	None	TBD	TBD	TBD
			13	*Schedule reserve needed for HST*	None	TBD	TBD	
			15	Congressional level of support for new space telescope (rank 1–5)	None	TBD		
			16	Congressional level of support for existing programs (rank 1–5)	None	TBD		
			17	Degree of searching extensibility available through S/W uploading	None	TBD		
			C (5–10) #6	Maintain a sufficient cadre…to support…operation of telescope and interpretation of data	None	TBD		
			C (5–10) #5	Maintain state-of-the-art facilities & equipment to support design, realization, & operation of the telescope	None	TBD		

(continued)

179

TABLE 4.19 (Continued)

Italic denotes repeated instances of leading indicators   Asterisk denotes secondary interfaces   Bold/enlarged denotes Hubble precedent

Objec. No.	Objective Description	Type of Influencing Scen.	Lead. Ind. No. or Influencing Objec. No.	Description of Leading Indicator or Influencing Objective	Composite Indicator	Lead. Ind. Concern or Objec. Aggr. Risk	Aggregate Risk of Objective	Roll-Up Rationale
E (>10) #1	Discover how the universe works, explore how it began and evolved, and search for life on planets around other stars	Risk	P (5–10) #4	* Design, build, deploy, & operate the next-generation telescope	None	TBD		
			P (5–10) #3	* Continue operating existing telescopes	None	TBD		
			10	*Complexity of design (rank 1–5)*	None	TBD	TBD	TBD
			11	*Complexity of integration and testing (rank 1–5)*	None	TBD		TBD
			12	**Cost reserve needed for HST**	None	TBD		
			13	**Schedule reserve needed for HST**	None	TBD		
			15	Congressional level of support for new space telescope (rank 1–5)	None	TBD		
			16	Congressional level of support for existing programs (rank 1–5)	None	TBD		
			C (5–10) #6	* Maintain a sufficient cadre…to support…operation of telescope and interpretation of data	None	TBD		
			P (5–10) #4	Design, build, deploy, and operate the next generation telescope	None	TBD		
			P (5–10) #3	Continue operating existing telescopes	None	TBD		

Palette for TBD Shaded Cells:

Green Risk:	−1	Tolerable	Yellow Risk:	−2	Marginal	Red Risk:	−3	Intolerable

180

NOTES

1. Additional templates for commercial TRIO enterprises will be developed in Chapter 6.
2. In addition to the sources cited in the bulleted list, the Jet Propulsion Laboratory published "James Webb Space Telescope Independent Comprehensive Review Panel Final Report," JPL D-67250, in October 2010. The report provides additional information on root causes of schedule and cost slippages, particularly those associated with the roles of NASA Headquarters and Goddard Space Flight Center in the 2010 time frame. The problems associated with establishing realistic budgets were particularly emphasized. NASA management responded to the recommendations in the report in "NASA's Detailed Response to the James Webb Space Telescope Independent Comprehensive Review Panel Report," presently available on the web under that title.
3. The organizational units called "mission directorates" and "centers" at NASA are equivalent to the organizational units referred to as "program directorates" and "technical centers" elsewhere in this book with respect to TRIO enterprises.
4. In Section 4.6.1, some additional cross-organizational interfaces between the objectives in Figure 4.4 will be identified and included in the development of the demonstration.
5. A demonstration of the roll-up process leading to this type of result will be presented in Section 4.6.5.
6. This will occur in Section 4.6.4.
7. This will be done in Section 5.2.4.

REFERENCES

Foust, Jeff. 2014. "NASA Facing New Space Science Cuts." (May 31). http://news .nationalgeographic.com/news/2014/05/140530-space-politics-planetary -science-funding-exploration/

Government Accountability Office (GAO). 2014b. GAO-15-100, Report to Congressional Committees, "James Webb Space Telescope: Project Facing Increased Schedule Risk with Significant Work Remaining." Washington, DC. Government Accountability Office (December). http://www.gao.gov/assets/670/667526 .pdf

Harwood, William. 2009. "The History of Hubble: A Grand Space Telescope." SpaceflightNow.com (May 9).

HubbleSite.org, 2016. "Team Hubble: Servicing Missions." http://hubblesite.org/the _telescope/team_hubble/servicing_missions.php

Leone, Dan. 2014. "Manufacturing Issues Plague James Webb Space Telescope." SpaceNews (November 14).

National Aeronautics and Space Administration (NASA). 2009. "Hubble Space Telescope Servicing Mission 4." http://www.nasa.gov/mission_pages/hubble/servicing/SM4/main/Summary_FS_HTML.html

National Aeronautics and Space Administration (NASA). 2014c. *FY 2014 Annual Performance Report and FY 2016 Annual Performance Plan.* Washington, DC. National Aeronautics Space Administration, http://www.nasa.gov/sites/default/files/atoms/files/fy14_apr-fy16_app.pdf

National Aeronautics and Space Administration (NASA). 2016b. "Explore James Webb Space Telescope." www.jwst.nasa.gov

Management and Implementation of EROM at the Institutional/Technical Level (Technical Centers or Directorates)

5.1   EROM FROM A TECHNICAL CENTER'S PERSPECTIVE

As discussed previously in Section 1.1.7, EROM can be applied separately to management units within a TRIO enterprise so long as the objectives of each management unit are consistent with the objectives of the enterprise as a whole, and the cross-cutting risks and opportunities are handled consistently. Since the top objectives of a technical center or technical directorate are derived from the TRIO enterprise's strategic objectives, the top objectives of the center are consonant with those of the enterprise in all areas where the center's roles align with the enterprise's responsibilities.

To support the TRIO enterprise's strategic objectives, technical centers may have multiple roles. They may act as managers of programs and projects that are assigned to them by the program directorates, as contributors to programs and projects as requested when another technical center has management responsibilities, as preservers of core competencies required to support programs and projects, as preservers of other core competencies mandated by the executive level, and as support agents for special needs levied on the enterprise by other entities such as the federal government. In the role of managers of programs and projects assigned to them, they may also act as integrators and arbitrators of an extended organization that includes other technical centers, prime contractors, other commercial suppliers, university partners, and international partners. Furthermore, as was illustrated in Figure 2.5, implementing a technical center's plan includes developing and managing the workforce, maintaining needed facilities and retiring unneeded ones, acquiring services and material, and off-loading responsibilities when appropriate to the partnering agencies and companies. Chapter 5 focuses on these areas in developing guidance for the conduct of EROM at the institutional/technical level—that is, technical centers.

The particular objectives of EROM at the technical center level vary as the roles of the center vary. For example, when the technical center is exercising its role as a manager of programs and projects, the principal objective of EROM is to integrate the risks and opportunities discovered by the multiple organizations contributing to the program/project, ensuring that they are handled consistently across the program/project and across the center, that cross-cutting risks and opportunities are accounted for, that the contributions of individual risk and opportunity scenarios are aggregated appropriately from lower levels to higher levels, and that responses such as mitigation of risks and exploitation of opportunities are coordinated. On the other hand, when it is exercising its role as preserver of core competencies, the principal EROM objective is its primary institutional objective: to optimize the acquisition, allocation, and retirement of the various assets available to the technical center, including human assets (the workforce), physical assets (facilities, equipment, systems, and software), and instructional assets (policies, requirements, standards, and guidance).

5.2   EXTENDED ENTERPRISES AND THE TECHNICAL CENTER'S EXTENDED ORGANIZATION

5.2.1   Overview

The example demonstration used in Chapter 4 is an instance of a project that involves multiple partners, or entities, with overlapping responsibilities. The collection of these entities is referred to herein as an *extended enterprise,* because in addition to contributing to the same project, each is an independent enterprise with its own set of strategic objectives and performance requirements. Consider, for example, the extended enterprise for the NASA JWST project, shown in Table 5.1. The center that manages the project (Goddard Space Flight Center) must communicate with the extended enterprise in a manner that satisfies the strategic objectives of the TRIO enterprise (NASA) while also respecting the strategic objectives of each of the contributing entities. Other centers within the extended enterprise (those identified in Table 5.1) also must communicate with the other entities they interface with.

TABLE 5.1 Distribution of Responsibilities among the Principal Entities within the JWST Project (Source: NASA 2016c)

Entity	Responsibility
NASA Centers:	
Goddard (GSFC)	Manages the JWST project and provides Integrated Science Instrument Module (ISIM) components
Jet Propulsion Lab (JPL)	Manages the Mid-Infrared Instrument
Ames (ARC)	Detector technology development
Johnson (JSC)	Provides observatory test facilities
Marshall (MSFC)	Mirror technology development and environmental research
Glenn (GRC)	Cryogenic component development
Industry Partners:	
Northrop Grumman (NGC)	Prime contractor
Ball Aerospace	In charge of building the mirrors
COM DEV International	In charge of the Fine Guidance Sensor (FGS)
Academic Partners:	
Space Telescope Science Inst.	Science and Operations Center at Johns Hopkins University
University of Arizona	In charge of building the Near Infrared Camera (NIRCam)
International Partners:	
European Space Agency (ESA)	Provides the Near Infrared Spectrograph, Mid-Infrared Instrument Optics Assembly, and the Ariane Launch Vehicle
Canadian Space Agency (CSA)	Provides the Fine Guidance Sensor/Near Infrared Imager and Slitless Spectrograph

As a rule, each technical center participates, either as manager or as a contributor, in many programs and projects and therefore has responsibilities to interface with many extended enterprises, as shown in Figure 5.1. For convenience, we refer to the collection of entities in all the extended enterprises that interact with a technical center as the center's "extended organization." The technical center's extended organization includes not only entities in the extended enterprises with which the center interacts on program planning and execution but also entities within the TRIO enterprise administration that provide direction and administrative support to the center.

The success of such extended-organization endeavors depends on the establishment of communication protocols that promote consistency of approach across the entities, sharing of information while protecting that which is proprietary, and seamless integration of the products.

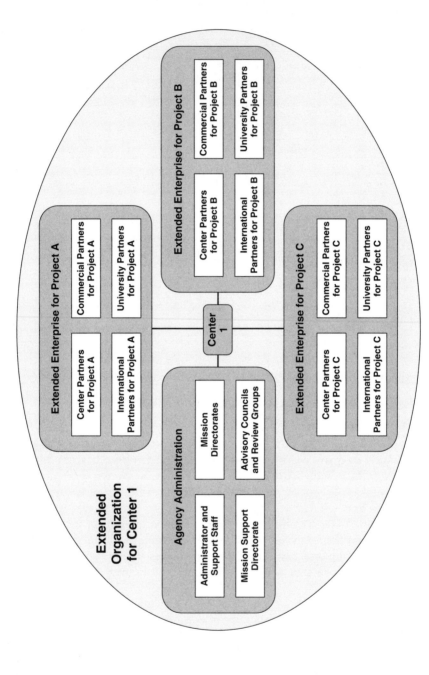

FIGURE 5.1 The extended organization for a NASA center

5.2.2 Relationship of Each Technical Center to the Other Entities in the Center's Extended Organization

In its multiple roles, each technical center within a TRIO enterprise acts as its own enterprise with its own set of objectives to be achieved, as an integrator of risk and opportunity information emanating from the other entities in the center's extended organization, and as an element of the extended enterprises charged with helping to ensure that the TRIO enterprise's strategic objectives are achieved.

These multiple roles are illustrated schematically in Figure 5.2, where NASA's strategic objectives are taken as an example of the executive-level objectives that each center supports. In this figure, the executive-level strategic objectives are divided into three types:

1. Those that are principally programmatic in nature and are allocated to centers by the mission directorates (program directorates)
2. Those that are more institutional in nature and are managed, by designation of the NASA administrator, within centers and within the Mission Support Directorate
3. Those that are required of all agencies in the federal government and are typically managed at the executive (NASA administrative) level

Correspondingly, the objectives of each technical center within a TRIO enterprise can be divided into three types that mirror the categories that apply to the higher-level strategic objectives:

1. Support of specific programs and projects that are assigned to the technical center in service of the TRIO enterprise's mission
2. Provisions for additional institutional capabilities needed to maintain the technical center's core competencies
3. Support of mandates that are required by the federal government or other sources

The risks, opportunities, and leading indicators associated with these types of objectives tend to cut across each technical center's extended organization. This cross-cutting aspect is illustrated in the lower part of Figure 5.2, which depicts the inputs from the center's extended organization that are needed to perform the roll-up, or aggregation, of risks and opportunities within the center. These risk and opportunity inputs are divided into the following categories:

- Individual risk scenarios, opportunity scenarios, and associated leading indicators that are unique to the technical center
- Individual risk scenarios, opportunity scenarios, and associated leading indicators that affect not only the technical center in question but also other entities in the center's extended organization

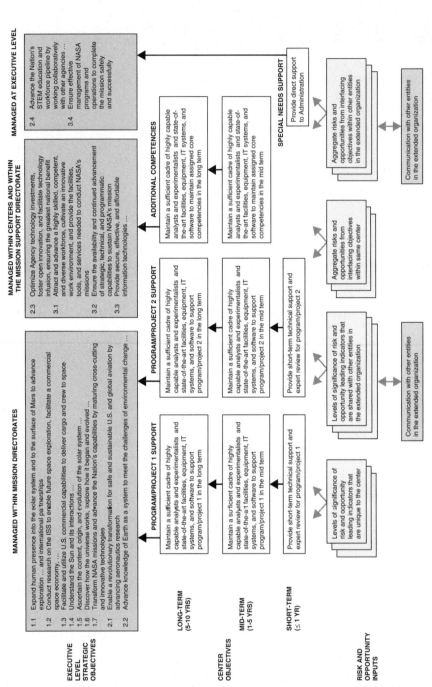

FIGURE 5.2 NASA example of how each center takes risk and opportunity inputs from a variety of entities and supports multiple strategic objectives of the agency

- Aggregate risks and opportunities for objectives that are unique to the technical center
- Aggregate risks and opportunities for objectives that emanate from or are shared with other entities in the center's extended organization

5.2.3   EROM Organizational Structure for a Technical Center's Extended Enterprises

Experience has shown that for EROM to be practiced successfully in enterprises that have multiple partners, there needs to be an EROM team for each extended enterprise that prepares the overall risk management plan and oversees the management of risk and opportunity (Holzer 2006). The team at the extended enterprise level is responsible for identifying risks that cross over the interfaces between entities (i.e., between technical centers, contractors, and other partners) and/or that emanate from those interfaces, for conducting preliminary analyses to assess the likelihoods and potential impacts, and for assigning primary ownership. When the origin of an interfacing or cross-cutting risk initiates from an action or inaction of a particular entity within the extended enterprise, ownership is typically assigned first to that entity. If the entity lacks authority to act on the risk, it is elevated to a higher level within the chain of authority. Frequently, risk ownership is assigned at program or project level if the process of resolving the risk requires action at that level. Thereafter, the EROM team monitors the resolution process, which may involve the improvement of existing internal controls, establishment of new internal controls, or formulation and implementation of a mitigation plan.

To flesh out and monitor interfacing and cross-cutting risks and opportunities, the EROM team may establish various subgroups. The number of subgroups or their particular names are not that important. What is important is that their responsibilities with respect to one another are clearly defined and the schedules under which they operate are coordinated.

For example, there may be separate working groups and management boards established for each organizational unit, for each program/project, and for each technical center, as shown in Figure 5.3. Risk and opportunity (R-O) working groups for each entity would have responsibility for identifying, analyzing, and recommending controls and mitigations to reduce risks pertaining to the entity's objectives in the extended enterprise. They would meet on a regular, scheduled basis with their corresponding R-O management board to share risks and opportunities that affect the entity and review decisions made by the management board about how to respond to them. They would also meet with the working groups of the other entities in the extended enterprise at regularly schedule meetings organized by the program/project, to discuss and evaluate risks and opportunities that are

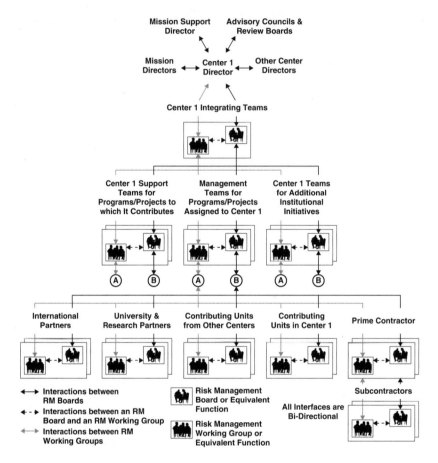

FIGURE 5.3 A representative EROM organizational chart for a technical center that manages extended enterprises

of mutual interest. Although not specifically shown in the figure, informal communications between the working groups of different entities could also occur between scheduled meetings when there is a need to discuss technical issues in an ad-hoc manner.

R-O management boards for each entity would have responsibility for prioritizing the risks and opportunities identified and reported by the entity's R-O working group, determining the kind of response needed, assigning ownership, monitoring progress, and approving changes of status. Typical responses for risks would include, for example, (1) accept and watch, (2) add controls, (3) mitigate, or (4) close-out. Changes of status would typically involve movement from one kind of response to another, and could involve elevating the response (e.g., from accept and watch to mitigate) or lowering the response (e.g., from accept and watch to close-out). They would also meet on a regularly scheduled basis with the management boards of the other entities at regularly scheduled meetings organized by the program/project to organize and adjudicate risks and opportunities that are of mutual interest.

The technical center, in addition to managing the extended enterprises that are assigned to it, has additional responsibilities that include contributing to other programs and projects, executing designated institutional initiatives to maintain its core competencies, and communicating with other technical centers that have similar responsibilities for other extended enterprises, with the program directorates that assign program/project responsibilities to the technical center, with the directorate that has institutional oversight at the executive level, and with the advisory councils and review boards that provide an evaluation function at the executive level. These interfaces are also shown in Figure 5.3.

The principal goal of the EROM structure, which cannot be overemphasized, is for all entities to be involved in the EROM process by having technical representation in a working group and/or managerial representation in a management board. This far-reaching intent is necessary to achieve the buy-in that is needed in all parts of the extended enterprise.

5.2.4 Challenges of Creating and Managing an Integrated Database

As discussed in Section 4.8.3, wherever there is a need for EROM oversight and communication between entities, there is also a need for an integrated database that incorporates EROM information across these entities. At the extended enterprise level, the integrated database should typically include the information in the risk and opportunity templates, the owner for each risk and opportunity, the organizational entities that are involved, corresponding working groups and management boards, change plans, change history, and status.

While ideally the integrated database for an extended enterprise should capture all risks and opportunities for all the participating entities, some entities may already have an established risk management process and database that they do not want to give up. To facilitate acceptance of the process, exceptions to the principle of a totally integrated database may have to be made. For example, some entities may need their own version of the database because they do not have network connectivity. Periodically (perhaps weekly), they might provide a copy of their database updates for uploading into the main database. Other entities may have concerns about proprietary information and not want to have all their data available to all participants. It may be decided that such entities may maintain their own separate database as long as they enter risks and opportunities into the main database that have the potential to degrade the capability performance at the program/project level. These entities would be aware of how their risk and opportunity data affect the extended enterprise by virtue of having access to the main database.

Because of the cross-cutting nature of enterprise risks and opportunities, there is also a need for reduced, summary databases that integrate EROM information at higher levels of the organization. For example, there should be a repository of data at the technical center level covering those aspects of EROM that cut across the extended enterprises within the center's extended organization. Similarly, there should be a data repository at executive level covering the aspects of EROM that cut across the technical centers, program directorates, support directorates, and management councils.

5.3   EROM-INFORMED BUDGETING OF RESOURCES ACROSS A TECHNICAL CENTER'S EXTENDED ORGANIZATION

5.3.1   Objectives-Based Distribution of Human, Physical, and Instructional Assets

An important function of EROM, in its institutional mode of operation, is to assist each technical center in the budgeting of key resources across the extended organization. The key resources to be budgeted, as shown in Figure 5.4, include human assets (personnel trained and experienced in different skill areas), physical assets (supporting facilities, IT systems, other systems, equipment, and software), and instructional assets (supporting policies, requirements, standards, and guidance documents). The budgeting involves more than costs. In addition to satisfying cost constraints, the final distribution of assets must reflect the intent of the TRIO enterprise's strategic objectives that are inherited by the technical center, including: successful execution of programs and projects that support the strategic objectives, maintenance of core competencies in specified strategic areas, promotion of strategic partnerships, and sharing with the public through strategic education initiatives. The tools for achieving this strategic distribution of assets are both quantitative and qualitative.

5.3.2   Representative Templates for Distributions of Allocated Assets

Representative templates that may be used for displaying the distribution of allocated assets are provided in Table 5.2. These templates include both

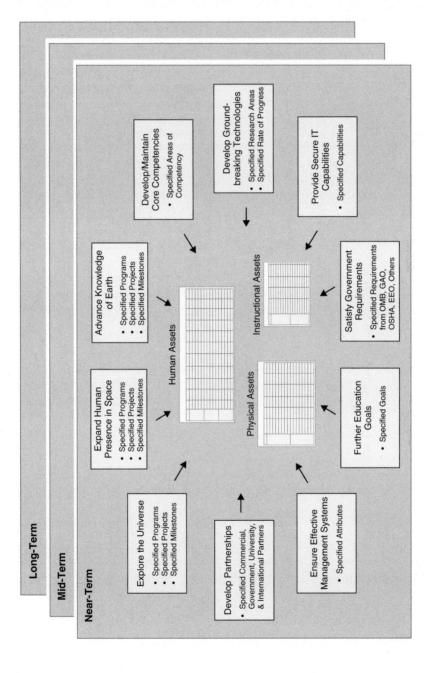

FIGURE 5.4 The success of a technical center's inherited strategic objectives is dependent on the "right-sizing" of the resources available to the center (NASA example)

193

TABLE 5.2 Templates for Distribution of Human (Workforce), Physical, and Instructional Assets

Long-Term

Mid-Term

Near-Term

(a) Current and Projected Workforce

Organizational Entities Included in the Compilation	Skill Area	Skill Levels	Current Number of Available EPs	Projected Number of EPs Available for Spec. Term
All Entities in Extended Organization	Area 1 (e.g., Propulsion Design)	All	XX	TBD
		3, 4, and 5	XX	TBD
		5 Only	XX	TBD
	Area 2 (e.g., Information Technology)	All	XX	TBD
		3, 4, and 5	XX	TBD
		5 Only	XX	TBD
	Etc.			
Center 1 (Center of Interest)	Same Breakdown of Skill Areas and Skill Levels			
Etc., as enumerated in (d)				

(c) Current and Projected Instructional Asset

Contributing Entity	Instructional Area	Instructional Asset	Current Content Relevant to Center 1 Objectives	Projected Content for Specified Term
All Entities in Extended Organization	Area 1 (e.g., Acquisition Management)	Policy Directive #1	XX	TBD
		Proc. Reqt. Doc. #1	XX	TBD
		Standard #1	XX	TBD
		Guidebook #1	XX	TBD
	Area 2 (e.g., Equal Opportunity)	Policy Directive #1	XX	TBD
		Proc. Reqt. Doc. #2	XX	TBD
		Standard #2	XX	TBD
		Guidebook #12	XX	TBD
	Etc.			
Center 1 (Center of Interest)	Same Breakdown of Operational Ability Measures, Support Areas, and Support Assets			
Etc., as enumerated in (d)				

(b) Current and Projected Physical Assets

Organizational Entities Included in the Compilation	Operational Ability Measure	Support Area	Support Asset	Current Ability Relevant to Center 1 Objectives	Projected Ability Relevant to Center 1 Objectives
All Entities in Extended Organization	Capability	Area 1 (e.g., Propulsion Testing)	Facility #1	XX	XX
			System #1	XX	XX
			Equipment Item #1	XX	XX
			Software Item #1	XX	XX
		Area 2 (e.g., Information Technology)	Facility #2	XX	XX
			System #2	XX	XX
			Equipment Item #2	XX	XX
			Software Item #2	XX	XX
	Availability	Area 1 (e.g., Propulsion Testing)	Facility #3	XX	XX
			System #3	XX	XX
			Equipment Item #3	XX	XX
			Software Item #3	XX	XX
		Area 2 (e.g., Information Technology)	Facility #4	XX	XX
			System #4	XX	XX
			Equipment Item #4	XX	XX
			Software Item #4	XX	XX
	Etc.				
Center 1 (Center of Interest)	Same Breakdown of Operational Ability Measures, Support Areas, and Support Assets				
Etc., as enumerated in (d)					

(d) Example Entities

Organizational Entities Included in the Compilation		
Center 1 (Center of Interest)	Contractor 1 (Onsite)	University Partner 1
Center 2 (Other Center)	Contractor 2 (Onsite)	University Partner 2
Center 3 (Other Center)	Contractor 1 (Offsite)	International Partner 1
Center 4 (Other Center)	Contractor 2 (Offsite)	International Partner 2
Etc.		

current and projected distributions. The projected distributions refer to the predicted allocation of assets in the near term (~1 year), mid-term (~5 years), and long term (~10 years), assuming the current plan is implemented. The specific entries in Table 5.2 are discussed in the following three subsections.

Human Asset (Workforce) Distribution   The success of any organization (whether an entity in a technical center's extended organization or the extended organization itself) depends on the ability to hire and maintain a skilled workforce. Since several of the strategic objectives inherited by technical centers pertain to diversification of the workforce through formation of partnerships with other domestic agencies, commercial enterprises, universities, and international agencies, it is necessary for the proper skills to be maintained in all the contributing entities of the center's extended organization. The particular skills to be preserved have to be matched to the needs of the programs and projects that the technical center is managing or contributing to, as well as to the additional core competencies that the technical center is required to maintain.

Table 5.2 (a) illustrates conceptually the type of information needed to evaluate the status of the workforce across the technical center's extended organization. It includes the number of experienced personnel (EP) at different skill levels for each skill area that is needed and for each entity that contributes. Skill level designations on the scale of 1 to 5 can be interpreted, for example, as follows (typical of Industry standards):

> *5 – Expert in area. Typically the area lead. Understands all aspects of system and has extensive practical experience.*
>
> *4 – Senior member of area. Knowledgeable in most aspects. Leads projects. Substitutes for area lead when needed. Self-starter. Understands most or all of system. High degree of practical experience.*
>
> *3 – Junior member of area. Owns specific areas of responsibility. Needs continuous coaching. Self-supporting once tasks assigned. Responsible engineer on some components. General knowledge of system.*
>
> *2 – Group apprentice. Minimal experience but shows competency in areas that have been tried. Does not work alone. Understands key aspects of system. Some practical experience.*
>
> *1 – Brand-new to area. Entry-level tasks. Minimal contribution. Some knowledge of the general workings of the system. Limited practical experience.*

Each combination of skill area, skill level, and contributing organizational entity is referred to herein as a workforce category.

Physical Asset Distribution Because the strategic objectives of the TRIO enterprise include both enterprise objectives (programs and projects) and, in the case of federal agencies, national policy objectives (e.g., the well-being of the TRIO enterprise's commercial, educational, and international partners), it is necessary not only for workforce allocations to be considered in a holistic manner across the extended organization, but also for the distribution and utilization of physical assets to be so considered. As mentioned earlier, physical assets in the present context include supporting facilities (including test facilities), IT and other systems, equipment, and software.

Table 5.2 (b) illustrates conceptually the type of information needed to evaluate the status of physical assets across the technical center's extended organization. It includes the capability and availability of each asset to be used to satisfy the technical center's objectives, broken out according to the support area that it addresses and the entity that owns it.

The specifications of capability and availability in this template are expressed verbally rather than numerically (although numerical information may be included in the verbal descriptions). This is different from the specification of EPs in the allocation of human assets, which is strictly numerical. Both terms, *capability* and *availability*, are specifically referenced to needs for satisfying the technical center's objectives. For example, the capability of a propulsion test facility to test small components is not a relevant capability if its use for the technical center is only for testing of full-up systems. Likewise, the availability of a propulsion test facility for purposes other than those needed by the technical center and its extended organization are not relevant and do not need to be tracked. In a large sense, the description of the capability and availability of a physical asset is equivalent to a statement of its ability to meet the technical center's performance and availability requirements.

Instructional Asset Distribution Since the TRIO enterprise's mission is dynamic and the means it uses to achieve its objectives change from time to time (e.g., as a result of the increasing complexity of its missions or the occurrence of breakthrough technology advancements), its instructional documents frequently need to be updated or superseded. Similarly, the instructional documents for entities that partner with the TRIO enterprise may need to be revised or superseded to be consistent with the TRIO enterprise's policies and requirements, and one of the TRIO enterprise's responsibilities will be to audit the contents of the partners' instructional documents. As noted earlier, instructional documents include policy directives, procedural requirements, standards, and guidance documents.

Table 5.2 (c) illustrates conceptually the information needed to characterize the status of instructional assets relevant to the center's operation and the operation of its partners. It includes the content required of instructional documents in various instructional areas over the near term, mid-term, and long term. Again, the content is expressed verbally rather than numerically, and only content relevant to the technical center's objectives need be entered in the template.

5.3.3   Asset Risks, Opportunities, and Risk/Opportunity Scenario Statements

In addition to the risks and opportunities associated with the successful performance of the technical center's designated programs and projects, there is a separate category of risks and opportunities associated with the center's human, physical, and instructional assets and its obligation to maintain its mandated core competencies. Both types of risk have to be considered in the overall assessment of whether a technical center is achieving all its objectives.

Risks of future asset shortages and imbalances can arise from various sources. Following, for example, is a list of risks that could affect the viability of the workforce by causing people to leave prematurely:

- If funding is cut or a program is retired earlier than expected, people might seek more stable work alternatives.
- If a program is extended beyond its planned time frame, the impact of retirements might become more important.
- If competition in-house for qualified persons increases, people might transfer to other organizations to increase their opportunities.
- If market competition for qualified persons increases, people might accept positions with other companies with higher pay.
- If local economic conditions degrade, people might move to another part of the country.
- If a contractor or partner develops financial problems, that entity might not be able to maintain its workforce.
- If people are required to work longer hours on a continuing basis, people might seek positions that are less stressful.

Other risks can affect the viability of the workforce by increasing the number of qualified persons that are needed to achieve the technical center's objectives beyond those that are available. For example:

- If domestic or international political priorities mandate an acceleration of the schedule or an increase in the scope of the objectives, there might be a need for more qualified people.
- If an important task in a project falls behind schedule because of unexpected difficulties, there might be a need for an increased allocation of people to that task to get it on schedule again.

There are also events that could lead to opportunities pertaining to the workforce. For example:

- If funding is increased due, for example, to favorable economic conditions, it may be possible to attract persons with unusually high qualifications by offering higher salaries or other monetary incentives.
- If market competition for qualified persons decreases, it may be possible to attract qualified persons without offering higher salaries or other monetary incentives.

Risks that could affect the viability of physical and instructional assets include the following:

- If a facility has to be shut down unexpectedly due to an accident, malfunction, or the mandate of a watchdog organization, its availability to the technical center may disappear.
- If another program that requires use of the facility suddenly gains high national priority, the availability of the facility for the technical center's use may decrease.
- If a catastrophic accident occurs in one of the TRIO enterprise's programs or projects, the TRIO enterprise's policies and procedural requirements may have to be changed to respond to findings of the ensuing review board.
- If a revolutionary new technology becomes available offering new opportunities previously not thought possible, the TRIO enterprise's standards and guidebooks may have to be rewritten to accommodate the new technology.

Obviously, the last of these encompasses both a risk and an opportunity, for while there is a risk that the instructional documents may have to be rewritten, leading to increased cost and/or schedule implications, there is simultaneously an opportunity for implementing improved technology.

For asset risks and opportunities, it is useful to expand on the risk and opportunity scenario statement structure presented in Section 3.4.2 to include information about the effect of the risk or opportunity on assets in the extended organization. Following is a specialized form of risk/opportunity scenario statement that satisfies the general format but is specifically applicable to risks and opportunities affecting assets in the technical center's extended organization:

Given [a specified set of current conditions and current/projected trends],
     …*there is a possibility that* [a specified departure event or set of departure events] *may occur,*

> ...*affecting the [[*envisaged or required*] availability, capability,* and/or content of specified human, physical, and/or instructional assets*],*
>
> ...*resulting in a noteworthy* [decrease or increase]
>
> ...*in the center's likelihood of being able to meet* [a specified center objective or set of objectives].

This risk/opportunity scenario statement recognizes that there are several ways in which a departure event can affect the viability of the human, physical, and/or instructional assets for the technical center's extended organization. The event can result, for example, in a positive or negative change in:

- The number of experienced personnel *available to* the extended organization in various workforce categories
- The number of experienced personnel *needed by* the extended organization in various workforce categories to meet the technical center's objectives
- The availability and capability of physical assets *under the purview of* the extended organization
- The availability and capability of physical assets *needed by* the extended organization to meet the technical center's objectives
- The content of instructional assets *needed by* the extended organization to meet the technical center's objectives

These variants are encompassed in the risk/opportunity scenario statement within the phrase [*envisaged or required] availability, capability, and/or content of specified human, physical, and/or instructional assets.* Note that while each of the variants is different from the others, they all lead to a common result: an imbalance or gap (either positive or negative) between the assets in the extended organization and the assets needed to satisfy the technical center's objectives.

5.3.4 Leading Indicators of a Technical Center's Health

In addition to the leading indicators cited in Sections 3.4.4 and 3.4.5 and those listed in Table 3.1, there is a separate category of leading indicators associated with the technical center's ability to maintain its mandated core competencies. For example, the following is a subset of workforce-related leading indicators recommended for NASA use by the National Academy of Public Administration (NAPA) (Harper et al. 2007):

- Median age of workforce
- Number of uncovered full-time equivalents (FTEs)

- Ratio of fresh-out hires to total hires
- Ratios of civil service persons to contractors and supervisors to staff
- Center-by-center use of workforce incentives such as flexible work schedule, bonuses, and subsidized student loan payments
- Percentage of people participating in training over the past year
- Number of turnovers and absenteeism
- Overall productivity rating
- Employee perceptions/assessments of management (e.g., from 360-degree feedback and *Best Places to Work* survey)
- Number and severity of disciplinary actions
- Number of unfair labor practices and Equal Employment Opportunity (EEO) complaints
- Ranking in *Best Places to Work in the Federal Government,* diversity element

These were devised by NAPA as being indicators of the health of a center, and in particular, indicators of the risk of not being able to maintain a robust workforce.

Similar lists can be postulated for physical assets and instructional assets. For example, the following list of attributes can be thought of as leading indicators of the health of a technical center with respect to the availability and capability of an organization's physical assets:

- Median age of facilities
- Maintenance history of facilities
- Scale factors for testing
- Unaddressed cybersecurity threats
- History of changes to policies and procedures

5.3.5 Correlations between Internal Leading Indicators and Gaps in the Distributions of Human, Physical, and Instructional Assets

Important correlations exist between leading indicators that were cited earlier, such as schedule and cost margins, and gaps in the distributions of human, physical, and instructional assets. These correlations make it possible to develop a risk- and opportunity-based plan for acquiring, allocating, and retiring a technical center's human, physical, and instructional assets.

To illustrate by way of example, suppose that there happens to be a shortage of skilled personnel available to the prime contractor for the JWST project in the area of cryogenics for cooling systems, and suppose that, based on current trends and expected future events, the shortage is projected to worsen during the next five years. When this information is factored into the scheduling for JWST development and testing, it may be found that the margin for the completion of the buildup of the integrated system is less than the trigger value for significant concern (i.e., the response trigger value as defined in Section 3.5.1). When this information is transferred to the risk roll-up template for JWST (Table 4.6), it may be found that there is an intolerable risk of not being able to satisfactorily achieve the following strategic objectives that the center is committed to:

- Objective 1.6: Discover how the universe works, explore how it began and evolved ...
- Objective 3.1: Attract and advance a highly skilled, competent, and diverse workforce ... needed to conduct NASA's missions

Observe in this example the following entry on the workforce template for the technical center's extended organization:

Number of people in skill category 4 or 5 in the skill area of cryogenics working for the prime contractor

is directly related to the following leading indicator:

Schedule margin for JWST integration

Thereby, it has been identified as causing two of the center's top objectives (listed above) as having an intolerable risk of not being satisfactorily achieved.

In addition, it should be apparent that the same sort of correlation can exist between entries on the physical and instructional asset template, the leading indicators pertaining to margins, and the technical center's top objectives. For example, if a certain testing facility is not available when needed or lacks certain needed capabilities, the schedule margin for completion of testing may be intolerably low, thereby having the same effect on the technical center's top objectives.

Likewise, the distributions of human, physical, and instructional assets can affect the ability to take advantage of opportunities that may arise in the future. For example, having a few skilled researchers available to conduct innovative research in a pioneering propulsion technology may lead to an opportunity to utilize that technology to expand the TRIO enterprise's objectives related to exploration of our solar system or to accomplish its current objectives more quickly or at less cost.

5.3.6   Optimization of the Acquisition, Allocation, and Retirement of Human, Physical, and Instructional Assets

Optimization of the plan for acquiring, allocating, and retiring human, physical, and instructional assets is an iterative process that utilizes the correlations between assets, leading indicators, and the technical center's objectives. The optimization process is summarized in Figure 5.5 and proceeds as follows:

- The technical center's objectives and associated risks, opportunities, and corresponding leading indicators are identified as in Chapter 4.
- An asset allocation plan that is postulated to meet cost constraints is proposed using the templates in Section 5.3.2.
- The effect of the allocation plan on the current and projected leading indicator values is evaluated based on the discussion in Section 5.3.5, using the Leading Indicator Evaluation Template (Table 4.3).
- The risks and opportunities are rolled up to the technical center's top-level performance objectives using the Risk and Opportunity Roll-Up Templates (Tables 4.6 and 4.9).
- The cost of implementation of the asset allocation is evaluated using traditional cost accounting methods.
- Modifications to the asset allocation plan are considered to determine whether the balance between overall risk and opportunity exposure and overall cost can be improved.

The iterative process may continue until any of the following conditions occurs:

- The overall risks to success cannot be further reduced within cost constraints.
- Additional significant opportunities cannot be availed within cost constraints.
- Costs cannot be reduced without significantly increasing the overall risk or sacrificing significant opportunities.

The iterative process is illustrated in more detail in Figure 5.6. As part of its graphical display, Figure 5.6 includes the Leading Indicator Evaluation Template originally presented in Table 4.3, modified to include not only performance risk indicators but also asset and UU risk indicators.

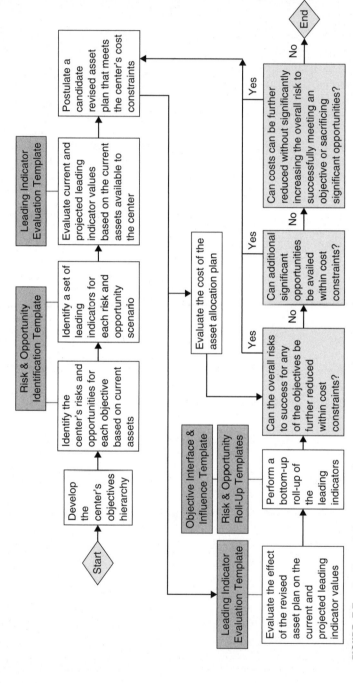

FIGURE 5.5 Outline of the steps in the iterative process for optimizing asset distributions based on costs and current and projected values of leading indicators

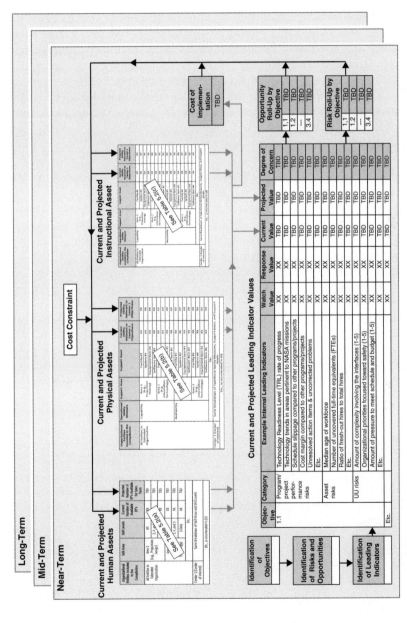

FIGURE 5.6 Illustration of iterative process for optimizing asset distributions based on costs and current and projected values of leading indicators

5.3.7 Relevance to Provider Acquisition Decisions Made by Technical Centers

The processes described earlier in Section 5.3 can be applied to assist the technical center in selecting providers such as prime contractors and other suppliers. The process of deciding between alternative providers is determined in large part by the amount of risk versus the amount of opportunity that each brings to the table in helping the technical center achieve its objectives. The steps that a technical center needs to implement in order to make a rational selection are similar to those described in the earlier subsections, but with a focus on the risks and opportunities that are brought by each provider. Very briefly, these steps are as follows:

1. Identify the risk and opportunity scenarios that are introduced by allocating the selected tasks to the provider.
2. Identify and evaluate the associated leading indicators.
3. Integrate the risk, opportunity, and leading indicator information for the provider with the corresponding risk, opportunity, and leading indicator information that is already in the EROM templates.
4. Perform the roll-up of risks and opportunities using the roll-up templates including the risks and opportunities introduced by the candidate provider.
5. Determine which candidate provider maximizes the likelihood of the technical center being able to achieve its objectives.

The steps are similar to those in Figure 5.5, except that new risk and opportunities introduced by a new candidate provider are taken into account and the iterative process is not exercised.

REFERENCES

Harper, Sallyanne, et al. 2007. "NASA: Balancing a Multisector Workforce to Achieve a Healthy Organization." A report by a panel of the National Academy of Public Administration (February). http://www.napawash.org/wp-content/uploads/2012/07/00-NASA-Report-2-20-07.pdf

Holzer, T. H. July 2006. "Uniting Three Families of Risk Management—Complexity of Implementation x 3," *INCOSE International Symposium* 16 (1): 324–336. Also available from National Geospatial-Intelligence Agency.

National Aeronautics and Space Administration (NASA). 2016c. "The James Webb Space Telescope Team." http://www.nasa.gov/mission_pages/webb/team/index .html

Special Considerations for EROM Practice and Analysis at Commercial TRIO Enterprises

6.1 OVERVIEW

The bulk of the discussions so far have focused on TRIO enterprises whose primary objectives concern the development and implementation of risky technologies aimed at scientific advancement for the benefit of the public. These enterprises tend to be government or nonprofit organizations. However, as discussed several times in earlier chapters, many of these government and nonprofit enterprises rely heavily on commercial partners, who often play the role of a prime contractor. Others take the role of subcontractors under the direction of a prime contractor, or under contract directly to the government or a nonprofit sponsoring organization. Thus, it is obviously in the interest of both the noncommercial and commercial enterprises to form EROM alliances and foster consistencies of approach that work for both.

The top objective of TRIO enterprises that operate for profit is ultimately to provide monetary gain for their companies and their share-holders. Like the objectives of a public enterprise, the financial objectives of a commercial TRIO enterprise involve short-term, mid-term, and long-term goals. The shorter-term financial objectives satisfy the more immediate needs of the shareholders, whereas the longer-term ones help ensure the via-bility of the company. Unlike noncommercial enterprises, however, the implementation of technical research, integration, and operations for com-mercial enterprises serves as means objectives rather than as a fundamental objective. The fundamental objective is financial gain.

Thus, a distinguishing feature of commercial TRIO enterprises, com-pared to noncommercial ones, is that their performance is evaluated in terms of quantitative measures such as dollars, rather than qualitative measures such as understanding the universe in which we live. At the same time, how-ever, the risks and opportunities that affect the likelihood of future success for commercial TRIO enterprises tend to be qualitative, similar to those that affect noncommercial TRIO enterprises. For example, risk issues such as recurrent management problems are fundamentally qualitative in nature (i.e., management performance may be rated on a qualitative scale such as excellent, good, fair, or poor), but their ultimate effect on a company's financial state is quantitatively measurable. This implies that the qualitative methods described in earlier chapters for analyzing risks and opportunities carry over to the commercial sector, but they have to be integrated with quantitative models for assessing the present and potential future states of the financial objectives of the organization.

This quantitative-qualitative duality is illustrated in Figure 6.1. The figure shows how the qualitative processes developed earlier, as exemplified by the templates in Chapter 4, act synergistically with the quantitative modeling needed for financial evaluation. For example:

- The treatment of risk and opportunity scenarios in the financial model is informed by the risk and opportunity scenarios developed in the templates.
- The key variables in the financial model are informed by the leading indicators and risk/opportunity drivers identified in the templates.
- The functional relationships between financial outcomes and key variables in the financial model are informed by the watch and response trigger values developed in the templates.
- The aggregation of financial factors in the financial model to evaluate cumulative monetary gain or loss is informed by the risk and opportunity aggregation rationale developed in the templates.

The feedback loop works in the other direction as well:

- Predicted values of financial gain or loss obtained from the results of the financial modeling can be used as leading indicators in the qualitative analysis.
- Modeling assumptions used in the financial quantitative analysis can help define the assumptions needing to be watched or controlled through internal controls.

Because of the fact that there may be large epistemic uncertainties (stemming mainly from incomplete knowledge) in the inputs to the quantitative models and in the models themselves, the quantitative assessment is often performed using different sets of assumptions. In many assessments, three different calculations referred to as (1) optimistic, (2) most likely, and (3) pessimistic are performed, as shown in Figure 6.1. In other assessments, referred

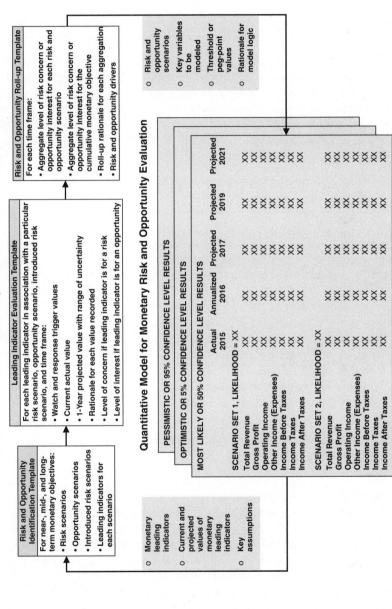

FIGURE 6.1 Integration of qualitative and quantitative modeling to evaluate the likelihood of success of a commercial TRIO enterprise

to generally as Monte Carlo assessments, thousands of mechanized calculations are performed to explore the effects of different parameter choices and/or modeling choices over their ranges of uncertainty on the financial model results. Monte Carlo assessment results are often presented in terms of mean values and values at different confidence levels (e.g., 5%, 50%, and 95%).

The following subsections discuss the nature of the risks, opportunities, and leading indicators that attend commercial TRIO enterprises and the ways in which the EROM templates described earlier can be applied along with quantitative modeling to evaluate the cumulative financial risks and opportunities, identify the risk and opportunity drivers, and deduce strategies for risk mitigation, opportunity action, and internal control.

6.2   RISK AND OPPORTUNITY SCENARIOS AND LEADING INDICATORS

6.2.1   Risk and Opportunity Taxonomies

The risks and opportunities that commercial TRIO enterprises face are as numerous and as diverse as those faced by noncommercial TRIO enterprises, if not more so. To illustrate, Figures 6.2 and 6.3, respectively, depict example taxonomies of enterprise risks and opportunities that might apply to a representative large commercial TRIO enterprise that serves as a prime contractor on large projects for commercial and noncommercial customers. Note that the diversity of second-level subcategories in Figures 6.2 and 6.3 is comparable to that in Figure 3-7.

The specific categories contained within the taxonomies would generally be different for different kinds of companies.

6.2.2   Risk and Opportunity Branching Events and Scenario Event Diagrams

In addition to the many categories of risk and opportunity they encounter, commercial TRIO enterprises often have to make rapid tactical management decisions on risks and opportunities to keep pace with changing conditions in the marketplace. For example, pricing decisions may have to be made quickly if a key competitor suddenly lowers their prices. The decision options appear as a branching event in the risk scenario. If management decides to lower its prices to compete with its competitor, its financial risk will be different from what it would be if it decides not to. In the near term there may be an increased risk of reduced profits, but in the longer term the overall financial risk may be lower.

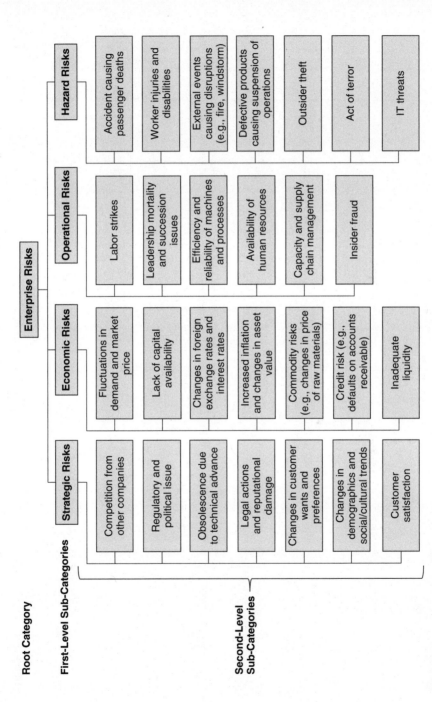

FIGURE 6.2 Example enterprise risk taxonomy for a commercial TRIO enterprise

Root Category

First-Level Sub-Categories

Second-Level Sub-Categories

Enterprise Risks

Strategic Risks

Competition from other companies

Regulatory and political issue

Obsolescence due to technical advance

Legal actions and reputational damage

Changes in customer wants and preferences

Changes in demographics and social/cultural trends

Customer satisfaction

Economic Risks

Fluctuations in demand and market price

Lack of capital availability

Changes in foreign exchange rates and interest rates

Increased inflation and changes in asset value

Commodity risks (e.g., changes in price of raw materials)

Credit risk (e.g., defaults on accounts receivable)

Inadequate liquidity

Operational Risks

Labor strikes

Leadership mortality and succession issues

Efficiency and reliability of machines and processes

Availability of human resources

Capacity and supply chain management

Insider fraud

Hazard Risks

Accident causing passenger deaths

Worker injuries and disabilities

External events causing disruptions (e.g., fire, windstorm)

Defective products causing suspension of operations

Outsider theft

Act of terror

IT threats

211

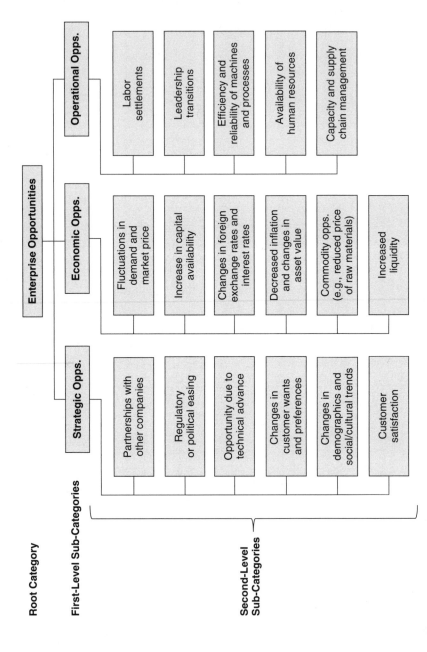

FIGURE 6.3 Example opportunity taxonomy for a commercial TRIO enterprise

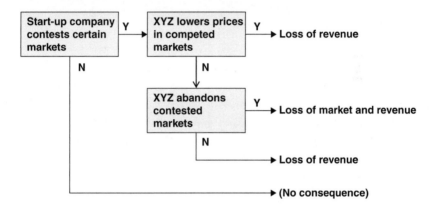

| **Competition from Other Companies** |

- **Risk:** [*Condition*] XYZ manufactures many products for the aerospace and defense industries. [*Departure*] A competitor might start a new manufacturing company, intending to take considerable market share from some of the key areas now served by XYZ. To compete, XYZ would have to either lower its prices in those markets or abandon them altogether. [*Consequence*] Either choice could result in significant loss of near-term and mid-term revenue.

  o **Leading Indicators:** Customer satisfaction in each market (1-5); management attention to cost saving in each market (1-5); adequacy of market analysis of competition (1-5); historical success of low-cost start-ups; diversity of customers served by XYZ

FIGURE 6.4 Example risk scenario statement and scenario event diagram for a risk in the taxonomic category "Competition from other companies"

Thus, for commercial TRIO enterprises, it is often advisable to generalize the risk and opportunity scenario statements discussed in Section 3.4.2 to include risk and opportunity scenario event diagrams. A simplified example of a scenario statement augmented by a scenario event diagram is shown in Figure 6.4. In this example, a prime contractor (named Company XYZ) that manufactures products and develops systems for the aerospace and defense industries identifies, as a risk, that a competitor might start a new manufacturing company, intending to take market share from some of the key areas now served by XYZ. To compete, XYZ determines that it would have to either lower its prices in those markets or abandon the markets altogether. Either choice could result in significant loss of revenue in the near- and mid-terms (e.g., one to three years). The scenario event diagram depicts these choices and identifies the financial consequences.

Similarly, Figure 6.5 depicts a risk scenario statement and accompanying scenario event diagram that pertains to the prime contractor for the next

Customer Satisfaction

- **Risk:** [*Condition*] The cryocooler subsystem development for the Next Generation Space Telescope project has experienced several missed milestones and overall management problems. The customer has expressed dissatisfaction. The best choice would be for Dr. XX to be transferred from being PM for Project AA to being PM for the space telescope project because of his experience and management strengths. [*Departure*] If Dr. XX is transferred out of Project AA, the customer for Project AA will be unhappy and may cancel the project. [*Consequence*] This would result in an immediate loss of revenue and would jeopardize future contracts with the customer, resulting in a loss of longer-term revenue and customer diversification.

  o **Leading Indicators:** Customer feedback (1-5); remaining schedule reserve for development of the cryocooler subsystem; difficulty of cryocooler issues yet to be resolved (1-5); flexibility of the Project AA customer with regard to a PM change (1-5); significance of potential future projects with each customer (1-5).

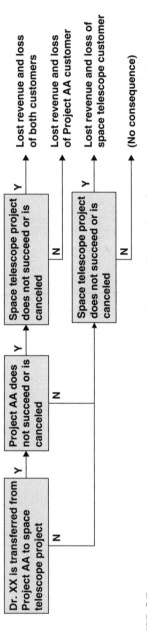

FIGURE 6.5 Example risk scenario statement and scenario event diagram for a risk in the taxonomic category "Customer satisfaction"

generation space telescope. This example, as it was developed in Chapter 4 from the point of view of the integrating government agency, identified schedule risks in the cryocooler subsystem development task that were exacerbated by management issues. From the viewpoint of the prime contractor, the most attractive solution is to move the project manager of another project (Project AA) to head the cryocooler development task in the space telescope project. But while reducing the risk of further missed milestones in the space telescope project, the proposed solution increases the risk of delays and added costs for Project AA. The possible consequences of making such a move involve lost revenue in the near term and lost customers in the long term. The latter leads to monetary loss in the long term. These choices and consequences are depicted in the scenario event diagram.

Other risks and opportunities that might be of concern to Company XYZ and the accompanying scenario event diagrams are illustrated in Figures 6.6 through 6.11.

6.2.3 Risk and Opportunity Templates

The evaluation of risks and opportunities at the pathway level, the scenario level, and the financial objective level can be qualitatively addressed by utilizing templates similar to those developed in Chapters 4 and 5. For purposes of these templates, each path that leads to a consequence is treated as though it were an individual scenario. Tables 6.1 and 6.2 illustrate, in abbreviated form, what the risk and opportunity identification and evaluation templates and the risk and opportunity roll-up templates of Chapter 4 might look like for the XYZ Company. As shown, the results start with a qualitative assessment of the degree of concern or interest associated with each leading indicator (Table 6.1), continue with the degree of concern or interest associated with each pathway through each scenario event diagram (Table 6.2 middle column), and end with the overall cumulative degree of concern or interest pertaining to the company's ability to meet its financial objectives rolled up over all pathways and scenarios (Table 6.2 right-hand-side).

When the objective being evaluated is monetary, each pathway in a scenario event diagram can also be evaluated quantitatively. The results of the quantitative analysis include an assessment of the likelihood of each pathway, often using event tree/fault tree techniques, and an assessment of the financial consequence of each pathway using financial models. As mentioned in Section 6.1, the qualitative results should be consistent with the quantitative results because the rationale used to obtain the former is carried over into the rationale used to obtain the latter (and vice versa).

Table 6.3 introduces a template designed to verify consistency between the qualitative and quantitative assessments. Referred to as the Risk and

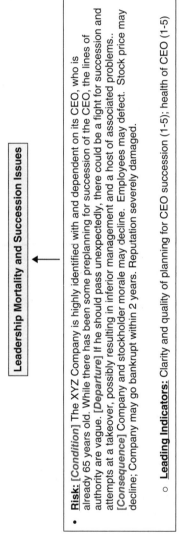

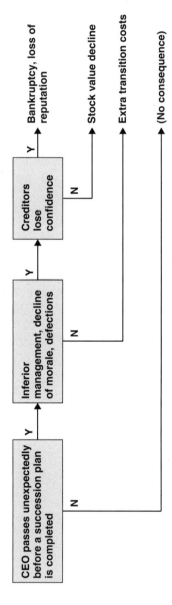

FIGURE 6.6 Example risk scenario statement and scenario event diagram for a risk in the taxonomic category "Leadership mortality and succession issues"

Accident Causing Human Deaths

- **Risk: [*Condition*]** Fatal accidents are always a possibility during aerospace and defense operations. XYZ's products have resulted in minimal fatalities so far. Stringent safety training programs are in place. XYZ has a large amount of liability insurance, a highly competent public relations department, and a high-quality manufacturing program. [*Departure*] A large, fatal accident due to a product defect may occur leading to high-stakes litigation by the victims' families and a reduction in orders for a period of time. XYZ may either attempt to contest the litigation in court or not contest it and seek out-of-court settlement. [*Consequence*] Large impact on revenue, mostly in the first year, and lasting damage to the company's reputation could result.

  o **Leading Indicators:** Historical probability of fatal accidents from similar products; frequency and potential severity of precursors for similar products; quality of XYZ's manufacturing processes (1-5); effectiveness of XYZ's public relations program (1-5); amount of XYZ's liability insurance.

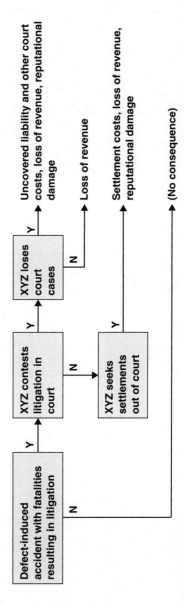

FIGURE 6.7 Example risk scenario statement and scenario event diagram for a risk in the taxonomic category "Accident causing human deaths"

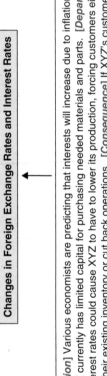

Changes in Foreign Exchange Rates and Interest Rates

- **Risk:** [*Condition*] Various economists are predicting that interests will increase due to inflation in the general economy. XYZ currently has limited capital for purchasing needed materials and parts. [*Departure*] A dramatic increase in interest rates could cause XYZ to have to lower its production, forcing customers either to extend the service life of their existing inventory or cut back operations. [*Consequence*] If XYZ's customers extend the service life of their existing inventory, there will be increased maintenance costs as well as a safety risk because of the aging of the components and materials.

  o **Leading Indicators:** Economists' predictions of the amount of interest rate inflation to occur over the next 5 years; amount of capital funds available for purchases of material and parts; liquidity of available funds

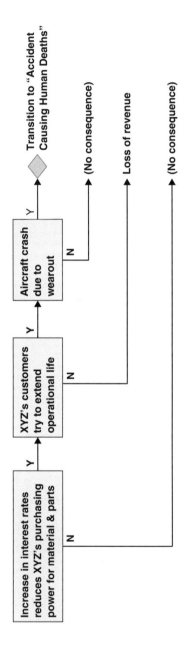

FIGURE 6.8 Example risk scenario statement and scenario event diagram for a risk in the taxonomic category "Changes in foreign exchange rates and interest rates"

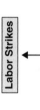

Labor Strikes

- **Risk: [*Condition*]** Raises for design and assembly personnel at XYZ for next year are projected to be lower than in previous years. Present wages and benefits are among the top 10% in the country [*Departure*] Union grievances could lead to an unanticipated strike and walkout of personnel. This could spark a sympathy walkout by supervising personnel, making it necessary to reduce production sharply and renegotiate labor contracts. Management may make tactical decision to use remaining supervisory staff to manufacture and assemble the products. This may stoke more resistance from labor union. It may also produce higher stress levels due to increased workload for supervisors. [*Consequence*] A walkout could result in a significant loss of revenue spread over 5 years, half of it in the first year. If XYZ requires supervisors to fill in for manufacturing and assembly personnel, there may be increased safety risks if the supervisors lack recent operational experience and if the stresses from the increased workload on them become excessive.

  - **Leading Indicators:** Employee concerns about salary expressed in employee job satisfaction questionaries (1-5); frequency of discussions between management and employees about job issues; attendance at such discussions; amount of insurance coverage for loss of business revenue due to a walkout; level of recent manufacturing and assembly experience among the supervisory staff.

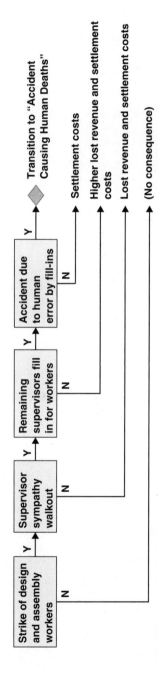

FIGURE 6.9 Example risk scenario statement and scenario event diagram for a risk in the taxonomic category "Labor strikes"

Exploitation of New Technology

- **Opportunity:** [*Condition*] A supplier has approached XYZ with an idea for developing a new technology that provides promise for better performance than current technology at lower operating cost. The supplier has proposed to share development costs and ownership of the new technology with XYZ. [*Departure*] XYZ may opt to support the new technology development with the intent of using it when it becomes available. [*Benefit*] Although the initial expenditure will result in a monetary loss at first, the increased performance at lower operating cost will ultimately result in a significant monetary gain.

  o **Leading Indicators:** Performance capability of new technology; Cost of developing the new technology. Cost of operating the new technology. Degree of trust between XYZ and the supplier.

- **Introduced Risk:** [*Condition*] Unanticipated technical problems, underappreciated costs, and undetected safety hazards have occurred in connection with similar new technologies. The supplier overall has a long history of successes. [*Departure*] It is possible that the new technology will not succeed, that it will cost much more than anticipated, or that it will produce a safety hazard that may not be detected until an accident occurs after deployment of the product. [*Consequence*]These departures could cause significant additional expenses and/or loss of revenue.

  o **Leading Indicators:** Amount of new technology incorporated into the new aircraft; quality of manufacturer's and supplier's verification and validation (1-5); amount of insurance coverage for liability and/or lost business; historical frequency of severe accidents and accident precursors for newly operationalized technology; historical rate of reliability growth with time in service

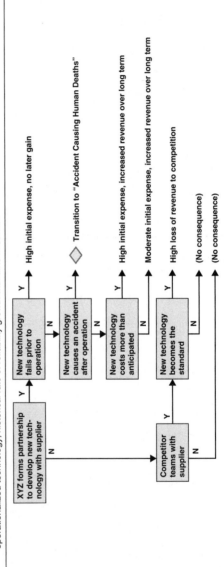

FIGURE 6.10 Example risk scenario statement and scenario event diagram for a risk in the taxonomic category "Exploitation of new technology"

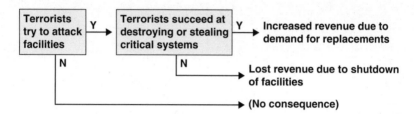

FIGURE 6.11   Example risk scenario statement and scenario event diagram for a risk in the taxonomic category "Act of terror"

Opportunity Roll-Up Comparison Template, it displays the results obtained from the qualitative and quantitative approaches at each stage of the roll-up. The qualitative results are depicted as "levels of concern" for risk scenarios and "levels of interest" for opportunity scenarios, and utilize the same color coding that was introduced in Chapter 4. Three sets of quantitative results are listed in this template and are labeled "optimistic," "most likely," and "pessimistic." If a Monte Carlo approach were to be used wherein the calculations would be performed in combination with a rigorous sampling process, the different sets of results obtained could then be associated with confidence levels (e.g., 5%, 50%, and 95%) rather than qualitative indicators such as "optimistic," "most likely," and "pessimistic."

6.2.4   Risk and Opportunity Matrices

Traditionally, rankings of individual risk scenarios have been an important part of risk management at the program/project level. The most commonly used display format for these rankings has been a 5 × 5 matrix, in which likelihood or probability, ranked on a scale of 1 to 5, comprises the rows in the matrix, and impact or consequence, similarly ranked on a scale of 1 to 5, comprises the columns. This type of display works well for enterprise risks and opportunities where the top-level objectives are monetary, since the

TABLE 6.1   Form of the Risk and Opportunity Identification and Evaluation Templates (Combined) for the Commercial TRIO Enterprise Example

Long-Term Monetary Risk and Opportunity

Mid-Term Monetary Risk and Opportunity

Short-Term Monetary Risk and Opportunity

Scenario Departure Event Description	Scenario Type	Scenario Path Description	Leading Indicator No. and Description	Lead. Ind. Watch Value	Watch Value Rationale	Lead. Ind. Response Value
Competitor start-up in XYZ's markets	Risk	XYZ lowers prices				
		XYZ abandons markets				
		XYZ takes no action				
Best project manager is moved from Project AA to space telescope project	Risk	Project AA fails or is canceled				
		Both projects fail or are canceled				
XYZ pursues new technology	Opportunity	Technology succeeds				
	Introduced Risk	Technology costs more than planned				
		Technology fails, leading to accident				
Etc.						

Palette for TBD (+/-) Shaded Cells:

−1 Green Risk: Tolerable   −2 Yellow Risk: Marginal   −3 Red Risk: Intolerable

Response Value Rationale	Lead. Ind. Current Value	Current Value Rationale	Lead. Ind. 1-Yr. Projected Value	Projected Value Rationale	Lead. Ind. Level of Concern or Interest
					(−)
					(−)
					(−)
					(−)
					(−)
					(−)
					(−)
					(−)
					(−)
					(−)
					(−)
					(−)
					(−)
					(−)
					(+)
					(+)
					(+)
					(−)
					(−)
					(−)
					(−)
					(−)
					(−)

+1	Beige Oppor.: Insignificant	+2	Violet Oppor.: Marginal	+3	Blue Oppor.: Significant

TABLE 6.2 Form of the Risk and Opportunity Roll-Up Templates (Combined) for the Commercial TRIO Enterprise Example

Long-Term Monetary Risk and Opportunity

Mid-Term Monetary Risk and Opportunity

Short-Term Monetary Risk and Opportunity

Scenario Departure Event Description	Scenario Type	Scenario Path Description	Leading Indicator No. and Description	Lead. Ind. Level of Concern or Interest	Lead. Ind. Level Rationale	Scen. Path Level of Concern or Interest
Competitor start-up in XYZ's markets	Risk	XYZ lowers prices		(−) (−) (−)		Cum. Risk Rating
		XYZ abandons markets		(−) (−) (−)		Cum. Risk Rating
		XYZ takes no action		(−) (−) (−)		Cum. Risk Rating
Best project manager is moved from Project AA to space telescope project	Risk	Project AA fails or is canceled		(−) (−) (−)		Cum. Risk Rating
		Both projects fail or are canceled		(−) (−) (−)		Cum. Risk Rating
XYZ pursues new technology	Opportunity	Technology succeeds		(+) (+) (+)		Cum. Opp. Rating
	Introduced Risk	Technology costs more than planned		(−) (−) (−)		Cum. Risk Rating
		Technology fails, leading to accident		(−) (−) (−)		Cum. Risk Rating
Etc.						

Palette for TBD (+/−) Shaded Cells:

−1 Green Risk: Tolerable   −2 Yellow Risk: Marginal   −3 Red Risk: Intolerable

Scen. Path Level Rationale	Scen. Dep. Event Level of Concern or Interest	Scen. Dep. Event Level Rationale	Cumulative Monetary Risk Level of Concern	Cumulative Monetary Opp. Level of Interest	Cumulative Monetary. Level Rationale
	Cum. Risk Rating				
	Cum. Risk Rating	Cum. Risk Rating	Cum. Opp. Rating		
	Cum. Opp. Rating				

+1 Beige Oppor.: Insignificant   **+2** Violet Oppor.: Marginal   **+3** Blue Oppor.: Significant

TABLE 6.3 Qualitative/Quantitative Risk and Opportunity Roll-Up Comparison Template for the Commercial TRIO Enterprise Example (Excerpt)

> **Long-Term Monetary Risk and Opportunity**
>
> **Mid-Term Monetary Risk and Opportunity**
>
> **Short-Term Monetary Risk and Opportunity**

Scenario Departure Event Description	Scenario Type	Scenario Path Description	Scen. Path Qual./Quant. Comparison			Qual. Level of Concern or Interest
			Qual. Level of Concern or Interest	Likelihood Prediction from Model	Gain or Loss Prediction from Model	
Competitor start-up in XYZ's markets	Risk	XYZ lowers prices	(–)	Optimistic: Most Likely: Pessimistic:	Optimistic: Most Likely: Pessimistic:	Cum. Risk Rating
		XYZ abandons markets	(–)	Optimistic: Most Likely: Pessimistic:	Optimistic: Most Likely: Pessimistic:	
		XYZ takes no action	(–)	Optimistic: Most Likely: Pessimistic:	Optimistic: Most Likely: Pessimistic:	
Best project manager is moved from Project AA to space telescope project	Risk	Project AA fails or is canceled	(–)	Optimistic: Most Likely: Pessimistic:	Optimistic: Most Likely: Pessimistic:	Cum. Risk Rating
		Both projects fail or are canceled	(–)	Optimistic: Most Likely: Pessimistic:	Optimistic: Most Likely: Pessimistic:	
XYZ pursues new technology	Opportunity	Technology succeeds	(+)	Optimistic: Most Likely: Pessimistic:	Optimistic: Most Likely: Pessimistic:	Cum. Opp. Rating
	Introduced Risk	Technology costs more than planned	(–)	Optimistic: Most Likely: Pessimistic:	Optimistic: Most Likely: Pessimistic:	
		Technology fails, leading to accident	(–)	Optimistic: Most Likely: Pessimistic:	Optimistic: Most Likely: Pessimistic:	
Etc.						

Palette for TBD (+/–) Shaded Cells:

| –1 | Green Risk: Tolerable | –2 | Yellow Risk: Marginal | –3 | Red Risk: Intolerable |

Scen. Dep. Event Qual./Quant. Comp.		Cumulative Qual./Quant. Comparison			
Likelihood Prediction from Model	Gain or Loss Prediction from Model	Cumulative Risk Qual. Level of Concern	Cumulative Opp. Qual. Level of Interest	Likelihood Prediction from Model	Gain or Loss Prediction from Model
Optimistic: Most Likely: Pessimistic:	Optimistic: Most Likely: Pessimistic:			Optimistic: Most Likely: Pessimistic:	Optimistic: Most Likely: Pessimistic:
Optimistic: Most Likely: Pessimistic:	Optimistic: Most Likely: Pessimistic:				
Optimistic: Most Likely: Pessimistic:	Optimistic: Most Likely: Pessimistic:	Cum. Risk Rating	Cum. Opp. Rating		

+1	Beige Oppor.: Insignificant	+2	Violet Oppor.: Marginal	+3	Blue Oppor.: Significant

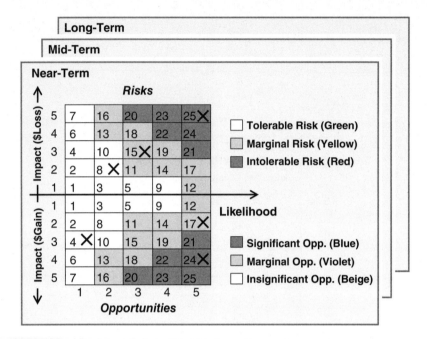

FIGURE 6.12 Example risk and opportunity matrix for quantitative financial objectives

measure of each objective is quantitative and interpreted consistently across objectives. It works less well when the top-level objectives are qualitative.

For enterprise risk and opportunity management, where risk and opportunity share complementary status, it is useful to include both risk and opportunity on separate mirror matrices, as shown conceptually in Figure 6.12. In that figure, each X represents a risk or opportunity scenario. The numbering of the cells from 1 to 25 provides the basis for rank-ordering the importance of each scenario. For example, the X in cell number 25 on the risk matrix is judged to be more important than any of the other risk or opportunity scenarios denoted by X's in the figure.

When the top objectives are monetary, as for a commercial TRIO enterprise, the meanings of the 1-to-5 rankings in Figure 6.12 are easy to interpret both qualitatively and quantitatively. Qualitatively, a ranking of 1, 2, 3, 4, or 5 translates to an assessment of "very low," "low," "moderate," high," or "very high," respectively. Quantitatively, the measures of 1-to-5 for likelihood and 1-to-5 for impact basically reflect the judgment of the decision maker(s) as to what constitutes "very low," "low," "moderate," "high," and "very high" for the objective being considered. They may therefore vary from objective to objective. For example, the decision maker's judgment about what constitutes "very high" monetary gain in the near-term may be very different than for long-term monetary gain.

A risk and opportunity matrix can be used as a mapping device for the likelihood and impact of each risk and opportunity scenario pathway developed in a scenario event diagram. The quantitative results recorded in the Risk and Opportunity Roll-Up Comparison Template (Table 6.3) can be used for this purpose. Illustrations of such mappings are provided in Figure 6.13 for a risk scenario and in Figure 6.14 for an opportunity scenario.

6.3   CONTROLLABLE DRIVERS, MITIGATIONS, ACTIONS, AND INTERNAL CONTROLS

Many of the risk and opportunity drivers for a commercial TRIO enterprise are shared with those for its noncommercial sponsors, and so it should not be surprising if the list of drivers, risk mitigations, opportunity actions, and internal controls for the former are the same as those of the latter. For example, the prime contractor for the next-generation space telescope will be just as concerned about depletions in schedule and cost reserve as the funding government agency.

In addition, however, a commercial TRIO enterprise will have many more risk and opportunity drivers that pertain to their financial well-being. Table 6.4 provides a representative list of such drivers for the XYZ Company. The term "controllable risk drivers" in the table refers to the fact that these drivers are amenable to responses such as risk mitigations, opportunity actions, and internal controls. Accordingly, an example or two of these potential responses are included in the table for each controllable driver.

Table 6.5 shows an excerpt from a Risk Mitigation, Opportunity Action, and Internal Control Identification Template that pertains to the XYZ example. The example entries that are included in this figure pertain to the risk and opportunity scenarios that were previously presented in Figures 6.4, 6.5, and 6.10. In Table 6.5, each listed driver constitutes a collection of driver constituents. None of the constituents in themselves constitutes a driver because no single constituent results in the cumulative risk or opportunity changing from one color to another. (See Section 3.6.1 for a discussion of why this criterion is one of the conditions defining the term *driver*.) As illustrated in the figure, it is the combination of constituents that causes the changing of the status of the cumulative risk or opportunity, as evidenced by its change of color.

Competition from Other Companies

- **Risk:** [*Condition*] XYZ manufactures many products for the aerospace and defense industries. [*Departure*] A competitor might start a new manufacturing company, intending to take considerable market share from some of the key areas now served by XYZ. To compete, XYZ would have to either lower its prices in those markets or abandon them altogether. [*Consequence*] Either choice could result in significant loss of near-term and mid-term revenue.

  - **Leading Indicators:** Customer satisfaction in each market (1-5); management attention to cost saving in each market (1-5); adequacy of market analysis of competition (1-5); historical success of low-cost start-ups; diversity of customers served by XYZ

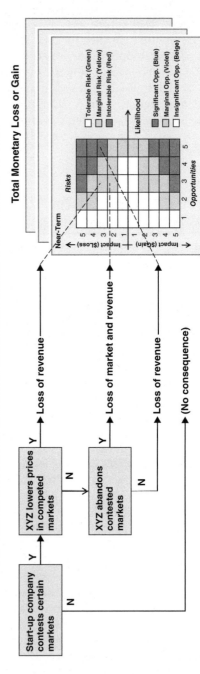

FIGURE 6.13 Example risk scenario statement, scenario event diagram, and scenario matrix for a risk in the taxonomic category "Competition from other companies"

Exploitation of New Technology

- **Opportunity:** *[Condition]* A supplier has approached XYZ with an idea for developing a new technology that provides promise for better performance than current technology at lower operating cost. The supplier has proposed to share development costs and ownership of the new technology with XYZ. *[Departure]* XYZ may opt to support the new technology development with the intent of using it when it becomes available. *[Benefit]* Although the initial expenditure will result in a monetary loss at first, the increased performance at lower operating cost will ultimately result in a significant monetary gain.

  o **Leading Indicators:** Performance capability of new technology; cost of developing the new technology; cost of operating the new technology. Degree of trust between XYZ and the supplier.

- **Introduced Risk:** *[Condition]* Unanticipated technical problems, underappreciated costs, and undetected safety hazards have occurred in connection with similar new technologies. The supplier overall has a long history of successes. *[Departure]* It is possible that the new technology will not succeed, that it will cost much more than anticipated, or that it will produce a safety hazard that may not be detected until an accident occurs after deployment of the product. *[Consequence]* These departures could cause significant additional expenses and/or loss of revenue.

  o **Leading Indicators:** Amount of new technology incorporated into the new aircraft; quality of manufacturer's and supplier's verification and validation (1-5); amount of insurance coverage for liability and/or lost business; historical frequency of severe accidents and accident precursors for newly operationalized technology; historical rate of reliability growth with time in service

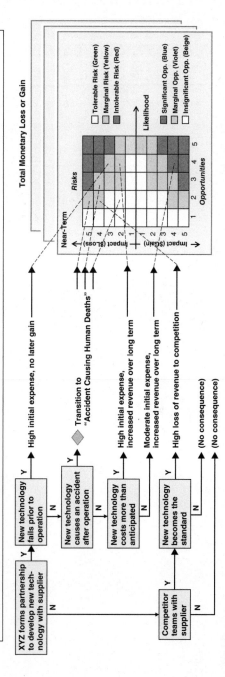

FIGURE 6.14 Example risk scenario statement, scenario event diagram, and scenario matrix for a risk in the taxonomic category "Exploitation of new technology"

TABLE 6.4 Example Controllable Drivers and Corresponding Existing Safeguards, Risk Mitigations, Opportunity Actions, and Internal Controls for XYZ Company

	Example Controllable Drivers		Example Existing Safeguard(s)		Example Mitigation/Action		Example Internal Control
CD1	Insufficient diversification of customers	ES1	Over 500 customers served	MA1	Close out nonprofitable contracts and market new customers	IC1	Monitor and report on revenue status/projections for each customer and potential customer
CD2	Insufficient capital funds and/or liquidity to purchase new materials and parts in an inflationary market	ES2	Available capital funds and liquidity sufficient for current market with 10% margin	MA2	Convert certain long-term investments to short-term investments or cash	IC2	Develop a robust and peer reviewed investment plan and continually monitor it
				MA3	Merge with a competing company (increases capital funds and/or liquidity)	IC3	Assess and report on track record of potential companies for merging
CD3	Insufficient insurance to allay unusually high liability costs	ES3	Current liability insurance covers up to $200M per incident	MA4	Increase deductible in order to increase maximum coverage	IC4	Continually monitor sufficiency of coverage
CD4	Insufficient insurance to cover cost of loss of business	ES4	Current loss-of-business insurance covers up to 6 months loss-of-business	MA4	Increase deductible in order to increase maximum coverage	IC4	Continually monitor sufficiency of coverage
CD5	Inadequate market analysis of competition	ES5	Market analysis is part of business plan	MA5	Hire market analysts as consultants	IC5	Assess and report on credentials and track record of candidate analysts
CD6	Inadequate strategy for competing in low cost market	ES6	Cost accounting system	MA6	Prepare a cost-cutting plan for contingency implementation	IC6	Vet cost-cutting plan with affected entities

CD		ES		MA		IC	
CD7	Insufficient public relations focus to bolster reputation in event of a crisis	ES7 ES8 ES9	Crisis outreach and hotline Community involvement Publicized donations to charities	MA7	Improve responsiveness to customers in everyday communication	IC7	Monitor and report on customer satisfaction
CD8	Lack of early discussions with labor to avert walkouts	ES10	Current wages and benefits in top 10% of Industry	MA8	Organize/attend social events with labor leaders	IC8	Monitor and report on labor leader views and sentiments
CD9	Inadequate problem-solving approach with labor	ES11	Problem solving and communication training for labor relations staff	MA9	Problem solving and communication training for managers	IC9	Monitor and report on managers' participation in training
CD10	Organization too dependent on CEO	ES12	CEO succession plan in place	MA10	Shift responsibilities to lower levels	IC10	Develop processes for overseeing delegation of responsibilities and effectiveness of execution
CD11	Stress levels causing human error	ES13	Employee assistance program	MA11	Track stress levels through employee questionnaires and reduce workload when stress is too high	IC11	Report to upper management on stress levels and worker error incidents

TABLE 6.5 Excerpt of the Risk Mitigation and Internal Control Template and the Opportunity Action and Internal Control Template for the Commercial TRIO Enterprise

Long-Term Monetary Risk and Opportunity

Mid-Term Monetary Risk and Opportunity

Short-Term Monetary Risk and Opportunity

Cumulative Monetary Risk/Opp. Level of Concern/ Interest	Cumulative Monetary Risk or Opp. if Driver Removed	Driver No.	Driver Constituent Type	Driver Constituent Description	Existing Safeguards/ Actions	Mitigation/ Action No.
−2 Yellow Marginal	−1 Green Tolerable	1	Risk	Insufficient diversification of customers	Over 500 clients served	1
			Risk	Negative customer feedback	Customer survey	2
	−1 Green Tolerable	2	Risk	Etc.		
+3 Blue Significant	+1 Beige Insignificant	3	Opportunity	Likelihood of game-changing new technology	R&D program	3
			Introduced Risk	Infant mortality	Developmental and integrated testing	4
						5
	+2 Violet Marginal	4	Opportunity	Etc.		

Risk and Opportunity Important Parameters and Proposed Mitigations/Controls						
Proposed Mitigation/ Action	Mitiga- tion/ Action Rationale	Internal Control No.	Type of Control	Deficiency Needing Control or Assumption Needing Watch	Proposed Internal Control	Internal Control Rationale
Close out unprofitable contracts and market new clients	XX	1	Assump.	Market analysis is accurate	Vet market analysis	XX
		2	Deficiency	Insufficient follow-up of new possibilities	Record follow-ups	XX

Examples of the Use of EROM Results for Informing Risk Acceptance Decisions

7.1 OVERVIEW

The purpose of Chapter 7 is to demonstrate how EROM can help inform risk acceptance decisions at key decision points for programs and projects that serve multiple strategic objectives. Such objectives (and the associated performance requirements) may span multiple mission execution domains (e.g., safety, technical performance, cost, and schedule) as well as multiple government or other stakeholder priorities (e.g., tech transfer, equal opportunity, legal indemnity, and good public relations). Since the risks of not meeting the top-level program/project objectives may imply risks of not meeting the enterprise's strategic objectives, risk acceptance decisions at the program/project level have to include consideration of enterprise-wide risk and opportunity management.

Two demonstration examples are pursued for this topic. The first is based on the Department of Defense's Ground-Based Midcourse Defense (GMD) program as it existed in an earlier time frame (about 14 years ago). In the time that has passed since then, a significant body of information about the GMD program has become available to the public through published reviews performed by the Government Accountability Office (GAO) and the DoD Inspector General (IG). The second is based on NASA's efforts to develop a commercial crew transportation system (CCTS) capability intended to transport astronauts to and from the International Space Station (ISS) and other low-earth-orbit destinations.

All information used for these examples was obtained from unclassified and publicly available reports, including government reviews and media reporting. Because of sensitivities concerning proprietary information, both examples are pursued only to the point where information is available to the public.

The GMD and CCTS examples are interesting when considered together because they are cases where the objectives are analogous but the plan to achieve them is different. Apart from the obvious differences in the mission objectives (one being defense against missiles, the other being space exploration), they share the following competing goals:

1. Develop an operational capability quickly
2. Make the system safe and reliable
3. Keep costs within budget
4. Develop partnerships with commercial companies
5. Maintain public support

However, in one case (GMD), the plan for achievement of the top program objective emphasizes the first goal (rapid deployment), whereas in the other case (CCTS), the plan emphasizes the second goal (safety and reliability). Taken together, they represent an interesting study of the importance of EROM in helping the decision maker to reach a decision that reflects his or her preference for one goal without neglecting the other goals.

7.2 EXAMPLE 1: DOD GROUND-BASED MIDCOURSE MISSILE DEFENSE IN THE 2002 TIME FRAME

7.2.1 Background

The GMD program was initiated in the early 1980s by the Reagan administration under a different name, and is now managed by the Missile Defense Agency (MDA) under DoD. The GMD is a system-of-systems designed to intercept and destroy enemy ballistic missiles during ballistic flight in the exoatmosphere after powered ascent and prior to reentry. The individual systems within the system-of-systems include ground and sea-based radars, battle management command, control, and communication (BMC3) systems, ground-based interceptor (GBI) boost vehicles, and exoatmospheric kill vehicles (EKVs). The main providers of these systems are Raytheon, Northrop Grumman, and Orbital Sciences, and the prime contractor is Boeing Defense, Space & Security. The program is now projected to cost $40 billion by 2017 (Wikipedia 2016), a sharp escalation from its initial cost estimate of $16 billion to $19 billion (Mosher 2000).

In 2002, in an effort to achieve the rapid deployment goals of the George W. Bush administration, the secretary of defense exempted MDA from following the Pentagon's normal rules for acquiring a weapons system (Coyle 2014). The upshot, according to the DoD Office of the Inspector General (IG) (2014a), was that the EKV did not go through the milestone decision review process and product development phase. These activities are normally mandated "to carefully assess a program's readiness to proceed to the next acquisition phase and to make a sound investment decision committing the DoD's financial resources." For the product development phase, the program is assessed "to ensure that the product design is stable, manufacturing processes are controlled, and the product can perform in the intended operational environment." As a result of waiving these processes for the GMD system, according to the IG, "the EKV prototype was forced into operational capability" before it was ready. Furthermore, according to the IG, "a combination of cost constraints and failure-driven program restructures has kept the program in a state of change. Schedule and cost priorities drove a culture of 'use-as-is' leaving the EKV as a manufacturing challenge."

Complicating the decision to suspend standard review and verification practices, the program was already subject to a variety of quality management deficiencies. Before and after that decision was announced, concerns had been expressed by the Government Accountability Office (GAO) (2015) about quality management within a number of DoD programs, including the GMD program. These concerns included nonconformances, insufficient systems engineering discipline, insufficient oversight of the prime contractor activities, and relying on subtier suppliers to self-report without effective oversight. These deficiencies, among others cited by GAO, led to the installation of defective parts, ultimately resulting in substantial increases in both schedule and cost.

The decision to proceed to deployment with an unproven EKG was made because of the primacy of Objective 1 at the time the decision was made. The operating assumption was that the system could be deployed in a prototype form and later retrofitted as needed to achieve reliability goals.

7.2.2 Top-Level Objectives, Risk Tolerances, and Risk Parity

For this example, the principal objective of the program is to rapidly achieve a robust, reliable, and cost-effective operating GMD system. That top objective (denoted as Objective 1) may be subdivided into the following three contributing objectives:

- Objective 1.1: Rapidly deploy a robust operational GMD system. In this context, the term *robust* implies a system that is able to withstand any credible environment to which it may be exposed prior to launch, during launch, and during intercept.
- Objective 1.2: Rapidly achieve a reliable operating GMD system. The term *reliable* refers to the ability of the system to identify, intercept, and destroy its targets with a high probability of success.

- Objective 1.3: Achieve a cost-effective operating GMD system. The term *cost effective* refers to the ability to deploy and maintain a robust operational system and achieve consistently high reliability within the established funding limits for the program.

Restating one of the main themes of this book, the framework for EROM calls for factoring risk tolerance into the analysis processes that accompany the development of requirements. To avoid imbalance between the competing goals that will later be regretted, it is necessary for there to be a process for eliciting the decision maker's risk tolerances in an objective, rational manner, and incorporating these tolerances into the evaluation of the plan. As discussed in Sections 3.3.1, 3.3.2, and 3.5.1, risk tolerance may be accounted for through the development of the following EROM-generated items:

- Risk parity statements
- Risk watch and response boundaries
- Leading indicator watch and response triggers

Risk parity statements are elicited from the decision maker. Each risk parity statement reflects a common level of pain from the decision maker's perspective. Thus, each reflects the decision maker's view of an even trade-off between objectives.

The objectives for this example and a suggested format for a cumulative risk parity table are illustrated in Figure 7.1. The following statements of cumulative risk, taken from the table in Figure 7.1, are parity statements because each of them corresponds to the same level of discomfort (i.e., rank 2):

- Risk Parity Statement 1 (Discomfort Level 2): We are 50 percent confident that it will take no more than *X1 months* to complete initial deployment of the system.
- Risk Parity Statement 2 (Discomfort Level 2): We are 80 percent confident that it will take no more than *X2 months* to complete initial deployment of the system.
- Risk Parity Statement 3 (Discomfort Level 2): We are 50 percent confident that it will take no more than *X3 months* before the system is 80 percent reliable.
- Risk Parity Statement 4 (Discomfort Level 2): We are 80 percent confident that it will take no more than *X4 months* before the system is 80 percent reliable.

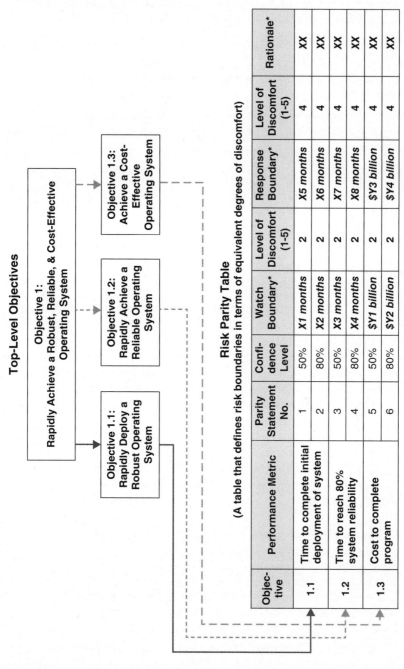

FIGURE 7.1 Objectives and hypothetical cumulative risk parity table for GMD example

- Risk Parity Statement 5 (Discomfort Level 2): We are 50 percent confident that the total cost to deploy the system and achieve 80 percent reliability will be no more than $Y1 *billion*.
- Risk Parity Statement 6 (Discomfort Level 2): We are 80 percent confident that the total cost to deploy the system and achieve 80 percent reliability will be no more than $Y2 *billion*.

Similarly, the following parity statements also evolve from the table in Figure 7.1 because of the fact that each statement results in a rank 4 level of discomfort:

- Risk Parity Statement 1 (Discomfort Level 4): We are 50 percent confident that it will take no more than $X5$ *months* to complete initial deployment of the system.
- Etc.

7.2.3   Risks and Leading Indicators

Based on the information provided in Section 7.2.1 for the GMD program, two risk scenarios suggest themselves. The first emanates from quality management control concerns in the 2002 time frame and affects all three objectives: rapid deployment, reliability attainment, and cost effectiveness. The second results from the suspension of standard controls, combined with the challenging nature of kinetic intercept at hypersonic speeds, and affects the latter two objectives.

Example risk scenario statements and corresponding example leading indicators are shown in Figure 7.2. The leading indicators for each risk are representative of the sources of concern cited by GAO and by the DoD IG, as summarized in Section 7.2.1. Those listed for the first risk scenario in Figure 7.2 are based on the following observation (IG 2014b):

"Quality management system deficiencies identified by GAO and DoD OIG reports include:

- Inconsistent process review at key decision points across programs,
- Quality metrics not consolidated in a manner that helps decision makers identify and evaluate systemic quality problems,
- Insufficient workforce knowledge,
- Inadequate resources to provide sufficient oversight, and
- Ineffective supplier oversight."

Those listed for the second risk scenario are based on technology readiness level (TRL) and experience from other programs and projects, which

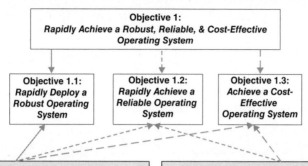

Objective 1:
Rapidly Achieve a Robust, Reliable, & Cost-Effective Operating System

Objective 1.1:
Rapidly Deploy a Robust Operating System

Objective 1.2:
Rapidly Achieve a Reliable Operating System

Objective 1.3:
Achieve a Cost-Effective Operating System

- **Risk 1:** Given that quality management control deficiencies have been a problem in the development of a number of predecessor systems, resulting in malfunctions of critical parts, deployment delays, and significant additional costs, and given that these deficiencies have not been adequately addressed according to independent review agencies, there is a possibility that quality control deficiencies will lead to reliability, schedule, and cost problems in the present program.

  Leading Indicators:

  1. Status of documentation and approval of quality management processes
  2. Thoroughness of quality process reviews at key decision points
  3. Clarity and quantifiability of quality metrics
  4. Sufficiency of workforce knowledge about quality requirements and processes
  5. Sufficiency of supplier oversight throughout the extended enterprise
  6. Adequacy of resources to provide continuing supplier oversight
  7. Frequency and severity of quality management problems experienced on predecessor programs
  8. Overall ranking of the organization's quality management by independent review agencies

- **Risk 2:** Given that high system reliability is very difficult to achieve because of the extremely challenging environments, and that standard procurement rules and testing standards are to be suspended for the sake of rapid deployment, it is possible that the achievement of an acceptable success reliability will require more integrated tests and design changes than expected and that substantial retrofits will be needed to achieve reliability after deployment, resulting in much more time and expense to achieve an acceptable level of reliability and the possibility that the program may be canceled by a future Administration as a result.

  Leading Indicators:

  9. Technology readiness level for the present program
  10. Complexity of technology development for the present program compared to other programs
  11. Number of design changes during development needed in other programs that depend on new technology to achieve an acceptable level of reliability
  12. Flight test successes versus failures for other programs requiring new technology development
  13. Number of UU flight test failures in other programs that depended on new technology
  14. History of costs and schedule slippages from retrofits in previous programs that depended on new technology

FIGURE 7.2　Risks and leading indicators for GMD example (2002 time frame)

can serve as an indicator of potential future problems for the present program. These indicators pertain to the principal factors that have tended to produce reliability, schedule, or cost impacts and UU risks for complex programs.

7.2.4   Leading Indicator Trigger Values

Parity between cumulative risks can be stated in terms of parity between leading indicators. As discussed in Section 3.5, trigger values for leading indicators of risk are developed by the EROM analysts and are used to signal when a risk is reaching a risk tolerance boundary that was established by a decision maker. When there are many leading indicators, as is typically the case, various combinations of the leading indicators are formulated to act as surrogates for the cumulative risks. These combinations were referred to as composite leading indicators in Section 4.6.4.

To simplify this example, we combine the leading indicators in Figure 7.2 into three composite indicators, as follows:

- Composite indicator A, termed "Quality Management Ranking": A composite of leading indicators 1 through 8 with a ranking scale of 1 to 5.
- Composite indicator B, termed "Technology Readiness Ranking": A composite of leading indicators 9 through 11 with a ranking scale of 1 to 5.
- Composite indicator C, termed "Previous Success Ranking": A composite of leading indicators 12 through 14 with a ranking scale of 1 to 5.

It is assumed that as a part of the EROM analysis, formulas have been derived for combining the 14 leading indicators in Figure 7.2 into these three composite indicators, but these formulas are left unstated for purposes of this example.

Figure 7.3 illustrates how parity statements for composite leading indicators may substitute for parity statements for cumulative risks. The lower table in the figure leads to the following leading indicator parity statements corresponding to watch triggers (level of discomfort rank 2):

- Leading Indicator Parity Statement 1 (Discomfort Level 2): The watch boundary for the time to complete initial deployment of the system is consistent with a value of 1.5 for the quality management composite indicator.

Risk Parity Table
(A table that defines risk boundaries in terms of equivalent degrees of discomfort)

Objective	Performance Metric	Risk Parity Statement No.	Confidence Level	Watch Boundary*	Level of Discomfort (1-5)	Response Boundary*	Level of Discomfort (1-5)	Rationale*
1.1	Time to complete initial deployment of system	1	50%	X1 months	2	X5 months	4	XX
		2	80%	X2 months	2	X6 months	4	XX
1.2	Time to reach 80% system reliability	3	50%	X3 months	2	X7 months	4	XX
		4	80%	X4 months	2	X8 months	4	XX
1.3	Cost to complete program	5	50%	$Y1 billion	2	$Y3 billion	4	XX
		6	80%	$Y2 billion	2	$Y4 billion	4	XX

Leading Indicator Parity Table
(A table that defines leading indicator trigger values in terms of equivalent degrees of discomfort)

Objective	Performance Metric	Lead. Ind. Parity Statement No.	Risk Parity Statement No.	Composite Leading Indicator	Comp. Lead. Ind. Description	Watch Trigger (1.0-.5.0)	Response Trigger (1.0-.5.0)	Rationale
1.1	Time to complete initial deployment of system	1	1, 2	A	Quality Mgmt.	1.5	1.0	XX
1.2	Time to reach 80% system reliability	2	3, 4	A	Quality Mgmt.	4.0	3.0	XX
		3	3, 4	B	Tech. Readiness	4.0	3.0	XX
		4	3, 4	C	Previous Success	4.0	3.0	XX
1.3	Cost to complete program	5	5, 6	A	Quality Mgmt.	3.5	2.5	XX
		6	5, 6	B	Tech. Readiness	3.5	2.5	XX
		7	5, 6	C	Previous Success	3.5	2.5	XX

* Entries elicited from stakeholders are highlighted in italics

FIGURE 7.3 Hypothetical composite leading indicator parity table for GMD example

- Leading Indicator Parity Statement 2 (Discomfort Level 2): The watch boundary for the time to reach 80 percent system reliability is consistent with a value of 4.0 for the quality management composite indicator.
- Leading Indicator Parity Statement 3 (Discomfort Level 2): The watch boundary for the time to reach 80 percent system reliability is consistent with a value of 4.0 for the technology readiness composite indicator.
- Leading Indicator Parity Statement 4 (Discomfort Level 2): The watch boundary for the time to reach 80 percent system reliability is consistent with a value of 4.0 for the previous success composite indicator.
- Leading Indicator Parity Statement 5 (Discomfort Level 2): The watch boundary for the cost to complete the program is consistent with a value of 3.5 for the quality management composite indicator.
- Leading Indicator Parity Statement 6 (Discomfort Level 2): The watch boundary for the cost to complete the program is consistent with a value of 3.5 for the technology readiness composite indicator.
- Leading Indicator Parity Statements 7 (Discomfort Level 2): The watch boundary for the cost to complete the program is consistent with a value of 3.5 for the previous success composite indicator.

Similar leading indicator parity statements evolve for level of discomfort rank 4:

- Leading Indicator Parity Statement 1 (Discomfort Level 4): The response boundary for the time to complete initial deployment of the system is consistent with a value of 1.0 for the quality management composite indicator.
- Etc.

The trigger values in the leading indicator parity table indicate that quality management is less of a concern for the objective of rapidly deploying a robust operating system than for the objectives of rapidly achieving a reliable operating system and of completing the project in a cost-effective manner. Thus, a quality management watch trigger value of 1.5 is posited to be adequate for achieving rapid deployment, whereas corresponding technology readiness and previous success watch trigger values of 4.0 are needed to rapidly achieve reliability goals. Furthermore, only slightly lower values are needed to keep operating costs down. These entries reflect the fact that the deployment plan calls for bypassing most obstacles that would normally impede early deployment (including quality management provisions such as milestone decision reviews), whereas quality management issues not addressed prior to deployment could create substantial risks after deployment. The above discussion, and any other pertinent observations, would normally be included as rationale in the last column of the table.

7.2.5   Example Template Entries and Results

Having developed risk scenario statements for each objective, the associated leading indicators, and the associated parity statements, it is now possible to develop templates similar to those in Sections 4.5 through 4.7 to complete the analysis. For example, Tables 7.1 and 7.2 show, respectively, how the Leading Indicator Evaluation Template and the High-Level Display Template might appear for the GMD example, based on the information provided in the preceding subsections. The results indicate that there was (in 2002) significant risk after deployment owing to the combination of quality management deficiencies, flight test failures for predecessor systems, the complexity of the EKV system, and the probable need for a substantial number of retrofits.

While hypothetical, the example results are consistent with the decision maker's belief that in addition to early deployment, long-term reliability and cost effectiveness are important objectives. To put it another way, the decision maker's parity statements are the main determinant of the outcome.

7.2.6   Implications for Risk Acceptance Decision Making

Results such as those in Table 7.2, based on the decision maker's risk tolerances, would seem to indicate that the aggregate risks for two of the three objectives are intolerable and that the program should probably not proceed as currently formulated. The results also indicate the principal sources (drivers) of the risks and the corrective actions (suggested responses) that would tend to make the intolerable risks more tolerable. The principal risk driver in the case of the GMD example would be the decision to exempt the managing organization from following certain standards and rules, including the verification and validation processes normally followed prior to deployment of a system. Inadequate qualification testing for the integrated system and lack of milestone reviews are two of the principal issues to be addressed by corrective action.

The next step would be to assess the aggregate risks for all three objectives assuming the corrective actions were implemented. If such evaluation indicated that none of the aggregate risks remained red (as, for example, in Table 7.3), a logical decision might be to request an iteration from the prime contractor and reschedule the key decision point to a later date.

To facilitate the identification of alternative decisions that might succeed better than the current one, the results in Table 7.2 include a list of risk drivers for each objective and a list of suggested responses to better control the drivers. The principal risk driver in this case would be the decision to exempt the managing organization from following certain standards and

TABLE 7.1 Leading Indicator Evaluation Template for GMD Example (2002 Time Frame)

Objective	Comp. Ind. No.	Comp. Ind. Descrip.	Risk, Opp., or Intr. Risk	Scen. No.	Comp. Ind. Watch Value	Rationale or Source	Comp. Ind. Resp. Value	Rationale or Source	Comp. Ind. Current Value	Rationale or Source	Comp. Ind. 1-Yr. Projected Value	Rationale or Source	Comp. Ind. Level of Concern
1.1 Rapidly deploy a robust oper. system	A	Quality	Risk	1	1.5	XX	1.0	XX	2.0	XX	2.0	XX	−1 Green Tolerable
1.2 Rapidly achieve a reliable operating system	A	Quality	Risk	1	4.0	XX	3.0	XX	2.0	XX	2.0	XX	−3 Red Intolerable
	B	Readiness	Risk	2	4.0	XX	3.0	XX	1.5	XX	2.0	XX	−3 Red Intolerable
	C	Prev. Succ.	Risk	2	4.0	XX	3.0	XX	2.0	XX	2.0 to 2.5	XX	−3 Red Intolerable
1.3 Achieve a cost-effective operating system	A	Quality	Risk	1	3.5	XX	2.5	XX	2.0	XX	2.0	XX	−3 Red Intolerable
	B	Readiness	Risk	2	3.5	XX	2.5	XX	1.5	XX	2.0	XX	−3 Red Intolerable
	C	Prev. Succ.	Risk	2	3.5	XX	2.5	XX	2.0	XX	2.0 to 2.5	XX	−3 Red Intolerable

TABLE 7.2 High-Level Display Template for GMD Example (2002 Time Frame)

Objective Index	Objective Description	Risk to Objective	Drivers	Suggested Responses
1.1	Rapidly Deploy a Robust Operating System	−1 Green Tolerable	None	None
1.2	Rapidly Achieve a Reliable Operating System	−3 Red Intolerable	XX	XX
1.3	Achieve a Cost-Effective Operating System	−3 Red Intolerable	XX	XX

TABLE 7.3 High-Level Display Template for GMD Example after Adopting Corrective Actions That Balance the Risks to the Top-Level Objectives

Objective Index	Objective Description	Risk to Objective	Drivers	Suggested Responses
1.1	Rapidly Deploy a Robust Operating System	−2 Yellow Marginal	XX	None
1.2	Rapidly Achieve a Reliable Operating System	−2 Yellow Marginal	XX	None
1.3	Achieve a Cost-Effective Operating System	−2 Yellow Marginal	XX	None

rules, including the verification and validation processes normally followed prior to deployment of a system. Inadequate qualification testing for the integrated system and lack of milestone reviews are two of the principal issues to be addressed by an alternative decision.

7.3 EXAMPLE 2: NASA COMMERCIAL CREW TRANSPORTATION SYSTEM AS OF 2015

7.3.1 Background

The objective of the second example is to develop the capability to use a commercially provided space system to transport crew to low-earth orbit, including to the ISS. This objective has faced several challenges over the past two or three years. As stated by the NASA Administrator (Bolden 2013), "Because the funding for the President's plan has been significantly reduced, we now won't be able to support American launches until 2017. Even this delayed availability will be in question if Congress does not fully support the President's fiscal year 2014 request for our Commercial Crew Program, forcing us once again to extend our contract with the Russians." Clearly, while safety and reliability has always been a priority at NASA, the Administrator was concerned about the problem of having to be dependent on the Russians for transport capability for longer than necessary, while facing budget cuts that could prolong the problem.

Conscious of these concerns, the NASA Commercial Crew Program (CCP) has devised an approach designed to ensure that safety and reliability receive high priority while the potential for schedule slippages and cost overruns are minimized. The approach in effect for this program is referred to as a "Risk-Based Assurance" process utilizing a "Shared Assurance" model (Canfield 2016, Kirkpatrick 2014).

Basically, the role of certifying that identified hazards are adequately controlled is shifted from NASA safety and mission assurance personnel to the cognizant commercial contractor(s). NASA personnel, however, audit and verify the results for hazards that are deemed to pose high or moderate risk. The criteria for ranking the risk each hazard poses are based on a set of criteria that includes design and process complexity, degree of maturation, past performance, and expert judgment.

Before a system can be developed and American launches can occur, it is necessary for there to be a stable set of certification requirements, including engineering standards, required tests, analyses, and protocols for verification and validation. The development and implementation of these requirements entails seven steps:

1. Consultation between NASA and the providers leads to a virtual handshake on the requirements to be implemented.
2. The set of requirements is reviewed by the NASA technical authorities and by independent review groups, such as the Aerospace Safety Advisory Panel (ASAP).
3. The NASA approval authority approves the set of requirements.
4. The providers implement the requirements.
5. The providers make the case that the requirements have been implemented correctly and successfully.
6. Technical authorities and independent review groups review the case.
7. NASA approval authority approves the implementation.

It is noteworthy that at its quarterly meeting with NASA on July 23, 2015, ASAP was highly supportive of the efforts of the Commercial Crew Program (CCP) in executing its responsibilities, while also being highly cognizant of the challenges. "This Program has all the challenges inherent in any space program; it is technically hard. In addition, it has the challenge of working under a new and untried business model—engaging with two commercial partners with widely varying corporate and development cultures, each bringing unique advantages and opportunities and each presenting differing aspects to be wrestled with. This challenge is compounded by budget and schedule pressures, appropriation uncertainties, the desire to remove crew transportation to the ISS from dependency on Russian transportation as soon as possible, and the fixed-price contract environment. Given all of these challenges, the Panel sees considerable risk ahead for the CCP. Fortunately, competent and clear-headed professionals (in whom the Panel has great confidence) are dealing with these risks. However, the risks will only increase over time and test the skills at all management levels" (ASAP 2015).

7.3.2 Top-Level Objectives, Risk Tolerances, and Risk Parity

For this example, we consider the principal objective of the program to be the rapid achievement of a certified, operational CCTS capability within reasonable cost. The following three contributing objectives apply:

- Objective 1.1: Develop, review, and approve a set of CCTS certification requirements within a designated near-term time frame (e.g., by 2015 or 2016).
- Objective 1.2: Develop and build an operational certified CCTS within a designated near-term time frame (e.g., by 2017 or 2018).
- Objective 1.3: Achieve a CCTS and perform a designated number of flights within a designated cost (e.g., the amount of funding expected from Congress).

These objectives and a corresponding hypothetical cumulative risk parity table are illustrated in Figure 7.4. The following statements of cumulative risk, taken from the table in Figure 7.4, are parity statements that correspond to a rank 2 level of discomfort:

- Risk Parity Statement 1 (Discomfort Level 2): We are 50 percent confident that it will take no more than *X1 months* to develop, review, and approve the certification requirements.
- Risk Parity Statement 2 (Discomfort Level 2): We are 80 percent confident that it will take no more than *X2 months* to develop, review, and approve the certification requirements.
- Risk Parity Statement 3 (Discomfort Level 2): We are 50 percent confident that it will take no more than *X3 months* to develop and build an operational certified CCTS.

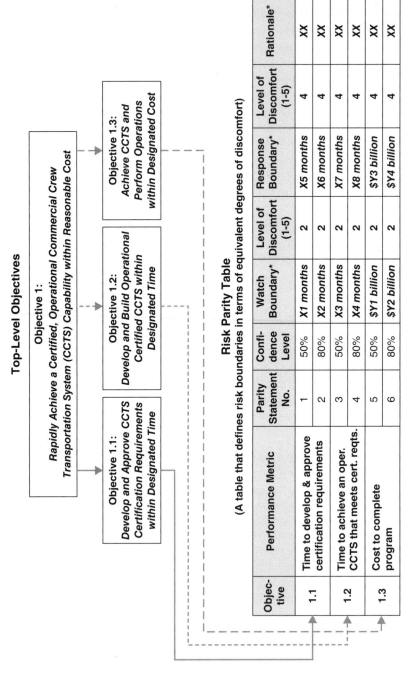

Top-Level Objectives

Objective 1:
Rapidly Achieve a Certified, Operational Commercial Crew Transportation System (CCTS) Capability within Reasonable Cost

Objective 1.1:
Develop and Approve CCTS Certification Requirements within Designated Time

Objective 1.2:
Develop and Build Operational Certified CCTS within Designated Time

Objective 1.3:
Achieve CCTS and Perform Operations within Designated Cost

Risk Parity Table

(A table that defines risk boundaries in terms of equivalent degrees of discomfort)

Objec-tive	Performance Metric	Parity Statement No.	Confi-dence Level	Watch Boundary*	Level of Discomfort (1-5)	Response Boundary*	Level of Discomfort (1-5)	Rationale*
1.1	Time to develop & approve certification requirements	1	50%	*X1 months*	2	*X5 months*	4	XX
		2	80%	*X2 months*	2	*X6 months*	4	XX
1.2	Time to achieve an oper. CCTS that meets cert. reqts.	3	50%	*X3 months*	2	*X7 months*	4	XX
		4	80%	*X4 months*	2	*X8 months*	4	XX
1.3	Cost to complete program	5	50%	*$Y1 billion*	2	*$Y3 billion*	4	XX
		6	80%	*$Y2 billion*	2	*$Y4 billion*	4	XX

* Entries elicited from stakeholders are highlighted in italics

FIGURE 7.4 Objectives and hypothetical cumulative risk parity table for CCTS example

- Risk Parity Statement 4 (Discomfort Level 2): We are 80 percent confident that it will take no more than *X4 months* to develop and build an operational certified CCTS.
- Risk Parity Statement 5 (Discomfort Level 2): We are 50 percent confident that the total cost to achieve an operational CCTS and perform 50 crewed flights will be no more than *$Y1 billion*.
- Risk Parity Statement 6 (Discomfort Level 2): We are 80 percent confident that the total cost to achieve an operational CCTS and perform 50 crewed flights will be no more than *$Y2 billion*.

Similarly, the following parity statements also evolve from the table in Figure 7.4 because of the fact that each statement results in a rank 4 level of discomfort:

- Risk Parity Statement 1 (Discomfort Level 4): We are 50 percent confident that it will take no more than *X5 months* to develop, review, and approve the certification requirements.
- Etc.

The first set of parity statements at rank 2 discomfort constitute watch boundaries for the cumulative risk, and the second set at rank 4 constitute response boundaries.

7.3.3   Remainder of Example 2

As foretold in Section 7.1, Example 2 will not be formally pursued beyond this point because of the proprietary nature of the data and the changing landscape within the program. It may be inferred, however, that the tasks to be pursued to complete Example 2 will be similar to those described in Section 7.2 to complete Example 1.

As a general comment reflecting this author's opinion, while assessing the risks associated with the risk-based assurance process and shared assurance model used in the CCP, close attention will have to be paid to the quality and degree of rigor applied to the communication between those responsible for assuring individual parts of the system. Without open and effective communication among the contractors and between the contractors and NASA, there could be a substantial risk that the assurance process will miss accident scenarios that emanate from interactions between subsystems, or will miss solutions that require a collaborative mindset. Furthermore, independence between the providers and those assuring the product is a best practice that needs to be maintained.

For these reasons, and because the risk-based assurance process and shared assurance model is a new approach to assurance at NASA, the approach itself will need to have a set of implementation controls to ensure that it is effective and efficient.

7.4 IMPLICATION FOR TRIO ENTERPRISES AND GOVERNMENT AUTHORITIES

Achievement of a balance between the competing objectives of timeliness, safety/reliability, and cost requires an honest appraisal of the decision maker's tolerances in each area. As Tables 7.1 and 7.2 show for the GMD example circa 2002, it is easy for decisions to be made based on what is perceived to be the most pressing objective at the time without considering the longer-term objectives that will become more pressing in the future. The use of EROM guards against this tendency, thereby making today's decisions more inclusive of short-term, mid-term, and long-term needs.

REFERENCES

Aerospace Safety Advisory Board (ASAP). 2015. "2015 Third Quarterly Meeting Report" (July 23). http://oiir.hq.nasa.gov/asap/documents/ASAP_Third_Quarterly_Meeting_2015.pdf

Bolden, Charles. 2013. "Launching American Astronauts from U.S. Soil." NASA (April 30). http://blogs.nasa.gov/bolden/2013/04/

Canfield, Amy. 2016. The Evolution of the NASA Commercial Crew Program Mission Assurance Process. NASA Kennedy Space Center. https://ntrs.nasa.gov/archive/nasa/casi.ntrs.nasa.gov/20160006484.pdf

Coyle, Philip. 2014. "Time to Change U.S. Missile Defense Culture," *Nukes of Hazard Blog, Center for Arms Control and Nonproliferation* (September 11).

Government Accountability Office. (GAO). 2015. GAO-15-345, *Missile Defense, Opportunities Exist to Reduce Acquisition Risk and Improve Reporting on System Capabilities*. Washington, DC: Government Accountability Office (May).

Inspector General (IG). 2014a. DODIG-2014-111, *Exoatmospheric Kill Vehicle Quality Assurance and Reliability Assessment—Part A*. Alexandria, VA: DoD Office of the Inspector General (September 8). http://www.dodig.mil/pubs/documents/DODIG-2014-111.pdf

Inspector General (IG). 2014b. DODIG-2015-28. *Evaluation of Government Quality Assurance Oversight for DoD Acquisition Programs*. Alexandria, VA: DoD Office of the Inspector General (November 3). http://www.dodig.mil/pubs/documents/DODIG-2015-028.pdf

Kirkpatrick, Paul. 2014. The NASA Commercial Crew Program (CCP) Shared Assurance Model for Safety. https://ntrs.nasa.gov/archive/nasa/casi.ntrs.nasa.gov/20140017447.pdf

Mosher, David. 2000. "Understanding the Extraordinary Cost of Missile Defense," *Arms Control Today*, December 2000. Also website http://www.rand.org/natsec_are/products/missiledefense.html

Wikipedia. 2016. "Ground-Based Midcourse Defense." Wikipedia (July 10).

CHAPTER 8

Independent Appraisal of EROM Processes and Results to Assure the Adequacy of Internal Controls and Inform Risk Acceptance Decisions

Given the complexity of the risks and opportunities that attend TRIO enterprises and the federal government's recent emphasis on applying EROM to the development, validation, and management of internal controls, independent evaluation of EROM processes and results is highly recommended. Such independent evaluations serve several purposes:

- In the case of federal agencies, they provide assurance to the executive and legislative branches of the government that significant risks and opportunities are recognized and are being effectively addressed.
- In the case of commercial enterprises, they provide the same assurance to the company's stockholders and creditors.
- In both cases, they provide the TRIO enterprise itself with a sense of assurance that decision making at all levels of the organization is being conducted in an informed, objective, and fully integrated manner.

8.1 BACKGROUND

8.1.1 OMB Motivation

The updated version of OMB Circular A-123 (2016), in a subsection entitled: "Role of Auditors in Enterprise Risk Management," states that: "Internal or external auditors conduct independent and objective audits, evaluations, and investigations of an Agency's programs and operations, which includes aspects of the internal control and risk management systems." Independent evaluation is stated as having special value, as follows: "Management and external auditors might have different interpretations of risks based on their respective roles and responsibilities. The agency risk function should seek to coordinate their roles so that the independence and scope of the external auditor's role is preserved while ensuring the continuing flow of risk information to the risk management function." In a later section, the updated Circular amplifies the importance of evaluating internal controls through the lens of ERM: "Agency managers must continuously monitor and improve the effectiveness of internal control associated with significant risks identified as part of their risk profile. This continuous monitoring, and other periodic evaluations, should provide the basis for the Agency Head's annual assessment of and report on internal control as required by the FMFIA." Through these statements, the Circular endorses independent periodic evaluations to ensure the integrity of the EROM approach and the completeness and accuracy of its analyses as they relate to the selection and implementation of internal controls and the associated required annual assurance report.

8.1.2   Department of Energy Guidance

The risk and internal control processes that the Department of Energy (DOE) uses are subject to independent evaluation through the financial statement audit conducted by DOE's external auditor and through normal quality assurance and peer review processes, according to the DOE FY 2014 guidance document on internal control evaluations (DOE 2014).

Also according to DOE, the determination of risk should drive not only the selection and placement of controls, but also the prioritization of controls testing. Controls designed for what would otherwise be intolerable risks should be tested more frequently than controls designed for marginal or tolerable risks. Example risks cited as being of concern to DOE in the context of internal controls (DOE 2014) are similar to those for other agencies. They fall within the following categories:

- "*Human Resources*—If the program does not have a sufficient number of qualified staff and managers available to effectively manage, oversee, and close out its projects, then project or program objectives will not be met.
- "*Contractor Oversight*—If federal staff is unable to manage issues with contractor or awardee performance, such as performance or quality shortcomings, cost or schedule overruns, or non-compliance with laws and regulations, then waste, or abuse of government funds may occur and program objectives will not be met.
- "*Acquisition or Procurement*—If a system is not in place to ensure competitiveness and fairness in contractor or awardee selection, then conflicts of interest may result.
- "*Budget Execution*—If the organization does not follow established policies and procedures for budget execution, then government funds

may be wasted, anti-deficiency violations may occur, and information regarding obligations, disbursements, and outlays may be inaccurate.

▪ "*Safeguards and Security*—If security procedures are not fully documented, supported by training for the appropriate personnel, and followed, then non-compliance with security requirements could occur and DOE property could be damaged or stolen or employee or public safety could be at risk" (DOE 2014, p. 9).

8.1.3 Institute of Internal Auditors Guidance

The United Kingdom's Institute of Internal Auditors (IIA, 2009) provides specific guidance on the desirable content of independent evaluations of ERM within an organization. According to IIA, audits of ERM practices should be performed to "provide objective assurance to the board [of directors of a company] on the effectiveness of risk management. Indeed, research has shown that board directors and internal auditors agree that the two most important ways that internal auditing provides value to the organization are in providing objective assurance that the major business risks are being managed appropriately and providing assurance that the risk management and internal control framework is operating effectively." The IIA report divides ERM activities into three categories: (1) those that fall under core internal audit roles, (2) those that fall under legitimate internal audit roles with safeguards, and (3) those not subject to internal audit, and it defines the ERM activities within each category as follows:

ERM Activities Falling under Core Internal Audit Roles
▪ Giving assurance on the risk management processes
▪ Giving assurance that risks are correctly evaluated
▪ Evaluating risk management processes
▪ Evaluating the reporting of key risks
▪ Reviewing the management of key risks

ERM Activities Falling under Legitimate Internal Audit Roles with Safeguards
▪ Facilitating identification and evaluation of risks
▪ Coaching management in response to risks
▪ Coordinating ERM activities
▪ Consolidated reporting on risks
▪ Maintaining and developing the ERM framework
▪ Championing establishment of ERM
▪ Developing risk management strategy for board approval

EROM Activities Not Subject to Internal Audit
▪ Setting the risk appetite
▪ Imposing risk management processes

- Management assurance on risks
- Taking decisions on risk responses
- Implementing risk responses on management's behalf
- Accountability for risk management

"In the case of ERM," according to the IIA paper, "internal auditing can provide consulting services so long as it has no role in actually managing risks—that is management's responsibility—and so long as senior management actively endorses and supports ERM."

8.2   QUERIES FOR AN INDEPENDENT APPRAISAL OF EROM IN THE CONTEXTS OF INTERNAL CONTROL AND RISK ACCEPTANCE

8.2.1   Overview

For an EROM approach based on the principles, recommendations, and templates provided in this book, an independent evaluation would need to be concerned with all the activities leading to the selection and implementation of risk mitigations, opportunity actions, and especially, internal controls informed by risk and opportunity drivers. Since there is a requirement for a statement of assurance regarding internal controls, the evaluation would also have to be concerned with whether the residual cumulative risks and opportunities after implementation of mitigations, actions, and controls are acceptable. Because these selections and decisions ultimately depend on the execution of all the processes discussed in the preceding chapters, the independent evaluation would have to be concerned with all of the following subjects:

- How the EROM team has been structured
- How the objectives hierarchy has been developed and the interfaces between objectives have been identified
- How risk tolerances and opportunity appetites have been derived from the decision makers' views of risk and opportunity parity
- How risk and opportunity scenarios have been identified
- How risk and opportunity leading indicators have been identified, monitored, and evaluated
- How risk and opportunity scenarios have been rolled up to aggregated risks and opportunities
- How risk and opportunity drivers have been identified and evaluated
- How risk mitigations, opportunity actions, and internal controls have been identified and evaluated based on the risk and opportunity drivers
- How asset distributions and risk/opportunity responses/controls have been optimized to achieve a desirable balance of aggregated risk and opportunity

■ How viable are the associated implementation plans

■ Whether to accept or reject the residual aggregated risks and opportunities

8.2.2 Template for Evaluating EROM Process and Results

Table 8.1 itemizes the queries that need to be addressed by the appraisal team for each evaluation category. Underneath each category, the template provides a list of queries and, for each query, results of the evaluation with respect to the subject of the query, recommendations for improvement (if any) in the treatment of the subject, and status of resolution if any is requested.

TABLE 8.1 Template for Evaluating EROM Process and Results

Item No.	Evaluation Item Description	Evaluation Result	Recommendation	Resolution Status
EROM Team Structure				
1	Are the scope and tasks of the enterprise-wide EROM team and each of the subteams appropriately defined?			
2	Do the enterprise-wide EROM team and each of the subteams have the proper depth and diversity of skills and experience to succeed in their tasks?			
3	Are the communications between the enterprise-wide EROM team and each of the subteams regularly scheduled, sufficiently frequent, and effective?			
4	Is there an enterprise-wide database of EROM information and is it sufficiently available to all participants, accounting for the need to protect sensitive and proprietary information where appropriate?			
5	Does the top-to-bottom management of each participating entity actively and vocally support the EROM effort?			
Development of Objectives Hierarchy and Identification of Interfaces				
6	Have all important sources of information pertaining to the definition and intent of the organization's objectives been identified and properly interpreted?			

(*continued*)

TABLE 8.1 (*Continued*)

Item No.	Evaluation Item Description	Evaluation Result	Recommendation	Resolution Status
7	Have all important organizational objectives been included in the hierarchy?			
8	Have all important interfaces between the objectives been identified and accurately represented?			
9	Has the rationale for identifying and interpreting interfaces between the objectives been clearly, completely, and accurately stated?			
Derivation of Risk Tolerances and Opportunity Appetites				
10	Have all significant stakeholders and decision makers been identified and queried to establish risk and opportunity parity statements for each top organizational objective?			
11	Have the responses of the stakeholders and decision makers been correctly interpreted and accurately converted into risk and opportunity watch and response boundaries for each objective?			
12	Has the rationale for establishing watch and response boundaries for each objective been clearly, completely, and accurately stated?			
Identification of Risk and Opportunity Scenarios				
13	Have all important sources of information pertaining to the organization's risks and opportunities been identified and correctly interpreted?			
14	Have all important risk and opportunity scenarios been included in the EROM analysis, including those that affect program/project success, core competencies, and organizational health?			
15	Have all significant risks that would be introduced by availing each identified opportunity been included in the EROM analysis?			
16	Have all important interfaces between the risk and opportunity scenarios and the organization's objectives been identified and accurately represented?			

TABLE 8.1 (*Continued*)

Item No.	Evaluation Item Description	Evaluation Result	Recommendation	Resolution Status
17	Has the rationale for identifying, interpreting, and assigning risk and opportunity scenarios to objectives been clearly, completely, and accurately stated?			
18	Have cross-cutting risk and opportunity scenarios been identified as such, and are they defined and handled consistently across the affected organizational units?			
19	Are there additional opportunities (not currently considered) to establish new objectives that significantly promote the organization's mission?			
Identification of Risk and Opportunity Leading Indicators				
20	Have all important leading indicators for each known risk and opportunity scenario been identified and included for consideration?			
21	Have the leading indicators that promote unknown and underappreciated (UU) risks been included for consideration?			
22	Have the functional relationships between the leading indicators and the objectives they pertain to been identified and correctly interpreted?			
23	Have cross-cutting risk and opportunity leading indicators been identified as such, and are they defined and handled consistently across the affected organizational units?			
Evaluation of Risk and Opportunity Leading Indicators				
24	Have correlations been established between the leading indicator values and the likelihood of success of each objective, and are these correlations transparent and verifiable?			
25	Have watch and response trigger values been established for all the leading indicators that affect each objective, and are they consistent with the risk and opportunity watch and response boundary values?			

(*continued*)

TABLE 8.1 (*Continued*)

Item No.	Evaluation Item Description	Evaluation Result	Recommendation	Resolution Status
26	Has the rationale for the leading indicator trigger values been clearly, completely, and accurately stated?			
27	Have all important sources of information pertaining to the status and trends of the leading indicators been identified and correctly interpreted?			
28	Have the status and trends of the leading indicators been accurately evaluated?			
29	Has the rationale for the evaluation of the leading indicator status and trends been clearly, completely, and accurately stated?			
30	Have cross-cutting leading indicators been evaluated consistently across the affected organizational units?			
Roll-Up of Risks and Opportunities				
31	Has there been a systematic roll-up of the risks and opportunities from the bottom to top level of the objectives hierarchy to determine aggregate risks and opportunities?			
32	Have the roll-ups accounted for all identified significant leading indicators and all identified significant interfaces between objectives?			
33	Have all important sources of information pertaining to the importance of each objective on other objectives and the mitigating effects of redundancies and workarounds been identified and correctly interpreted?			
34	Have the risk and opportunity roll-ups accurately reflected all important interfaces, redundancies, and workarounds?			
35	For commercial enterprises, are results from the quantitative and qualitative roll-ups of monetary risks and opportunities consistent with one another?			
36	Has the rationale for the roll-ups been clearly, completely, and accurately stated?			

TABLE 8.1 (*Continued*)

Item No.	Evaluation Item Description	Evaluation Result	Recommendation	Resolution Status
	**Identification and Evaluation of Risk and Opportunity Drivers**
37	Has the derivation of risk and opportunity drivers included consideration of hardware response, software response, human response, controls, assumptions, and organizational factors, singly and in combination, as opposed to just hardware and software responses?			
38	Is each derived risk and opportunity driver responsible for a change in level of importance of the aggregate risk or opportunity of a top objective (e.g., a change from a green/tolerable risk to a yellow/marginal or red/intolerable risk)?			
39	Do the identified risk and opportunity drivers accurately reflect the stated rationale in the risk and opportunity identification template, the leading indicator identification and evaluation template, the objectives interface template, and the risk and opportunity roll-up templates?			
40	Does the risk and opportunity driver list comprise a complete set of drivers for each top objective?			
	**Identification of Risk Mitigations, Opportunity Actions, and Internal Controls**
41	Have all existing internal controls been identified and correctly characterized?			
42	Have all significant flaws in the existing internal controls been identified?			
43	Have alternative sets of risk mitigations and opportunity actions been suggested?			
44	Do the suggested risk mitigations and opportunity actions address all the risk and opportunity drivers?			
45	Have all significant assumptions in the assessment of risk mitigations and opportunity actions been identified and correctly characterized?			
46	Have alternative sets of new internal controls and/or modifications to existing internal controls been identified?			

(*continued*)

TABLE 8.1   (*Continued*)

Item No.	Evaluation Item Description	Evaluation Result	Recommendation	Resolution Status
	Preliminary Evaluation of Risk Mitigations, Opportunity Actions, and Internal Controls			
47	Is each suggested set of risk mitigations, opportunity actions, and internal controls practicable?			
48	Do the suggested new/modified internal controls protect the viability of all significant assumptions and correct or obviate all significant current flaws?			
	Optimization Analyses and Associated Implementation Planning			
49	Have sensitivity analyses or iterations been conducted on the risk and opportunity roll-ups using risk and opportunity driver results as a guide?			
50	Has a near-optimal distribution of human, physical, and instructional assets been derived from these analyses?			
51	Has a near-optimal selection of risk mitigations, opportunity actions, and internal controls been derived from these analyses?			
52	Has a plan been prepared to implement the near-optimal distribution of human, physical, and instructional assets and the near-optimal set of risk mitigations, opportunity actions, and internal controls?			
	Risk Acceptance Decision-Making Support			
53	Is the cumulative risk and opportunity for each objective acceptable at the present time based on the stakeholders' risk tolerance and opportunity appetite?			
54	Is it possible to make the cumulative risk and opportunity even more acceptable over all objectives by introducing new risk mitigations, opportunity actions, and/or internal controls?			
55	Have processes for monitoring all important leading indicators been identified and are they being implemented?			
56	What is the recommendation for proceeding forward?			

REFERENCES

Institute of Internal Auditors (IIA) of the UK. 2009. "IIA Position Paper: The Role of Internal Auditing in Enterprise-Wide Risk Management." (January).

Office of Management and Budget (OMB). 2016. OMB Circular A-123 "Management's Responsibility for Enterprise Risk Management and Internal Control" (July 15).

US Department of Energy (DOE). 2014. "Internal Controls Evaluations: Fiscal Year 2014 Guidance." (February 10).

Brief Overview of the Potential Integration of EROM with Other Strategic Assessment Activities

Many TRIO enterprises form separate, interorganizational teams to evaluate progress and recommend changes in a variety of areas, including: (1) technical capabilities and the associated distribution of assets, (2) implementation of strategies for fulfilling the mission of the enterprise, and (3) cross-organizational execution and integration of programs, projects, activities, and initiatives. We refer to these enterprise-level teams, respectively, as technical capability assessment (TCA) teams, strategic assessment review (SAR) teams, and portfolio performance review (PPR) teams, although different organizations may have different terms. The question may arise whether the formation and implementation of an integrated set of EROM teams operating more-or-less in parallel with these other teams facilitates and enhances the important work of the TCA, SAR, and PPR teams or merely duplicates it. The short answer is that the integrated EROM team provides a key service to these other teams by introducing risks and opportunities into the overall discussion and rigorously accounting for them in the assessment and review processes. This chapter elaborates briefly on how the interaction between EROM and the other interorganizational teams works.

9.1 TECHNICAL CAPABILITY ASSESSMENT (TCA)

TCA teams are empaneled to examine the alignment of the TRIO enterprise's technical capabilities with the enterprise's long-term strategic needs, the program directorates' near-term needs, and the technical centers' identity and values. The purpose of the TCA team is to establish a more efficient operating model for maintaining a minimum set of technical capabilities that meets current and future mission needs while accommodating portfolio changes that occur periodically.

As shown on the upper part of Figure 9.1, the TCA approach may be based on a three-dimensional model that includes technical capabilities as

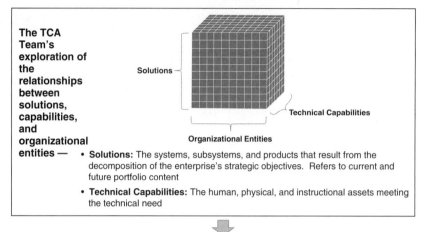

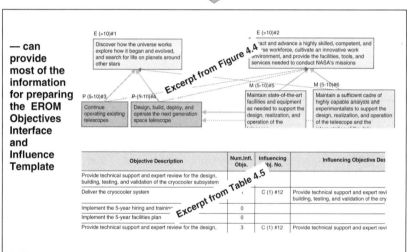

FIGURE 9.1 Relationship between the TCA process and the EROM objectives interface and influence template

one dimension, organizational entities as a second dimension, and solutions as a third dimension. In this context, technical capabilities include all of the human resources (workforce and contractors) and physical assets (equipment and facilities) utilized to meet the TRIO enterprise's technical objectives. Solutions refer to the current and future portfolio content (programs, projects, systems, subsystems, activities, initiatives) that results from decomposition and implementation of the enterprise's objectives. Analytical models may be used to assist the TCA team in the right-sizing of the enterprise's workforce and physical assets.

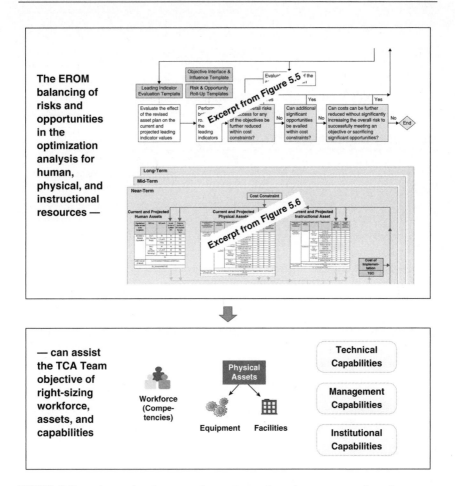

FIGURE 9.2 Relationship between the EROM risk-and-opportunity-based asset optimization process and the TCA asset right-sizing objective

There are two ways in which the EROM approach described in this book can interact synergistically with a typical TCA approach. One involves a transfer of information from TCA to EROM, wherein the TCA team provides the EROM team with an understanding of all the interfaces that exist between the technical centers' institutional initiatives, the technical centers' mission support activities, the program directorates' programs and projects, and the TRIO enterprise's strategic objectives. The other involves a transfer of information in the opposite direction, wherein EROM provides TCA with an assessment of how risks and opportunities contribute to the right-sizing of the workforce and other assets. A high-level schematic view of the mechanics of these two interactions is provided in Figures 9.1 and 9.2, respectively.

The EROM focus on incorporating a means for balancing risks and opportunities into the right-sizing process is unique to EROM. The planning for future workforce and other assets should include a reasonable assessment of the uncertainties reflected in risks and opportunities, and therefore, EROM should be an essential part of this TCA function.

9.2 STRATEGIC ANNUAL REVIEW (SAR)

For federal agencies, the Strategic Annual Review (SAR) process is the TRIO enterprise's response to the GPRA Modernization Act requirement that each agency conduct an annual review of its performance goals and objectives. Based on its strategic plan, each agency assesses progress toward the accomplishment of its strategic objectives by considering the status of multiyear and annual performance objectives, performance indicators, risks and associated risk indicators, external factors, and other events that may have affected the outcomes or threaten to affect them in the future.

As stated in OMB Circular A-11, Section 270.10 (2014): "Progress toward achieving individual quantitative performance goals related to the strategic objective[s] is one important consideration, but alone is not representative of the scope, complexity, or external factors that can influence program results and outcomes toward which Federal agencies are working." It goes on to state that agencies should consider, among other things:

- Whether desired changes have occurred in the ultimate outcomes the agency seeks to improve and whether these outcomes are directly measureable or must be assessed through proxies or other means of evaluation
- Evaluations, research studies, data and policy analysis or other assessments relevant to the strategic objective or the related programs
- Lessons learned from past efforts to continuously improve service delivery and resolve management challenges, especially in coordinating across organization components and with delivery partners
- Identification, assessment, and prioritization of probable risks that may impact program delivery or outcomes significantly in the coming year or two
- Budgetary, regulatory, or legislative constraints that may have an impact on progress

In addition, as stated in Section 270.11:

- "To support the identification, assessment and prioritization of probable risks that may impact program delivery or outcomes and are likely to impact the strategic objectives, agencies are encouraged to leverage any existing Enterprise Risk Management efforts when conducting strategic reviews."

A reasonable interpretation of this last bullet is that OMB, consistent with the use of an EROM approach, is encouraging agencies to look not only at probable risks that may impact program delivery or outcomes significantly in the coming year or two, as stated in one of the above bullets, but also at longer-term risks that may impact the strategic objectives farther into the future. It would be fair to say, however, that at the present time, the development of a longer-term perspective is encouraged but not mandated.

The EROM templates in Chapters 4 through 7 contain information on individual risks and opportunities, as well as on key leading indicators, which can significantly facilitate the SAR evaluation of strategies, performance goals, risks, opportunities, and associated indicators. In particular, the templates provide reports both for the near-term performance objectives that are required by the GPRA Modernization Act and by OMB Circular A-11, and for the longer-term objectives that are important to a TRIO enterprise's strategic evaluations.

In addition to improving the evaluation of status at each level of the objectives hierarchy, the EROM roll-up templates offer the capability of providing insights into how the risks and opportunities at lower levels affect the likelihood of success in meeting the strategic objectives. Because the roll-up process accounts for the plethora of individual risk and opportunity scenarios that affect each strategic objective in a rational and transparent way, the information in the roll-up templates can lead to significantly greater assurance that the SAR evaluation of the success of each strategic objective is defensible.

Figures 9.3 and 9.4 schematically illustrate the manner in which the EROM templates provide information useful to the SAR process.

9.3 PORTFOLIO PERFORMANCE REVIEW (PPR)

The portfolio performance review (PPR) is a recurring senior performance management review of programs, projects, and activities within the TRIO enterprise. Its intentions are to integrate TRIO enterprise-wide communication of performance metrics and analysis results, to highlight cross-cutting issues that impact performance and affect risk, and to enable senior management to quickly address issues. For federal agencies, the PPR meets requirements for quarterly progress reviews contained in GPRAMA and in OMB Circular A-11 Section 6.

For most TRIO enterprises, the PPR tends to concentrate on current issues much more than risks (potential future problems), and accordingly

Completion of the EROM Risk and Opportunity Identification and Leading Indicator Identification and Evaluation Templates —

Excerpt from Table 4.2

Scenario Statement	Leading Indicator Number	fLeading Indicator Description
...m subcontractor's less-than-adequate ...ding several missed milestones and overall ...ere may be a significant delay in the delivery date	1	Remainin... ...edule reserve for cryocooler development
	2	Re... reserve for the program that can be alloc...
	3	...solved technical issues for cryo developm...
		...uation of cryocooler development problems (sc...
...ed trends in the attrition of experienced pers... ...cted state of competition for the most hi... ..., the available technical resources... ...5-year plan resulting in capabilit...		...umber of retirements of qualfied optics analysis & test
		Number of retirements of qualfied integated analysis &...
	7	Number of qualified optics analysis & testing recent grad...
	8	Competition for recent optics graduates, e.g. from the m...
...eeded technology for the space tele...ope and the ...test facilities, facility needs 5 years from now may ...e 5-year plan resulting in capability shortcomings	9	Number of significant design modifications required to d...
	10	Complexity of design (rank 1-5)
	11	Complexity of integration and testing (rank 1-5)

Excerpt from Table 4.3

Leading Indicator Description	Risk, Opp., or Intr. Risk	Scen. No.	Lead. In...	Rationale or Source	Lead. Ind. Resp. Value	Rationale or Source
schedule reserve for cryocooler development			XX	XX	XX	XX
cost reserve that can be allocated to cry...	1		XX	XX	XX	XX
unresolved technical issues for c...	Risk	1	XX	XX	XX	XX
...tion of cryocooler development ... ...s	Risk	1	XX	XX	XX	XX
...ements of qualif. optics anal. & testing experts	Risk	2	XX	XX	XX	XX
...ements of qualif. integr. anal. & testing experts	Risk	2	XX	XX	XX	XX

— can provide significantly greater assurance about the SAR evaluation of risks, opportunities, and leading indicators (and vice versa)

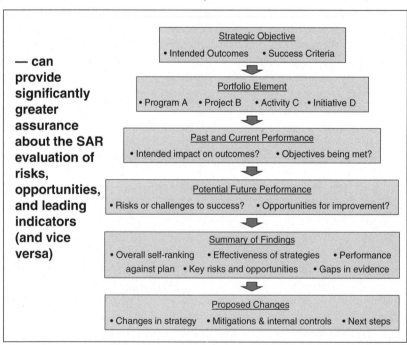

FIGURE 9.3 Relationship between the EROM risk and opportunity identification and leading indicator evaluation templates and the SAR process

Completion of the EROM Risk and Opportunity Roll-Up Templates —

Lead. Ind. No. or Influencing Objec. No.	Description of Leading Indicator or Influencing Objective	Composite Indicator	Lead. Ind. Concern or Objec. Aggr. Risk	Aggregate Risk of Objective	Rollup Rationale
None	None	None	None	None	No risks entered
1	Remaining schedule reserve for cryocooler development	...e	TBD	TBD	TBD
2	Remaining cost reserve for the program allocatab!~	None	TBD		
3	Severity of unresolved tech issues for cry~	None	TBD		
4	GAO evaluation of cryocooler dev~' (scale 1-5)	None	TBD		
C (1) #12	Provide tech support & exper' ~n, ... of cryo subsys.	None	None		
5	No. of retirements of qualified ~nalysis & testing experts	None	TBD	TBD	TBD
6	No. of retirements of qualified integated analysis & testing experts	None	TBD		
7	No. of qualified optics analysis & testing recent graduates	None	TBD		
8	Competition for recent optics graduates, e.g., from the military	None	TBD		

Excerpt from Table 4.6

Lead. Ind. No. or Influencing Objec. No.	Description of Leading Indicator or Influencing Objective	Composite Indicator	Lead. Ind. Significance or Objec. ~. Opp.	Aggregate Opp. of Objective	Roll-Up Rationale
18	Tech. readiness level for improved resolution IR cameras	N~	~ (+)	TBD (+)	TBD
19	Readiness level for SLS/ Ori~ including docking capa~'	~	TBD (+)		
20	Predicted P(LOC) fo. ~un	None	TBD (−)		
21	Predicted P(LOM) for ~LS	None	TBD (−)		
22	Predicted cost for a rendezvous mission	None	TBD (−)		

Excerpt from Table 4.9

— can provide greater assurance that the SAR evaluation of the success of each strategic objective is defensible

Strategic Objective Number	Strategic Objective Description	Rating (Red, Yellow, or Green)	Explanation for the Rating
		Green	
		Green	
		Green	
		Red	
		Yellow	
		Green	

FIGURE 9.4 Relationship between the EROM risk and opportunity roll-up templates and the SAR process

it tends to have a shorter-term focus than the TCA initiatives and the SAR reviews. According to Smalley (2013), "The BPR [NASA's equivalent of a PPR] is the culmination of all of the agency's regular business rhythm performance monitoring activities, providing ongoing performance assessment between key decision points." The BPR/PPR "is 'action-oriented' to improve performance and inform agency decision authorities of issues needing attention."

EROM tends to have a longer-term focus than the PPR, but there is also a component of it that deals with short-term performance objectives, as measured by success or failure in achieving *annual performance goals* (see Section 3.1.1). Therefore, the relevance of EROM to PPR as traditionally practiced is mainly directed at short-term performance. For TRIO enterprises where the PPR process has a longer-term, more strategic performance evaluation perspective, the interfaces between EROM and PPR have an accordingly larger scope.

Within the more tactical approach to performance evaluation, there are several areas where EROM and PPR can interface. The activities of the PPR process include information gathering, generally obtained both through questionnaires sent to all areas within the TRIO enterprise and through person-to-person interactions at the actual review meetings. These data can help populate the EROM templates dealing with risk, opportunity, and leading indicator identification and evaluation as well as the risk and opportunity roll-up process. Most importantly, information about the status of leading indicators and about existing margins within each mission execution domain (cost, schedule, technical, and safety) and their trends over time are valuable to the EROM process.

EROM can also provide useful information to the PPR process in the area of aggregating the assessment from program/project level to program directorate and technical center levels. As discussed throughout this book, the EROM process can be exercised not only for the TRIO enterprise as a whole but also for individual management units within the TRIO enterprise. The EROM roll-up and high-level display templates, when exercised at the program directorate and technical center levels, lead to rankings of the likelihood of success in achieving each top objective of each directorate and center. These rankings can provide useful information to the PPR in its attempt to provide an assessment aggregate roll-up for each directorate and center.

The manner in which the PPR process can provide information to the EROM process, and vice versa, is similar to the schematics of the TCA-EROM interface in Figure 9.1 and EROM-SAR interface in Figure 9.4.

REFERENCES

Office of Management and Budget (OMB). 2014. OMB Circular A-11. "Preparation, Submission, and Execution of the Budget." https://www.whitehouse.gov/sites/default/files/omb/assets/a11_current_year/a11_2014.pdf

Smalley, S. 2013. "Baseline Performance Review: NASA's Monthly Performance Update and Independent Assessment Forum," Presentation to National Defense Industrial Association, NASA Office of Chief Engineer.

CHAPTER 10

An Integrated Framework for Hierarchical Internal Controls

10.1 INTERNAL CONTROL PRINCIPLES AND THE INTEGRATION OF INTERNAL CONTROL, RISK MANAGEMENT, AND GOVERNANCE

This chapter explores how internal controls for TRIO organizations can be fully integrated with enterprise risk and opportunity management (EROM). It provides an extension and follow-up to earlier sections in this book (notably Sections 3.6 and 4.7) and is intended to be responsive to the recently issued requirements of the Office of Management and Budget (OMB) in Circular A-123 (OMB 2016) concerning EROM and internal controls. It also recommends innovative approaches that exceed the minimum OMB requirements in several areas.

In a nutshell, the following key principles for internal controls are advocated in this book:

- Internal controls should be derived from the organization's strategic objectives, tactical objectives, and core standards of operation and from considerations of the risk and opportunity drivers that affect the organization's ability to meet those objectives and standards.
- The drivers are determined from the factors that most significantly affect aggregate risks and opportunities rather than just from individual risks and opportunities.
- The identification and evaluation of internal controls focus largely on protection of the assumptions and/or correction of the actual and potential weaknesses that need to be addressed for the aggregate risks and opportunities to be effectively and efficiently controlled within the decision maker's risk tolerance and opportunity appetite.

- Internal controls should be the result of organizational staff members thinking about what could go wrong and what can be done to monitor and prevent it from going wrong.

Originally, control theory was developed for mechanical systems to ensure that they achieve their operational objectives while operating within predetermined constraints. In the case of mechanical systems, the constraints normally are defined by physical variables such as pressure, temperature, and flow rate. The system is regulated by feedback loops, referred to as control loops, which ensure that these variables are monitored and adjusted when needed through mechanical actuators to keep them within their designed operating range.

The implementation of control theory based on the use of control loops has been applied more recently in the context of internal control for organizations. The following principle of internal control for organizations is posited herein and developed formalistically in Section 10.2.1:

- Internal control loops can and should generally be derived and implemented in a *hierarchical* manner, wherein each level of the organization contributes to the overall internal control framework in a synergistic manner.[1]

Hierarchical control structures are analogous to organizational structures in a large company or agency. They contain a primary control loop, similar to the executive function in a company or agency, and a nested series of subordinate control loops, similar to a company's or agency's hierarchical structure of organizational entities and subunits. However, the control loop hierarchies do not exactly mirror the organizational hierarchies, as they are designed to address control needs that may transcend organizational hierarchies. The following principle applies here:

- There should be a clear mapping between the internal control structures within an organization and the organizational management structures so that the roles and responsibilities for formulating and implementing controls are clearly defined in terms of organizational entities.

That said, the principles for creating hierarchical control structures are similar to the principles for creating hierarchical organizational structures in the following senses:

- Hierarchical internal control structures should promote the defining of roles and responsibilities so as to ensure that all important controls have a champion or owner as well as an oversight authority.
- They should cause lower-level organizational units to be aware that they have control responsibilities that are intended to support the higher-level controls that exist at higher levels of the organization.
- They should be well-suited for integration with hierarchical EROM structures.

As discussed earlier in Sections 2.4.2 and 4.8.2, organization-wide risk and opportunity management works best when EROM teams are established for each unit of the organization, with frequent communication between the teams both horizontally and vertically. The same is true for internal control structures. In this way, risks and opportunities and internal controls can be treated consistently at each level of the organization and can be easily aggregated from bottom to top.

The relationship between the key organizational management functions of internal control, risk management, and governance is discussed in OMB Circular A-123. As illustrated in Figure 2.8, the OMB Circular views internal control as being a part of program/project risk management, program/project risk management as being a part of enterprise risk management, and enterprise risk management as being a part of governance.

For purposes of this discussion, the principal elements contained within each of these organizational management functions and the interfaces between them are illustrated in Figures 10.1 and 10.2. Figure 10.1, which is notionally similar to Figure 2.6 but reformatted to highlight overall relationships in the present context, applies to strategic planning, whereas Figure 10.2, which is notionally similar to Figure 2.7, applies to performance evaluation. Both are equally important functions of the agency that are subject to governance, risk management, and internal control.

The relationships between the various levels of the organization in conducting these organizational management functions are depicted in a very simplified form in Figure 10.3. The reader may want to refer back to Section 3.6.6 for a comparison of the bidirectional integration of internal controls and EROM advocated in this book to the more unidirectional approach advocated by COSO.

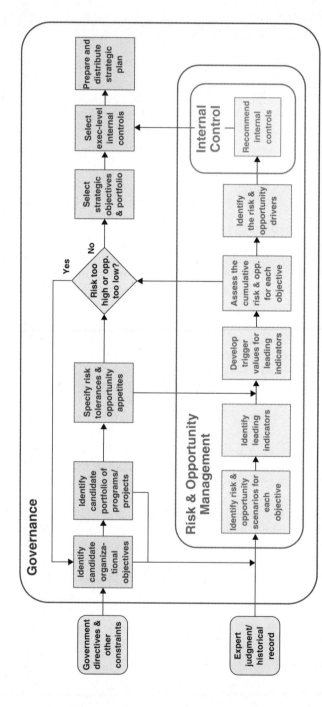

FIGURE 10.1 Conceptualization of the relationship between governance, risk management, and internal controls: strategic planning

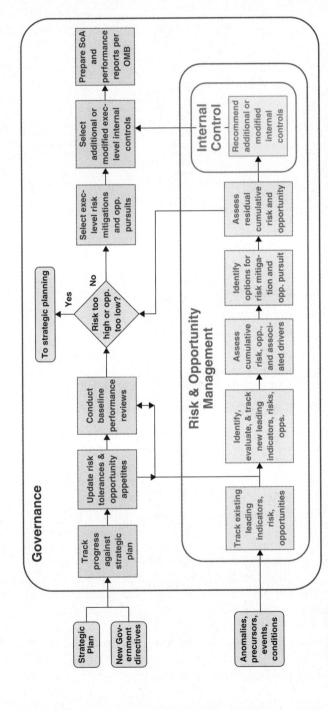

FIGURE 10.2 Conceptualization of the relationship between governance, risk management, and internal controls: organizational performance evaluation

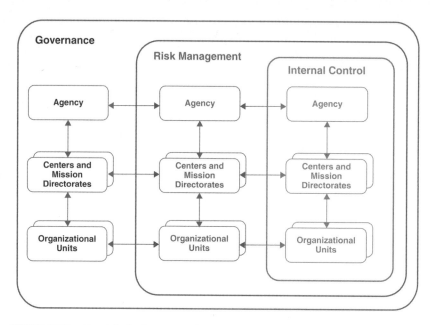

FIGURE 10.3 Simplified schematic of the interfaces between organizational management functions and organizational management levels

10.2 METHODOLOGICAL BASIS

10.2.1 Hierarchical Control Loops

A control loop is, by Merriam-Webster's definition, "an operation, process, or mechanism that is regulated by feedback." The feedback loops in Figures 10.1 and 10.2 are used to inform a process but not specifically to regulate it, and are therefore not control loops by Webster's definition.

Figure 10.4 shows a simplified representation of a control loop based on a model presented by Leveson (2011). The controller obtains information about the process state from measurable variables and uses this information to initiate action by manipulating controlled variables to keep the process operating within predefined limits or set points. A separate control loop of this form is typically provided for each of the organization's near-term, mid-term, and long-term objectives that are considered key to its mission.

The original formulation of control loops was intended for mechanical systems, such as that shown in Figure 10.5. In this simple example, a forced-air heating/cooling system (control mechanism) is used to keep the temperature of an enclosed space within comfortable temperature limits (control process output).

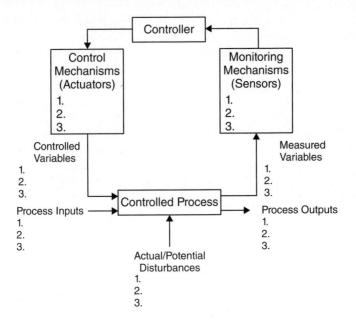

FIGURE 10.4 Standard control loop form

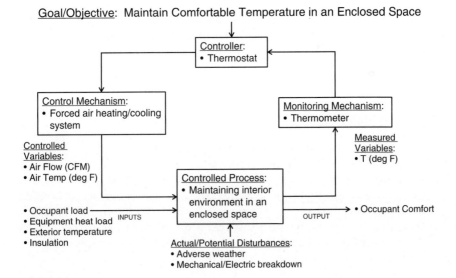

FIGURE 10.5 Example simple control loop for a mechanical system

The temperature (measured variable) is measured by a thermometer (monitoring mechanism) and the heating/cooling system is actuated by a thermostat (controller). The system controls the flow rate and temperature of air going into the enclosure (controlled variables). The necessary flow rate and air temperature are affected by the occupant load, equipment heat load, outside temperature, and amount of insulation in the walls (process inputs). The system is subject to various hazards that could lead to its failure, including adverse weather and mechanical/electrical breakdown (actual/potential disturbances).

When used for purposes of internal control in a TRIO enterprise, it is useful to think of the internal control structure as being composed of a hierarchy of control loops, as shown in Figure 10.6. The important features are as follows:

- The primary control loop emanates from an objective of the organization, derives from risk or opportunity drivers, and follows the format of Figure 10.4.
- Each monitoring and control mechanism in the primary control loop is considered to be an activity that may in itself need to be controlled via a secondary control loop. A secondary control loop would be necessary if there are risky elements of the activity (referred to in the figure as "control needs") that need to be monitored and, when appropriate, acted upon.
- Likewise, each monitoring and control mechanism in the secondary control loop is considered to be an activity that may need to be controlled via a tertiary control loop, based on risks that apply to it. The development of the hierarchy of control loops may continue to lower levels if needed.

10.2.2   RACI Matrices

Each activity in the hierarchy that spawns a lower-level control loop is assigned to an appropriate entity in the organization, has appropriate management oversight, and is communicated among other entities that have an interest or obligation that interfaces with that activity. A favored means for doing this is to develop a *RACI matrix* (Smith, 2005), which defines the organizations and people who are Responsible, Accountable, Consulted, and Informed on each activity (hence the acronym). An example form for a RACI matrix is shown in Table 10.1.

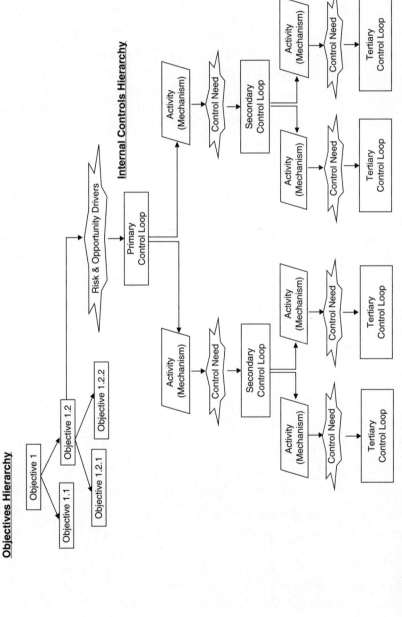

FIGURE 10.6 Example form of a hierarchical system of internal control loops

TABLE 10.1 Example form of a RACI matrix

RACI Definitions:

<u>R</u>esponsible = person or role responsible for ensuring that the item is completed
<u>A</u>ccountable = person or role responsible for actually doing or completing the item
<u>C</u>onsulted = person or role whose subject matter expertise is required in order to complete the item
<u>I</u>nformed = person or role that needs to be kept informed of the status of item completion

Control Loop	Monitoring or Control Activity	Responsible		Accountable		Consulted		Informed	
		Org	Person	Org	Person	Org(s)	Person(s)	Org(s)	Person(s)

10.3 EXAMPLES

10.3.1 Example 1: Institutional Responsibility for Risk Management and System Safety

In this example, we consider a safety and mission assurance (SMA) organization within a TRIO enterprise whose main responsibilities are to promote, promulgate, and help implement a unified risk management structure and a unified system safety structure within the enterprise. The SMA organization is charged with developing and helping to implement policy and standards that account for all strategically important enterprise activities within the risk management and system safety structures, including all applicable risks and interactions, and integrating the management of risks and system safety across organizational boundaries. Its charter includes the application of engineering and management principles, criteria, and techniques to optimize risk management and safety within the constraints of operational effectiveness, time, and cost.

Based on this charter, a rather simplified primary control loop for the SMA organization's role in risk management and system safety is shown in Figure 10.7. The principal controller in this case is the SMA organization. The control activities (or mechanisms) selected here for display include the development and updating of risk management and system safety policies, procedures, standards, and guides; provision of risk management and system safety training; counseling on risk mitigation options; and reliance on a technical authority to ensure technical quality.

For the control loop to work in the best manner, secondary control loops may be needed for several, if not all, of the monitoring activities and control activities of the primary control loop. For example, the control activity "Develop/update RM & SS policies, procedures, standards, guides" in Figure 10.7 requires a control loop to ensure that the activity is initiated when needed and that the products fulfill the needs of the enterprise. In order to develop a meaningful secondary control loop for this activity, it is useful first to devise a process diagram depicting the various activities that are involved in developing and updating RM and SS policies, procedures, standards, and guides. Such a diagram is shown in the lower half of Figure 10.8 on Pages 288 and 289. A control loop that reflects the principal elements in the process diagram is presented in Figure 10.9 on Pages 290 and 291. The control activities for the secondary loop include ensuring that the stakeholders' views are represented, that the policy and procedures are applicable and comprehensive, and that that they are compatible with other policies in the TRIO enterprise.

Similarly, there can be tertiary control loops designed to ensure that each activity in the secondary loop works as intended. For example, the monitoring activity "Oversight of review" in Figure 10.9 may require a control to

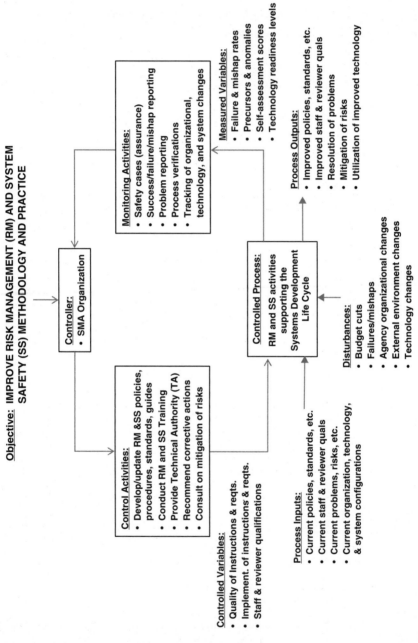

Objective: IMPROVE RISK MANAGEMENT (RM) AND SYSTEM SAFETY (SS) METHODOLOGY AND PRACTICE

Controller:
- SMA Organization

Control Activities:
- Develop/update RM &SS policies, procedures, standards, guides
- Conduct RM and SS Training
- Provide Technical Authority (TA)
- Recommend corrective actions
- Consult on mitigation of risks

Controlled Variables:
- Quality of Instructions & reqts.
- Implement. of instructions & reqts.
- Staff & reviewer qualifications

Process Inputs:
- Current policies, standards, etc.
- Current staff & reviewer quals
- Current problems, risks, etc.
- Current organization, technology, & system configurations

Controlled Process:
RM and SS activities supporting the Systems Development Life Cycle

Disturbances:
- Budget cuts
- Failures/mishaps
- Agency organizational changes
- External environment changes
- Technology changes

Monitoring Activities:
- Safety cases (assurance)
- Success/failure/mishap reporting
- Problem reporting
- Process verifications
- Tracking of organizational, technology, and system changes

Measured Variables:
- Failure & mishap rates
- Precursors & anomalies
- Self-assessment scores
- Technology readiness levels

Process Outputs:
- Improved policies, standards, etc.
- Improved staff & reviewer quals
- Resolution of problems
- Mitigation of risks
- Utilization of improved technology

FIGURE 10.7 Example primary control loop for the objective of improving risk management and system safety methodology and practice within the enterprise

ensure that the competency of the review group remains high despite possible turnovers within the group, changes in the areas of experience and expertise needed to be a reviewer, and/or changes in the manager that has the authority to grant budget and allocation of human resources toward the review process. A process diagram and tertiary control loop resulting from these considerations is shown in Figure 10.10.

The results of the hierarchical devolvement of control loops may be summarized in a table similar to Table 10.2. Persons and organizations responsible for, accountable for, consulted about, and informed about the status of and results from each monitoring and control activity may be documented in a table similar to Table 10.3. There needs to be an entry in each cell of Table 10.3 in order for the control structure to be considered free of gaps.

10.3.2   Example 2: NASA Commercial Crew Program Risk-Based Assurance Process and Shared Assurance Model

As discussed in Section 7.3.1, the objective of the NASA Commercial Crew Program (CCP) is to develop the capability to use a commercially provided space system to transport crew to low-Earth orbit, including to the International Space Station (ISS). To operate within mandated constraints, the CCP has adopted an approach designed to promote safety and reliability while minimizing schedule slippages and cost overruns. As mentioned in Section 7.3.2, the approach is referred to as a risk-based assurance (RBA) process utilizing a shared assurance model (Canfield 2016; Kirkpatrick 2014). The shared assurance approach takes advantage of each support organization's unique skills and areas of expertise while minimizing organizational overlap and still maintaining an appropriate level of checks and balances. Based on a set of factors that include design and process complexity, degree of maturation, past performance, and expert judgment, a decision is made about which of the hazards identified by the provider(s) need to be analyzed by NASA personnel and which do not. The ones that need to be overseen by NASA are assigned to NASA's list of product assurance actions (PAAs).

Because the RBA process and shared assurance model is a new approach to assurance at NASA, the approach itself needs to have a set of implementation controls to ensure that it is effective and efficient. The controls particularly need to address the quality and degree of rigor applied to the communication between those responsible for assuring individual parts of the system and assure that cross-cutting and system-wide concerns are adequately addressed.

Figure 10.11 depicts a candidate primary control loop that could serve this purpose while maintaining the RBA process and shared assurance model

PRIMARY CONTROL LOOP   Objective: IMPROVE RISK MANAGEMENT (RM) AND SYSTEM SAFETY (SS) METHODOLOGY AND PRACTICE

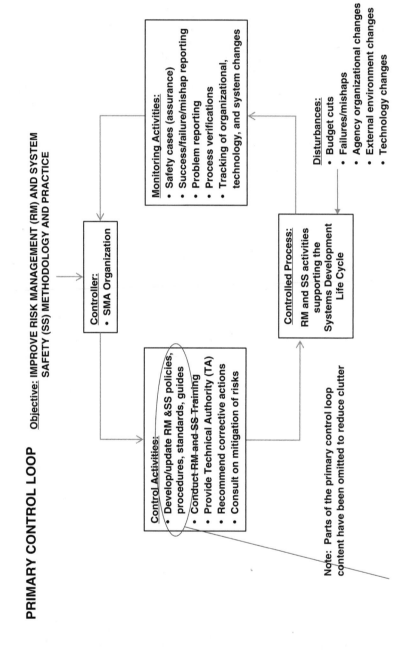

Controller:
- SMA Organization

Monitoring Activities:
- Safety cases (assurance)
- Success/failure/mishap reporting
- Problem reporting
- Process verifications
- Tracking of organizational, technology, and system changes

Control Activities:
- Develop/update RM &SS policies, procedures, standards, guides
- Conduct RM and SS Training
- Provide Technical Authority (TA)
- Recommend corrective actions
- Consult on mitigation of risks

Controlled Process:
RM and SS activities supporting the Systems Development Life Cycle

Disturbances:
- Budget cuts
- Failures/mishaps
- Agency organizational changes
- External environment changes
- Technology changes

Note: Parts of the primary control loop content have been omitted to reduce clutter

PROCESS DIAGRAM

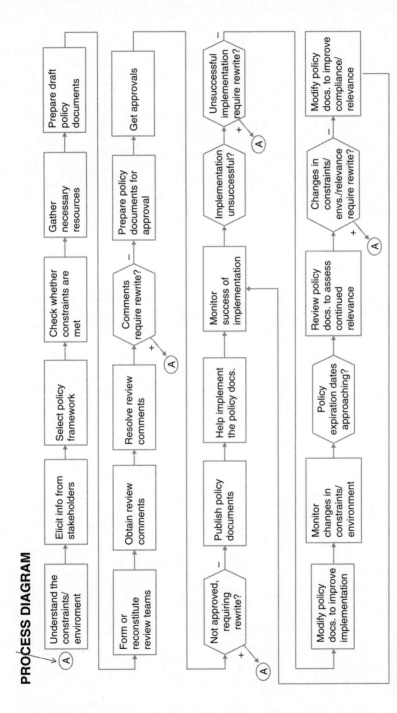

FIGURE 10.8 Process diagram for the selected control activity: "Develop and update risk management and system safety policies, procedures, standards, and guides"

PROCESS DIAGRAM

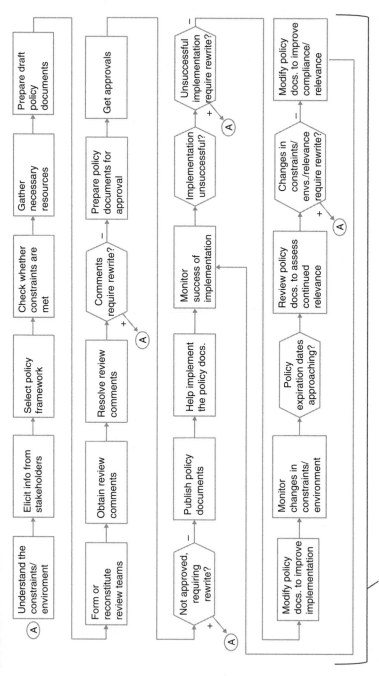

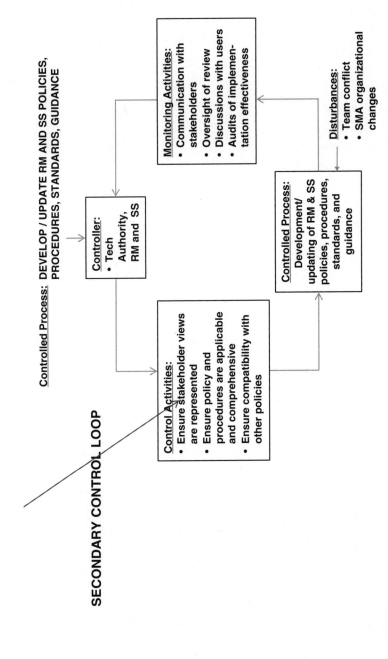

FIGURE 10.9 Secondary control loop for the selected control activity: "Develop and update risk management and system safety policies, procedures, standards, and guides"

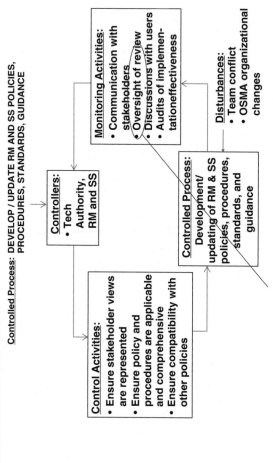

SECONDARY CONTROL LOOP

Controlled Process: DEVELOP / UPDATE RM AND SS POLICIES, PROCEDURES, STANDARDS, GUIDANCE

Controllers:
• Tech Authority, RM and SS

Monitoring Activities:
• Communication with stakeholders
• Oversight of review
• Discussions with users
• Audits of implementationeffectiveness

Disturbances:
• Team conflict
• OSMA organizational changes

Controlled Process: Development/ updating of RM & SS policies, procedures, standards, and guidance

Control Activities:
• Ensure stakeholder views are represented
• Ensure policy and procedures are applicable and comprehensive
• Ensure compatibility with other policies

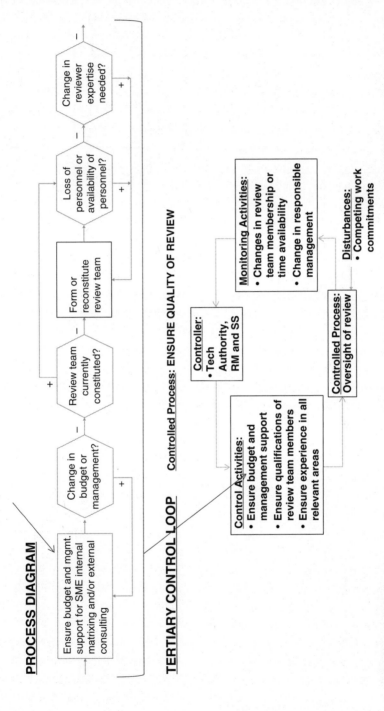

PROCESS DIAGRAM

Ensure budget and mgmt. support for SME internal matrixing and/or external consulting

Change in budget or management? (+)

Review team currently constituted? (−)

Form or reconstitute review team

Loss of personnel or availability of personnel? (−) (+)

Change in reviewer expertise needed? (−) (+)

TERTIARY CONTROL LOOP   Controlled Process: ENSURE QUALITY OF REVIEW

Controller:
• Tech Authority, RM and SS

Monitoring Activities:
• Changes in review team membership or time availability
• Change in responsible management

Disturbances:
• Competing work commitments

Controlled Process:
Oversight of review

Control Activities:
• Ensure budget and management support
• Ensure qualifications of review team members
• Ensure experience in all relevant areas

FIGURE 10.10 Process diagram and tertiary control loop for the selected control activity: "Develop and update RM and SS policies, procedures, standards, and guides"

293

TABLE 10.2 Example summary chart of cascading activities, weaknesses, and controls for the SMA organization example

Objective	Risk or Opportunity Driver	Primary Control Loop	Activity (M/C)*	Actual or Potential Weakness	Secondary Control Loop	Activity (M/C)*	Tertiary Control Loop	Actual or Potential Weakness	Activity (M/C)*
Improve risk management and system safety methodology and practice	Out-of-date documentation of RM & SS policies, procedures, standards, guides (risk)	Fig. A	Develop/ update RM & SS policies, procedures, standards, guides (C)	Stakeholders' and users' views may not be accurately represented	Fig. B	Communicate regularly with stakeholders and users (M)			
						Ensure stakeholders' views are represented (C)			
				Policies and procedures may be incomplete, incompatible, or inapplicable	Fig. C	Oversee review (M)	Fig. D	Insufficient budget and/or lack of support for matrixed staff	Ensure budget and management support (C)
									Monitor changes in responsible management (M)
								Review team qualifications and/or experience incompatible with need	Ensure qualifications of review team members (C)
									Ensure experience in all relevant areas (C)
									Monitor changes in review team membership or time availability (M)
	Ineffective or inefficient implementation of RM & SS policies, etc. (risk)	Fig. A	Improve RM & SS training (C)	Etc.					
Etc.									

*M = Monitoring Activity, C = Control Activity

TABLE 10.3 Example RACI chart for the SMA example

Control Loop	Monitoring (M) or Control (C) Activity	Responsible		Accountable		Consulted		Informed	
		Org	Person	Org	Person	Org(s)	Person(s)	Org(s)	Person(s)
Fig. B	Communicate regularly with stakeholders and users (M)	X	X	X	X	X	X	X	X
	Ensure stakeholders' views are represented (C)	X	X	X	X	X	X	X	X
Fig. D	Ensure budget and management support (C)	X	X	X	X	X	X	X	X
	Monitor changes in responsible mgmt. (M)	X	X	X	X	X	X	X	X
	Ensure qualifications of review team members (C)	X	X	X	X	X	X	X	X
	Ensure experience in all relevant areas (C)	X	X	X	X	X	X	X	X
	Monitor changes in review team membership or time availability (M)	X	X	X	X	X	X	X	X
Etc.									

Objective: ACHIEVE ACCEPTABLE SAFETY WITHIN COST CONTRAINTS USING
THE RISK BASED ASSURANCE PROCESS AND SHARED ASSURANCE MODEL

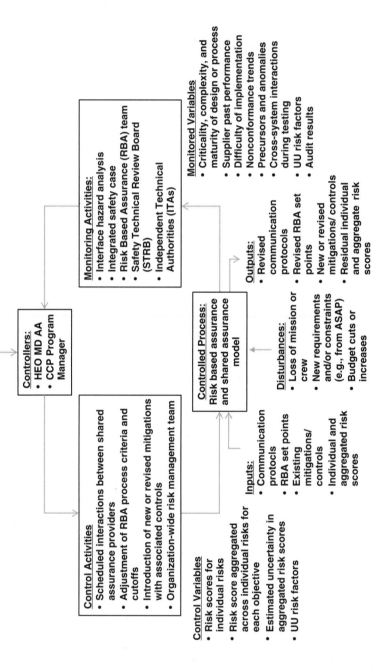

FIGURE 10.11 Example primary control loop for CCP's objective of achieving acceptable safety within schedule and budget using the RBA process and shared assurance model

intact. The control loop is labeled as "candidate" because it attempts to provide the needed monitoring and control actions but has not yet been vetted. The inputs to the control process are the existing communication protocols, risk set points for assigning individual hazards to BAAs, mitigations and associated internal controls upon those mitigations, risk scores for individual hazards, and aggregate risk for each of the CCP's objectives. The outputs are a revised set of communication protocols, risk set points, mitigations with associated internal controls, residual risk scores for each hazard, and residual aggregate risk for each objective. The primary monitoring activities include analyses (interface hazard analyses and integrated safety cases), monitoring teams (the RBA team and the Safety Technical Review Board), and independent technical authorities (ITAs). The primary control activities include communication protocols (scheduled interactions among entities), adjustments in risk set points, introduction of mitigations, and investiture of an organization-wide risk management team that includes both provider and NASA personnel.

As demonstrated earlier for Example 1, it is possible to devise secondary, tertiary, and even lower-level control loops for each monitoring and control activity. While attempting to do so in this example would be premature (mainly because it would need a level of detail that would require the participation of CCP personnel), it is possible to provide an outline of the kinds of monitoring and control variables and activities that might be included in these lower-level control loops. Such an outline is presented in Table 10.4.

10.4 INCORPORATION OF INTERNAL CONTROL PRINCIPLES INTO THE CONTROL LOOP APPROACH

Existing frameworks for internal control emphasize not only the strategic and/or top-level objectives of the organization as the starting point for the development of control loops but also principles of good practice. For example, the GAO Green Book (GAO 2014) provides 17 principles that are intended to guide the evaluation of an organization's internal controls. The formulation in the Green Book is similar to that in the COSO Internal Controls Integrated Framework (COSO 2013), which also is based on adhering to 17 principles. The Green Book essentially tailors the COSO principles to make them applicable to government agencies.

As shown in Table 10.5, these principles cover integrity and ethical values, management oversight, delegation of responsibility and authority, staff competency, development of policies, communication, and other practices. Underlying each principle is a set of means for accomplishment (referred to

TABLE 10.4　Candidates for secondary and tertiary control loops for CCP risk-based assurance process and shared assurance model

Controlled Process	Monitored Variables	Control Mechanisms
1. Maintenance of competent personnel	▪ Staff attrition ▪ Staff availability ▪ Staff areas of expertise	▪ Hiring program ▪ Incentives ▪ Staff-matrixing ▪ Training programs
2. Maintenance of a competent review team	▪ Reviewer availability ▪ Reviewer expertise ▪ Reviewer affiliations	▪ Inter-organizational agreements ▪ Sharing agreements with external entities
3. Maintenance of needed policy and procedures	▪ Changes in environment, organization, or technology ▪ Implementation success	▪ Periodic reviews of environment, organization, and technology ▪ Budget allocation for document updates
4. Maintenance of IT capability	▪ Bandwidth needs ▪ Cyber threats ▪ Aging of IT equipment	▪ Periodic reviews of cyber threats ▪ Budget allocation for IT system improvement
5. Provisions for incentivizing good communication	▪ Implementation of communication protocols ▪ Attendance at interdisciplinary meetings	▪ Communication training ▪ Management support for cross-organizational communication
6. Access to externally produced information	▪ Links to information sources ▪ Access to proprietary or sensitive information	▪ Periodic reviews of available sources ▪ Nondisclosure agreements
7. Effective and timely precursor and anomaly tracking	▪ Efficiency/effectiveness of tracking system ▪ Adherence to best practices	▪ Comprehensive, accessible, and user-friendly database ▪ Reporting protocol for precursors and anomalies
8. Effective and timely precursor and anomaly tracking	▪ Efficiency/effectiveness of tracking system ▪ Adherence to best practices	▪ Comprehensive, accessible, and user-friendly database ▪ Management oversight
9. Effective and timely implementation of waivers/exceptions	▪ Time taken for related waivers and exceptions ▪ Lessons learned from other programs	▪ Incentives for timely waiver submittals and approvals ▪ Protocols for elevation of waiver decisions
10. Effective and timely approval process	▪ Time taken to approve related submittals ▪ Approval backlog	▪ Clear assignment of approval responsibility ▪ Close coordination with approval authority

TABLE 10.5   GAO green book principles for internal control (GAO 2014)

1. *The oversight body and management should demonstrate a commitment to integrity and ethical values.*
2. *The oversight body should oversee the entity's internal control system.*
3. *Management should establish an organizational structure, assign responsibility, and delegate authority to achieve the entity's objectives.*
4. *Management should demonstrate a commitment to recruit, develop, and retain competent individuals.*
5. *Management should evaluate performance and hold individuals accountable for their internal control responsibilities.*
6. *Management should define objectives clearly to enable the identification of risks and define risk tolerances.*
7. *Management should identify, analyze, and respond to risks related to achieving the defined objectives.*
8. *Management should consider the potential for fraud when identifying, analyzing, and responding to risks.*
9. *Management should identify, analyze, and respond to significant changes that could impact the internal control system.*
10. *Management should design control activities to achieve objectives and respond to risks.*
11. *Management should design the entity's information system and related control activities to achieve objectives and respond to risks.*
12. *Management should implement control activities through policies.*
13. *Management should use quality information to achieve the entity's objectives.*
14. *Management should internally communicate the necessary quality information to achieve the entity's objectives.*
15. *Management should externally communicate the necessary quality information to achieve the entity's objectives.*
16. *Management should establish and operate monitoring activities to monitor the internal control system and evaluate the results.*
17. *Management should remediate identified internal control deficiencies on a timely basis.*

in the Green Book as attributes). As shown in Table 10.6, these means for accomplishment principally consist of a set of best practices and standards.

Work by Nancy Leveson et al. at MIT (2005) also bases the starting point for an internal control framework on a set of principles (referred to by Leveson et al. as system safety requirements), and for each principle, means of accomplishment (referred to by Leveson et al., as constraints). As shown in Table 10.7, the principles and means for accomplishment are largely based on best practices.

Principles such as those in the Green Book and the MIT work are usually qualitative in nature, and the success of an organization in satisfying the principles is usually measured using a qualitative rating scheme (e.g., green, yellow, or red). In order to obtain a rating for the status of each principle, the organization first rates the status of each means of accomplishment (e.g., using the green, yellow, and red format). An aggregation scheme is

TABLE 10.6   GAO green book means of accomplishment for principle 1 (GAO 2014)

---

1. The oversight body and management should demonstrate a commitment to integrity and ethical values.

   a. The oversight body and management demonstrate the importance of integrity and ethical values through their directives, attitudes, and behavior.

   b. The oversight body and management lead by an example that demonstrates the organization's values, philosophy, and operating style. The oversight body and management set the tone at the top and throughout the organization by their example, which is fundamental to an effective internal control system. In larger entities, the various layers of management in the organizational structure may also set "tone in the middle."

   c. The oversight body's and management's directives, attitudes, and behaviors reflect the integrity and ethical values expected throughout the entity. The oversight body and management reinforce the commitment to doing what is right, not just maintaining a minimum level of performance necessary to comply with applicable laws and regulations, so that these priorities are understood by all stakeholders, such as regulators, employees, and the general public.

   d. Tone at the top can be either a driver, as shown in the preceding paragraphs, or a barrier to internal control. Without a strong tone at the top to support an internal control system, the entity's risk identification may be incomplete, risk responses may be inappropriate, control activities may not be appropriately designed or implemented, information and communication may falter, and results of monitoring may not be understood or acted upon to remediate deficiencies.

   e. Management establishes standards of conduct to communicate expectations concerning integrity and ethical values. The entity uses ethical values to balance the needs and concerns of different stakeholders, such as regulators, employees, and the general public. The standards of conduct guide the directives, attitudes, and behaviors of the organization in achieving the entity's objectives.

   f. Management, with oversight from the oversight body, defines the organization's expectations of ethical values in the standards of conduct. Management may consider using policies, operating principles, or guidelines to communicate the standards of conduct to the organization.

   g. Management establishes processes to evaluate performance against the entity's expected standards of conduct and address any deviations in a timely manner.

   h. Management uses established standards of conduct as the basis for evaluating adherence to integrity and ethical values across the organization. Management evaluates the adherence to standards of conduct across all levels of the entity. To gain assurance that the entity's standards of conduct are implemented effectively, management evaluates the directives, attitudes, and behaviors of individuals and teams. Evaluations may consist of ongoing monitoring or separate evaluations. Individual personnel can also report issues through reporting lines, such as regular staff meetings, upward feedback processes, a whistle-blowing program, or an ethics hotline.

   i. Management determines the tolerance level for deviations. Management may determine that the entity will have zero tolerance for deviations from certain expected standards of conduct, while deviations from others may be addressed with warnings to personnel. Management establishes a process for evaluations of individual and team adherence to standards of conduct that escalates and remediates deviations. The oversight body evaluates management's adherence to the standards of conduct as well as the overall adherence by the entity. Management addresses deviations from expected standards of conduct timely and consistently. Depending on the severity of the deviation determined through the evaluation process, management, with oversight from the oversight body, takes appropriate actions and may also need to consider applicable laws and regulations. The standards of conduct to which management holds personnel, however, remain consistent.

TABLE 10.7 MIT-conducted NASA independent technical authority study: system safety principles for internal control and means of accomplishment (Leveson et al. 2005)

1. Safety considerations must be first and foremost in technical decision-making.
   a. State-of-the art safety standards and requirements for NASA missions must be established, implemented, enforced, and maintained that protect the astronauts, the workforce, and the public.
   b. Safety-related technical decision making must be independent from programmatic considerations, including cost and schedule.
   c. Safety-related decision making must be based on correct, complete, and up-to-date information.
   d. Overall (final) decision making must include transparent and explicit consideration of both safety and programmatic concerns.
   e. The Agency must provide for effective assessment and improvement in safety-related decision making.
2. Safety-related technical decision making must be done by eminently qualified experts, with broad participation of the full workforce.
   a. Technical decision making must be credible (executed using credible personnel, technical requirements, and decision-making tools).
   b. Technical decision making must be clear and unambiguous with respect to authority, responsibility, and accountability.
   c. All safety-related technical decisions, before being implemented by the Program, must have the approval of the technical decision maker assigned responsibility for that class of decisions.
   d. Mechanisms and processes must be created that allow and encourage all employees and contractors to contribute to safety-related decision making.
3. Safety analyses must be available and used starting in the early acquisition, requirements development, and design processes and continuing through the system life cycle.
   a. High-quality system hazard analyses must be created.
   b. Personnel must have the capability to produce high-quality safety analyses.
   c. Engineers and managers must be trained to use the results of hazard analyses in their decision making.
   d. Adequate resources must be applied to the hazard analysis process.
   e. Hazard analysis results must be communicated in a timely manner to those who need them. A communication structure must be established that includes contractors and allows communication downward, upward, and sideways (e.g., among those building subsystems).
   f. Hazard analyses must be elaborated (refined and extended) and updated as the design evolves and test experience is acquired.
   g. During operations, hazard logs must be maintained and used as experience is acquired. All in-flight anomalies must be evaluated for their potential to contribute to hazards.
4. The Agency must provide avenues for the full expression of technical conscience (for safety-related technical concerns) and provide a process for full and adequate resolution of technical conflicts as well as conflicts between programmatic and technical concerns.
   a. Communication channels, resolution processes, and adjudication procedures must be created to handle expressions of technical conscience.
   b. Appeals channels must be established to surface complaints and concerns about aspects of the safety-related decision-making and technical conscience structures that are not functioning appropriately.

used to synthesize the rating of the principle from the rating of the means of accomplishment that pertain to it. An example template for such an aggregation is shown in Table 10.8.

In the current context, attainment of a green rating for each principle can be thought of as a type of operational objective of the organization, in that the principles generally have a shorter-term focus than strategic objectives. Since principles are a type of objective, it is possible to build a hierarchy of control loops for principles in the same way as was illustrated for objectives in Figure 10.6.

A generic example for the primary control loop addressing the achievement of a principle labeled as "X" is illustrated in Figure 10.12. The monitored variables consist of a rating for each means of accomplishment and an aggregated rating. The monitoring mechanisms include self evaluations and independent evaluations of the status of the principle based on the ratings for the means of accomplishment and the aggregated rating. In the event that the aggregation results in a rating other than green, the evaluators would provide recommendations for how to rectify that problem. The control mechanisms consist of the implementation of some or all of the recommendations resulting from the self and independent evaluations. The controlled variables are the means of accomplishment.

Secondary and tertiary control loops should follow the approach discussed earlier in Sections 10.2 and 10.3, and will generally comprise both case-specific and generic controls. Case-specific controls are so-called because their design depends on the specifics of the control mechanisms identified in the primary loop. Generic controls, on the other hand, provide integrity to control processes in general. The candidate secondary and tertiary control loops listed in Table 10.4 would be applicable here as generic controls.

Figure 10.13 illustrates an instantiation of Figure 10.12 for the particular case of Principle 1: Demonstration of a commitment to integrity and ethical values by the oversight body and management. The means of accomplishment for this example are extracted from Table 10.6.

10.5   SUMMARY OF OBSERVATIONS

Internal controls should be derived from the organization's hierarchy of objectives and standards of operation and from considerations of the risk and opportunity drivers that affect the organization's ability to meet those objectives and standards. The risk and opportunity drivers are determined from the factors that most significantly affect aggregate risks and opportunities rather than just from individual risks and opportunities. The identification and evaluation of internal controls focus largely on protection of the

TABLE 10.8 Example template for aggregating means of accomplishment to principles

Principle No.	Principle Description	Means of Accomplish-ment No.	Means of Accomplishment Description	Means of Accomplishment Rating (G/Y/R)	Rating Rationale for Means of Accomplishment	Aggregated Principle Rating (G/Y/R)	Aggregated Rating Rationale
1		a					
		b					
		c					
2		d					
		e					
		f					
Etc.							

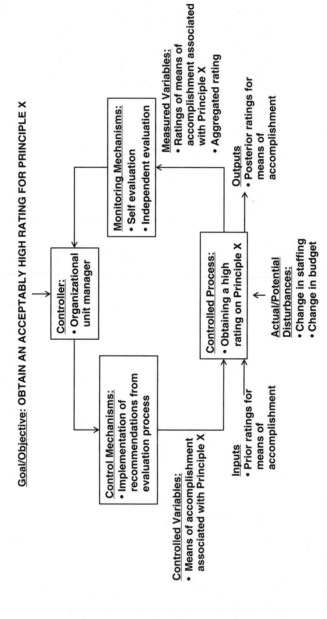

FIGURE 10.12 Example generic primary control loop for achievement of internal control principles

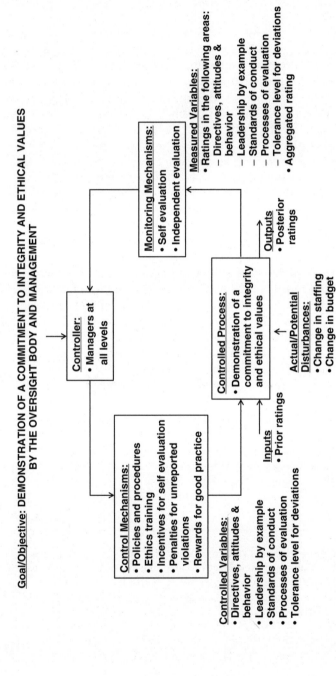

Goal/Objective: DEMONSTRATION OF A COMMITMENT TO INTEGRITY AND ETHICAL VALUES BY THE OVERSIGHT BODY AND MANAGEMENT

Controller:
• Managers at all levels

Control Mechanisms:
• Policies and procedures
• Ethics training
• Incentives for self evaluation
• Penalties for unreported violations
• Rewards for good practice

Controlled Variables:
• Directives, attitudes & behavior
• Leadership by example
• Standards of conduct
• Processes of evaluation
• Tolerance level for deviations

Inputs
• Prior ratings

Controlled Process:
• Demonstration of a commitment to integrity and ethical values

Actual/Potential Disturbances:
• Change in staffing
• Change in budget

Outputs
• Posterior ratings

Monitoring Mechanisms:
• Self evaluation
• Independent evaluation

Measured Variables:
• Ratings in the following areas:
  – Directives, attitudes & behavior
  – Leadership by example
  – Standards of conduct
  – Processes of evaluation
  – Tolerance level for deviations
  – Aggregated rating

FIGURE 10.13 Example primary control loop for demonstration of a commitment to integrity and ethical values

assumptions and/or correction of the weaknesses that need to be addressed for the aggregate risks and opportunities to be effectively and efficiently controlled within the decision maker's risk tolerance and opportunity appetite.

Structures of control loops may be derived and implemented in a hierarchical manner. Such structures should contain a primary control loop and a nested series of subordinate control loops. Hierarchical control loops can be developed starting from an organization's strategic objectives to enhance the likelihood of meeting those objectives. They can also be developed from the principles of internal control espoused in various prior references such as the GAO Green Book to enhance the likelihood of meeting those principles.

The benefits of creating hierarchical control structures are the same as the benefits for creating hierarchical organizational management structures. First, they promote the definition of roles and responsibilities to ensure that all-important controls have a champion or owner as well as an oversight authority. This causes lower-level organizational units to be aware that they have control responsibilities that are intended to support the higher-level controls that exist at higher levels of the organization. Furthermore, hierarchical control structures have the advantage of being well-suited for integration with EROM structures, which also are hierarchical in nature.

Hierarchies of control loops are similar in concept to organizational hierarchies but do not have to mirror the organizational hierarchies. All that is necessary is that there be a mapping between the two so that the roles and responsibilities for formulating and implementing controls are clearly defined in terms of organizational entities.

The approach advocated here differs philosophically somewhat from the approach taken in the COSO framework for internal controls. The COSO framework posits that internal controls are an input to enterprise risk management (ERM) but that ERM is not necessarily an input to internal controls. The framework herein suggests a more bidirectional integration of internal controls and EROM, which is more suitable for organizations whose objectives are more technical than financial in nature.

NOTE

1. The idea of developing hierarchical control loops in the organizational context is somewhat akin to the subject of cascading controls for mechanical systems (VanDoren, 2014). Surprisingly, however, the treatment of internal control loops as hierarchical within a hierarchical organizational structure appears to be mostly unexplored prior to this book.

REFERENCES

Bolden, C. 2013. "Commercial Crew Development." Wikipedia website (April). http://blogs.nasa.gov/bolden/2013/04/

Canfield, A. 2016. "The Evolution of the NASA Commercial Crew Program Mission Assurance Process," NASA Kennedy Space Center. https://ntrs.nasa.gov/archive/nasa/casi.ntrs.nasa.gov/20160006484.pdf

Committee of Sponsoring Organizations of the Treadway Commission (COSO). 2004. "Enterprise Risk Management—Integrated Framework."

Committee of Sponsoring Organizations of the Treadway Commission (COSO). 2013. "Internal Control—Integrated Framework."

Government Accountability Office. (GAO). 2014. GAO-14-704G, *The Green Book, Standards for Internal Control in the Federal Government*. Washington, DC: Government Accountability Office.

Kirkpatrick, P., and Vassberg, N. 2014. "The Evolution of the NASA Commercial Crew Program (CCP) Safety Process." Proc. of 7th IAASS Conference: "Space Safety Is No Accident."

Leveson, N. 2011. *Engineering a Safer World: System Thinking Applied to Safety.* Cambridge, MA: The MIT Press.

Leveson, N., et al., 2005. "Risk Analysis of NASA Independent Technical Authority." Massachusetts Institute of Technology. website sunnydat.mit.edu.

National Aeronautics and Space Administration (NASA). 2011. NASA/SP-2011-3422. "NASA Risk Management Handbook." Washington, DC.

Office of Management and Budget (OMB). 2016. Circular A-123. "*Management's Responsibility for Enterprise Risk Management and Internal Control.*" Washington, DC.

Smith, M., and Erwin, J. 2005. "Role & Responsibility Charting (RACI)," PMForum.org.

VanDoren, V. 2014. "*Fundamentals of Cascade Control.*" Control Engineering. Website http://www.controleng.com/single-article/fundamentals-of-cascade-control/bcedad6518aec409f583ba6bc9b72854.html

Acronyms

AFR	Annual financial report
APG	Annual performance goal, or agency priority goal
API	Annual performance indicator
APR	Annual performance report
ASAP	Aerospace Safety Advisory Panel
BPA	Blanket purchase agreement
CCP	Commercial crew program
CCTS	Commercial crew transportation system
CEO	Chief operating officer
COSO	Committee of Sponsoring Organizations
CRM	Continuous risk management
CRO	Chief risk officer
DM	Decision maker
DoD	Department of Defense
DOE	Department of Energy
EKV	Exoatmospheric Kill Vehicle
EP	Experienced personnel
ERM	Enterprise risk management
EROM	Enterprise risk and opportunity management
ES&H	Environmental safety and health
EXT	External
FMFIA	Federal Managers' Financial Integrity Act
GAO	Government Accountability Office
GMD	Ground-based midcourse defense
GPRA	Government Performance and Results Act
GPRAMA	GPRA Modernization Act
HST	Hubble Space Telescope
IG	Inspector general
IIA	Institute of Internal Auditors

INT	Internal
IR	Infrared
IRM	Institutional risk management
ISL	Information Systems Laboratories, Inc.
ISS	International Space Station
IT	Information technology
ITAR	International Traffic in Arms Regulations
JPL	Jet Propulsion Laboratory
JWST	James Webb Space Telescope
KPI	Key performance indicator
LOC	Loss of crew
LOM	Loss of mission
MDA	Missile Defense Agency
NASA	National Aeronautics and Space Administration
OIG	Office of Inspector General
OMB	Office of Management and Budget
P(LOC)	Probability of loss of crew
P(LOM)	Probability of loss of mission
PMC	President's Management Council
PPR	Portfolio performance review
PRA	Probabilistic risk assessment
RIDM	Risk-informed decision making
RACI	Responsible, Accountable, Consulted, Informed
RM	Risk management
R-O	Risk and opportunity
SAR	Strategic annual review
SLS	Space Launch System
SMA	Safety and Mission Assurance
SoA	Statement of assurance
SOAR	Strategic objectives annual review (referred to externally as simply "strategic review")
SOFIA	Stratospheric Observatory for Infrared Astronomy
STEM	Science, technology, engineering, and mathematics
TBD	To be determined
TCA	Technology capability assessment
TRIO	Technical Research, Integration, and Operations
TRL	Technology readiness level
UK	United Kingdom
US	United States
UU	Unknown and/or underappreciated
WBS	Work breakdown structure

Definitions

Annual performance indicator   A desirable outcome within the agency's objectives hierarchy having a time frame of one year or less.

Continuous risk management   A specific process for the management of risks associated with implementation of designs, plans, and processes throughout the life of a program or project.

Cumulative opportunity   The likelihood and benefit of being able to meet a specified element in the agency's objective hierarchy more satisfactorily than originally planned, or to meet a new goal or objective that better promotes the agency's mission.

Cumulative risk   The likelihood of not being able to meet a specified element in the agency's objective hierarchy, and the degree to which the element is not satisfied.

Enterprise risk and opportunity management   The methods and processes used by organizations to manage risks and seize opportunities related to the achievement of their objectives.

Extended enterprise   A program, project, or coordinated activity that involves multiple partners, or entities, with overlapping responsibilities. In addition to contributing to the same program/project/activity, each partner is an independent enterprise with its own set of strategic objectives and performance requirements.

Extended organization   The collection of organizational units that interact with a center. The center's extended organization includes the entities in all the extended enterprises with which the center interacts on program/project planning and execution, as well as other entities within or outside the agency that provide direction and administrative support to the center.

Internal controls   The set of policies and procedures that management uses to help programs, projects, and other activities within the organization to achieve results and safeguard the integrity of their operation.

Lagging indicator   A traceable measure that is quantifiable and correlates with the past performance of the organization with respect to one or more of its objectives.

Leading indicator   A traceable measure that is quantifiable, correlates as a predictor of the likelihood of future success of one or more of the agency's objectives, and is actionable.

Multiyear performance goal A desirable outcome within the agency's objectives hierarchy having a timeframe of one to five years (commonly referred to at NASA as simply performance goal).

Objectives hierarchy A tree-like structure of desired outcomes starting at the top with long-term strategic goals and progressing down to short-term tactical accomplishments (commonly referred to at NASA as strategic performance framework).

Opportunity The possibility of an existing goal, objective, or desired outcome being met more efficaciously, or a new goal, objective, or desired outcome becoming feasible.

Opportunity scenario A specific sequence of possible events that, if they should occur, would lead to an opportunity to either increase the likelihood of achieving an element in the agency's objectives hierarchy or open the possibility of defining a new objective that coincides with the agency's mission.

Opportunity scenario statement A statement characterizing an opportunity scenario in terms of one or more conditions, enabling events or potential advances, affected entities, actions, benefits, and objectives affected.

Parity statement A statement that defines risk and opportunity boundaries in terms of equivalent levels of discomfort or comfort.

Performance indicator A type of lagging indicator that measures the efficiency and effectiveness of past actions with respect to accomplishing performance objectives.

Portfolio A set of programs, projects, institutional assets, and other activities and resources that implement the high-level goals and objectives within the strategic plan.

Portfolio performance review An internal, bottom-up assessment of how well the agency has performed against its strategic goals and other performance metrics, such as cost, schedule, contract, and technical commitments.

Response boundary A measure of the likelihood and severity of a risk scenario or the likelihood and potential benefit of an opportunity scenario that would suggest that an action is imminently needed. A risk-response boundary marks the boundary between "marginal" and "intolerable" risk, and an opportunity response boundary marks the boundary between "marginal" and "significant" opportunity.

Response trigger value A measure of a leading indicator that would suggest that an action is immediately needed. A leading indicator response trigger signals when a risk is progressing from "marginal" to "intolerable" or when an opportunity is progressing from "marginal" to "significant."

Risk The possibility of a goal, objective, or desired outcome not being met.

Risk-informed decision making The use of risk analysis results to inform the selection of decision alternatives and to assure effective approaches for achieving goals and objectives.

Risk scenario A specific concern, characterized as a sequence of possible events, that is perceived as presenting a risk to the ability to achieve an element of the objectives hierarchy.

Risk scenario statement A statement characterizing a risk scenario in terms of one or more conditions, departure events, affected entities, and consequences.

Strategic goal A desirable strategic outcome within the agency's objectives hierarchy having a time frame of 10 years or beyond.

Strategic objective A desirable strategic outcome within the agency's objectives hierarchy having a time frame of 5 to 10 years or less.

Strategic performance evaluation The evaluation of an organization's performance with respect to the achievement of its strategic goals and objectives.

Strategic plan A document used to communicate with the organization the organization's goals and objectives, the actions needed to achieve them, the means for implementing those actions, and all of the other critical elements developed during the planning exercise.

Strategic planning An organization's process of defining its strategy, or direction, and making decisions on allocating its resources to pursue this strategy. It may also extend to control mechanisms for guiding the implementation of the strategy.

Watch boundary A measure of the likelihood and severity of a risk scenario or the likelihood and potential benefit of an opportunity scenario that would suggest that an action should be considered but is not imminently needed. A risk watch boundary marks the boundary between "tolerable" and "marginal" risk, and an opportunity watch boundary marks the boundary between "insignificant" and "marginal" opportunity.

Watch trigger value A measure of a leading indicator that would suggest that an action should be considered but is not imminently needed. A leading indicator watch trigger signals when a risk is progressing from "tolerable" to "marginal" or when an opportunity is progressing from "insignificant" to "marginal."

About the Companion Website

A full-color version of all the figures found in *Enterprise Risk and Opportunity Management,* is available on the book's companion website at www.wiley.com/go/enterpriserisk. Enter the password: risk17.

About the Author

ALLAN S. BENJAMIN, PHD

Dr. Allan Benjamin is a Senior Scientist Fellow for Information Systems Laboratories, Inc., an independent consultant, and a provider of risk management and system safety technical services to NASA headquarters. He has about 50 years of experience in the design and analysis of aerospace systems, nuclear reactor systems, nuclear weapon systems, ballistic missile systems, and military satellite systems. His fields of expertise include risk management, probabilistic risk assessment, uncertainty analysis, reliability analysis, aerodynamic analysis, and thermal analysis. In addition to NASA, he has worked for and/or consulted for the Departments of Energy and Defense, the Nuclear Regulatory Commission, Sandia National Laboratories, Los Alamos National Laboratories, the Missile Defense Agency, the Pantex Plant, Boeing, Lockheed Martin, Northrop Grumman, Orbital Sciences, and various smaller companies. His advanced degrees are from Brown University and the University of California at Los Angeles.

Index